FAITH FOR THE HEART

FAITH
for the
HEART

A "CATHOLIC" SPIRITUALITY

THOMAS H. GROOME

Paulist Press
New York / Mahwah, NJ

"Poem for Anne Gregory" from *The Winding Stair and Other Poems* by William Butler Yeats and George Bornstein. Copyright © 1933 by The Macmillan Company. Copyrights renewed © 1961 by Bertha Georgie Yeats. Reprinted with the permission of Scribner, a division of Simon & Schuster, Inc. All rights reserved.

Grateful acknowledgment goes to the Kavanaugh Trust for use of "The Long Garden" from *The Great Hunger* by Paddy Kavanaugh.

The Scripture quotations contained herein are from the New Revised Standard Version: Catholic Edition, Copyright © 1989 and 1993, by the Division of Christian Education of the National Council of the Churches of Christ in the United States of America. Used by permission. All rights reserved.

Cover background vector image by alevtinakarro/depositphotos.com
Cover design by Tamian Wood
Book design by Lynn Else

Library of Congress Cataloging-in-Publication Data
Names: Groome, Thomas H., author.
Title: Faith for the heart : a Catholic spirituality / Thomas H Groome.
Description: New York : Paulist Press, 2019.
Identifiers: LCCN 2018056138 (print) | LCCN 2019021961 (ebook) | ISBN 9781587688621 (ebook) | ISBN 9780809154661 (pbk. : alk. paper)
Subjects: LCSH: Spirituality—Catholic Church.
Classification: LCC BX2350.65 (ebook) | LCC BX2350.65 .G76 2019 (print) | DDC 248.4/82—dc23
LC record available at https://lccn.loc.gov/2018056138

ISBN 978-0-8091-5466-1 (paperback)
ISBN 978-1-58768-862-1 (e-book)

Published by Paulist Press
997 Macarthur Boulevard
Mahwah, New Jersey 07430
www.paulistpress.com

Printed and bound in the
United States of America

AUG 1 2 2019

Contents

Prelude

Hungers of the Heart

FOR A FEW FRIENDS

I write this book for a few friends I've met along the way, confident that they represent a larger readership.

The first one lists herself as *none* now when asked to declare a religious identity because she generally considers herself an atheist—maybe! Yet when we speak about it, she says she misses being part of a faith community of some kind, if only for the weddings and wakes. She readily admits that there are times when she finds herself praying somehow, like an old habit that won't quit, and she wonders if life lived with faith might be richer than life lived without it. Of course, she cannot simply give it to herself by dint of her own effort; as St. Paul explained, faith is "the gift of God" (Eph 2:8). But God offers the gift—somehow—to every person and is ever taking the initiative to draw my friend into the ambit of God's unconditional love. I offer some suggestions here, not so much for how she can *find* God again, but how she might allow herself to be *found*.

The second is a young adult friend who volunteers that he is "spiritual but not religious." I actually hear this claim, so common now, as having great potential to encourage a religious faith, precisely because the claimants are listening to their heart's desires and recognizing themselves as spiritual beings. However, when I inquire—gently and with respect—how he nurtures his soul, what stories or symbols or practices

1

or community he draws upon to sustain his spiritual journey, what he names seems to me very nebulous and without center. And I inquire only because I know from experience that it is simply not possible for one's spirituality to flourish without well-tested and reliable resources. I have some for him to consider from the deep treasury of "Catholic" spirituality.

The third friend is among the more than thirty-five million people in the United States alone who describe themselves as *former Catholics*. And there is comparable fall away from all mainline Protestant churches. So many now seem to be "dones"—at least with church— more than "nones." An older person now, she has personally suffered from negative experiences of the institutional Church and is deeply scandalized by the abominable crime of clergy sex abuse of children and minors. I certainly do not blame *her* for leaving. Nonetheless, it is possible to distinguish between the sins and crimes of some leaders in an ecclesial institution and the spiritual resources that the Church bears as the Body of Christ in the world. Though always carried in "earthen vessels," I invite her to reclaim from her old faith what still "belongs to God" (1 Cor 3:23).

Then, I write for all *"practicing* Catholics," who, like myself, are still not very good at it. Even in good times and especially in bad—and ours may be as bad as it gets (I refer again to the clergy sex abuse scandal still unfolding)—it is imperative that we remember the "pearl of great value" (Matt 13:46) that is ours and recognize afresh its inestimable value for living well and wisely. In many ways this whole book is an attempt to keep hope alive for Catholic Christians as we are led by the Holy Spirit into the needed Church reforms and renewals. Meanwhile, all of us can keep on *practicing* and we might get better at *living* faith.

Finally, I write for all Christians who belong by baptism to this shared Body of Christ, be they Catholic or Protestant, and of whatever intensity. Though I reflect from my own backyard of Catholic faith (I could not do otherwise), I am confident that every Christian person and community can find rich spiritual resources here. Just as the good example of Protestant brothers and sisters can encourage Catholics to deepen our knowledge and love of Scripture, perhaps we have a gift to return from the abundant spiritualities of Catholicism.

WHY THE HEART AND ITS HUNGERS?

I have crafted this book and its chapter themes around some great hungers of the human heart, deep desires that persist throughout our pilgrim way. Though one could well add others to what is here, all the heart's hungers are variations of a theme; they come together like a great symphony to constitute our ultimate desire. I propose that the hungers are implanted by divine design; God intends them to lead us to lives of faith, hope, and love, and ultimately to draw us home to Godself. *For God* is our ultimate hunger, the One who subsumes and alone can fulfill all the rest.

Hungers permeate every aspect of our human *being*, ascending from the purely physical to the highest spiritual, with all intertwined. So we have *bodily* appetites for food and drink, relief and rest, sex and pleasure, shelter, safety, and good health. We have *personal* needs to be agents of our own decision-making, to exercise our creativity, to make our own choices, and to shape how we live. We have *communal* needs for family and friendship, for love and intimacy, for life-giving relationships, for compassion and care, for empathy and esteem. We have *social* needs to be included with a sense of belonging, to be treated with dignity, respect, and justice, to participate in and contribute to our society. All of these felt needs feed into and seek satisfaction as desires of the heart.

Reflecting them all and reaching beyond them, we have hungers that we might describe as distinctly spiritual. They arise primarily from the human soul and are prompted by its transcendent reach. And though we come to realize that their fulfillment is never more than partial for now, this reach of soul prompts us to hunger for an ultimate fullness of life, for complete happiness, for unconditional love, for unwavering faith, for unshakable hope, for authenticity as persons, to enjoy true freedom, to realize justice for all, that our lives be meaningful and worthwhile. Ultimately, everything in life depends on how we go about satisfying such hungers of the heart, with the spiritual ones to guide and subsume fulfillment of the rest.

Regarding the heart, however, the Bible offers a wise caution. There are few defining terms used more often in the Bible than *heart*; it appears about a thousand times. In Hebrew, the most frequent term is *leb* (or a variation of it), and in Greek, it's *kardia*. While we now associate the heart only with emotions, biblically it is our very center, the sum of all that we are as human beings. For the Bible, the heart is first and foremost the physical organ that gives us life (Prov 4:23). And then it is the seat of our emotions (Ps 4:7), the source of our moral conscience (1 Sam 24:5), and the power of our intellectual ability (Isa 6:10). For the Bible, then, *heart* represents the whole person, all our capacities and desires.

The Bible also repeatedly makes clear—as we can attest from our own lives—that our hearts can lead us aright or lead us astray, depending on how we respond to their hungers. In and of themselves, the desires of the heart are good, implanted in us by God. However, God also made us free agents who are capable of pursuing our heart's desires in ways that are life-giving or life-destroying. They can lead us to freedom by placing first in our lives the one, true, loving, and life-giving God, or they can cause us to worship idols—fame or fortune, power or pleasure. And all false gods enslave.

Jesus, too, cautioned wisely about the desires of the heart. On the one hand, those with "an honest and good heart" hear the word of God "and bear fruit with patient endurance" (Luke 8:15). On the other hand, "it is from within, from the human heart, that evil intentions come," and Jesus then listed some of our worst sins (Mark 7:21). Within a few verses in his Sermon on the Mount, Jesus recognized that "the pure in heart...will see God" (Matt 5:8) whereas our hearts can also cause lust and adultery (Matt 5:28). In a summary New Testament text, the Epistle of James recognizes that the heart can be the source of "gentleness born of wisdom," resulting in works of justice and peace, whereas it can also be "unspiritual, devilish" (3:13–18).

The key seems to be what we choose as the ultimate treasure of our hearts—the core of what we most cherish and desire. Again here, Jesus advises, "For where your treasure is, there your heart will be also" (Matt 6:21). He explained further, "For out of the abundance of the heart the mouth speaks. The good person brings good things out of a good treasure, and the evil person brings evil things out of an evil treasure" (Matt 12:34–36). Clearly, then, what we make the treasure of our hearts shapes everything about our lives in the world.

That our heart's desires can lead us to life or destruction, toward fullness or emptiness, signals that we need reliable spiritual resources to prompt, guide, and nurture their fulfillment so as to be life-giving for all—oneself and others. In this book, I raise up some of the rich spiritual assets of Catholic Christian faith and invite their consideration to lend such guidance and resource.

So, each chapter will focus on some deep spiritual desire of the heart and how we might fulfill it wisely and well from the resources of "Catholic" spirituality. Alongside the symphony analogy, each of our desires is like the facets of a diamond—the flat planes that make up its outer face. Each facet allows light into the inner crystalline structure of the diamond—might we say the soul—and brings it out again with increased luster. All the facets work together to make up the sparkling beauty of the diamond.

Let us imagine, then, that God has crafted the desires of the human heart like a multifaceted diamond, with all the planes working in concert to realize the spiritual potential and beauty of the person. While we do not review all the facets—hungers—here, we address enough central ones to make the point that Christian faith offers rich spiritual resources that can help any person to realize their desires in ways life-giving for themselves and for the common good of all.

AN OLD APPROACH RENEWED

Appealing to people's desires to attract to Christian faith is not a new approach. Indeed, we could say that for the first thousand years of the Church's history, its dominant mode of appeal was to people's hearts. The great St. Augustine (354–430) championed this approach, convinced that Christian faith can most readily attract when crafted to address people's desires. He summarized this well in his immortal phrase, "Our *hearts* are restless 'till they find rest in God" (*Confessions*, Book 1, 1). And having learned this from his own experience, Augustine was a master at crafting the heartthrob of Christian faith.

Even while appealing primarily to desire, we will not neglect the time-honored role of reason in Christian faith and its spirituality. Faith and reason are essential partners for a life in faith. Without the monitor of critical reason, faith can even become dangerous. However, without faith, reason can lead to total relativism, as if there is no ultimate measure of truth or ethic. And we can unite desire and reason in the affair of Christian faith because, as my colleague Michael Himes likes to say, it both "brings joy and makes sense."

If the Church crafted the appeal of Christian faith to people's desires for the first thousand years, we might say that the second thousand appealed primarily to reason. The great Thomas Aquinas (1225–74) was the epitome of the more reasoned approach. There are signs, however, that modernity's unbounded confidence in reason to solve all our problems has faded. Sociologists tell us that there is a deep skepticism now, especially among millennials and young adults, about purely rational arguments for anything, and, by contrast, a greater openness to the experiential and affective.

A fresh appeal to desire on behalf of Christian faith and its spirituality seems like a wise strategic move at this difficult time—maybe long overdue. Because our hearts are hurting now more than our heads, returning to their hungers with the spiritual resources of Catholic faith seems more likely to renew our hope. We will so proceed here, even while honoring the rich tradition of *theology* as "faith seeking understanding" (definition of St. Anselm, 1033–1109).

A "CATHOLIC" SPIRITUALITY—IN QUOTES?

As alerted already, I write from my Catholic Christian home-in-faith, what I know best. Yet in the book's subtitle, and sometimes when referring to particularly generic aspects, I portray its spirituality as "Catholic" in quotes. Let me explain why.

First, I signal that I intend its adjectival meaning of "all are welcome." When at its best, this particular Christian tradition is "catholic" in that any and every person can learn from and be enriched by its spiritual wisdom for life, even if they do not embrace it as their identity in faith. The etymology of *kata holos* literally means "to include all" and is usually translated as universal. "Catholic" faith is universal in that all people of goodwill can draw upon its treasury of spiritual wisdom for life. I will sometimes use the quotation marks, especially in part 2, to highlight when a spiritual practice might appeal to more than self-identified Catholics. As James Joyce proposed in *Finnegan's Wake*, "Catholic means, 'here comes everybody.'"

Then, I put it in quotes to signal that even for people who so identify—using it as a noun—there may be a new spin offered here that is not their first connect with being *Catholic*. I have a friend who likes to play association of ideas at social gatherings. When he focuses around religious denominations and says "Baptist," people tend to say, "Bible"; if he says "Evangelical," people say, "Jesus"; if he says, "Catholic," people typically say "church"—or something related (pope, parish, etc.). While based on very anecdotal data, this rings true to me; the first association of most Catholics with their faith is *church*, whereas it should be *discipleship to Jesus*.

Pope Francis suggests that "to actually reach everyone without exception or exclusion, the [gospel] message has to concentrate on the essentials, on what is most beautiful, most grand, most appealing and at the same time most necessary. The message is simplified, while losing none of its depth and truth, and thus becomes all the more forceful and convincing" (*Evangelii Gaudium* 35). When we wonder "what is most beautiful, most grand, most appealing and at the same time most necessary" about Christian faith and its spirituality, we must first say—with Pope Francis—"Jesus Christ."

My hope with this text, then, is to help shift the reader's consciousness, as needed, to first associate being "Catholic" with living as a disciple of Jesus Christ, the whole intent of its spirituality. This will be reflected throughout every chapter (not just 3, 4, and 5 that focus on Jesus). The four Gospels will be the primary texts cited, adding, of course, from the rest of the New Testament and the Hebrew Bible. We might say that *Faith for the Heart* reflects an *evangelical* Catholic spirituality as based first on the good news (*evangelion*) of the gospel. This evangelical emphasis is not typically people's first association with being "Catholic"—and thus the quotation marks.

To focus on Jesus is very much encouraged by the Catholic Church at this time and epitomizes the pontificate of Pope Francis. The

Catechism of the Catholic Church (promulgated 1992, hereafter *CCC*) teaches well all the constitutive aspects of Catholicism—sacraments and symbols, dogmas and doctrines, values and virtues, creeds and moral codes. Yet it offers this moving summary of the essential core of Christian faith: "At the heart…we find a Person, the Person of Jesus of Nazareth, the only Son from the Father" (*CCC* 426). So our first association with being Christian of any kind should be discipleship to Jesus, that carpenter from Nazareth who was also the Christ, God among us as one of ourselves.

As the *Catechism* summary encourages, Catholics, like all Christians, must ground their faith identity in *both* the *Jesus of history* and the *Christ of faith*, in "*Jesus of Nazareth*" *and* "the only Son from the Father." To state the patently obvious, they are one and the same person and yet with two natures, fully human and fully divine. All Christian faith must be grounded in and defined by both the historical person and the risen Savior. The first is the model for Christians to follow and the second is the ultimate catalyst of God's abundant grace that enables us to do so.

So, all Christians are called to embrace *the way* modeled by the historical and fully human person, Jesus of Nazareth: the One who taught the in-breaking of God's reign of unconditional love, inviting disciples to radical love in response, even of enemies; who cared for all in need with great compassion, especially for the least, the lost, and the last; who reached out to sinners with unbounded mercy; who worked miracles to feed the hungry, cure the sick, expel evil, and console the grieving; who welcomed all to the table.

Equally, we need the same Jesus to be for us the *Christ of faith*, the Son of God, the Second Person of the Blessed Trinity, who was truly God's presence-in-person to effect liberating salvation within human history. For it is by his life, death, and resurrection that humankind is liberated from the powers of sin, personal and social, even from "the sting" of death (1 Cor 15:55). And God's saving work in Jesus now continues through the Holy Spirit. It is only by God's "abundance of grace…through the one man, Jesus Christ" (Rom 5:17) that we have the help we need to live as Jesus's disciples.

Focusing first and foremost on Jesus Christ simply means that he shapes our interpretation of every other aspect of Christian faith, and that discipleship to him is the heart of our spirituality. In other words, centering on Jesus is not to fall into a heresy from the early Church called "Christomonism"—as if the whole of Christian faith begins and ends with him. Instead, Jesus is the lens through which we interpret every other aspect.

So it is through Jesus, who he was and what he stood for, that we can know and imagine the One he called "Father"; as he said himself, "Whoever has seen me has seen the Father" (John 14:9). It is through the memory of Jesus that we can interpret and respond to the movements of the Holy Spirit whom he sent as promised and who now continues God's saving work in the world. It is in light of Jesus that we are to understand our triune God, the Church, the sacraments, the commandments, the dogmas, the social doctrine, and every aspect of Christian faith.

Traditional Catholics like myself might well ask, But what is new here? Surely our faith and spirituality have always focused on Jesus Christ. I suggest that while Catholics well emphasized the risen Christ, we paid far less attention to the historical Jesus—that Jewish carpenter-turned-prophet from Nazareth. The residue of Reformation polemics discouraged Catholics from reading their Bible, certainly not nearly as faithfully as our Protestant brothers and sisters do (we have improved a little since Vatican II).

Our inattention to the historical Jesus may be best explained, however, by the pattern of traditional Catholic catechesis. In the popular catechisms (Baltimore, Maynooth, etc.) that dominated catechetics from the Council of Trent (1545–63) until the Second Vatican Council (1962–65), the doctrinal summary was based on the Apostles Creed. So the catechisms took each article of the Creed and catechized it in a question and answer format to be memorized. But recall that the Creed's article "born of the virgin Mary" is followed immediately by "suffered under Pontius Pilate." As a result, the traditional catechisms—and their effect still lingers—skipped over Jesus's public ministry, going immediately from his birth to his death, as if these were all we need to know.

So, we find not a mention in the *Baltimore Catechism* about Jesus feeding the five thousand, welcoming tax collectors and prostitutes, being touched by and healing the woman with a hemorrhage, hugging and curing lepers, nor the great stories that he told like the good Samaritan, the prodigal son, Lazarus and the rich man, the persistent widow, and so on. When you add in that the Church made it seem as if access to God's "abundant grace" in Jesus Christ depends entirely on its mediation and ministry—no salvation without the Church—you can see why we Catholics tend to "think church" first before we "think Jesus" as the core of our faith and its spirituality. I use "Catholic" then to signal a new pattern for many of us to first think discipleship to Jesus, the Christ, as the heart of our faith and spirituality.

THE APPROACH OF LIFE TO FAITH TO LIFE

I intend the approach of this book to reflect the tone and flow of a conversation, like what Jesus had with a Samaritan woman (rejecting the cultural prejudices of racism and sexism) at a water well in Samaria, some two thousand years ago (check out John 4). I will try to honor the promise he made to her and to Christians ever after that his gospel should be like "a spring of water gushing up to eternal life" (John 4:14). Though we have done our share of making Christian faith seem like stagnant water—which kills—here I attempt to access it as Jesus intended, as the best of fresh and life-giving water.

Then, recall that Jesus's encounter with the Samaritan woman unfolds as a give-and-take conversation between them. Their meeting occurs because Jesus is tired and thirsty, sits down to rest by a well, and the woman comes to draw water. From their shared situation in life, Jesus initiates their conversation by requesting, "Give me a drink." The back-and-forth that follows eventually reaches the point where her questioning prompts Jesus to instruct her in his gospel message, climaxed by identifying himself to her as the Messiah. Her incipient faith response was to wonder if he might indeed be the Promised One. In John's Gospel, the Samaritan woman of five husbands becomes Jesus's first evangelizer—to her own people.

As I will elaborate in the postlude at the end of the book, Jesus's conversation with the Samaritan woman was typical of his pedagogy throughout his public ministry. Most often he began by referring to some life situation or experience of his hearers, taught his gospel into their everyday lives, and then invited them to *living* faith as disciples. Jesus's approach can be summarized as inviting people *from life to Faith to life* (in Faith).

Following this pattern, I begin each chapter by focusing on a particular hunger of the heart that marks our present situation in life. I then ask you (the reader) to pause and reflect on the theme in your own experience, and as if in conversation, at least with yourself and perhaps with God. Turning to experience is not simply to stimulate interest but reflects that this is how God—like Jesus—most often reaches out to us personally. As Karl Rahner proposed, all Christians now need to become "mystics," and the mystical—encountering God's outreach—is primarily through our own human experiences.

Thereafter, the body of each chapter makes proposals of how a "Catholic" spirituality responds to the focused hunger, offering further pauses throughout for reflection on the implications for a life of *living* faith. Toward the end of each chapter, we turn to the hope that its proposals might lend to our hearts. I, then, invite you to make decisions for your own life-in-faith and conclude with some spiritual practice(s) to help satisfy the particular hunger.

For now, I invite you to enter into the dynamic and, rather than skipping the *Pause for Reflection* inserts, stop and engage these experience-focused questions before moving on. If reading in a book group, share your reflections together. As always for disciples of Jesus, the intent of our spirituality is to integrate our lives and Christian faith into *living* faith. Such conversation—with your own experience, with neighbors or with God—will heighten the potential of bringing your life to faith in ways that encourage bringing your faith to life.

CLARIFYING TERMS AND LANGUAGE PATTERNS

Because we focus on the heart/soul throughout this book, its core theme is spirituality. Happily, if surprisingly, spirituality is enjoying a renaissance in our time, now called *postmodern*—as compared to the previous *modern* era (I elaborate later). However, there is little agreement on the meaning of the term *spirituality*. Let me at least clarify what I mean by it here.

We can think about spirituality on two levels, the generic and the specific, or in theory and in practice. So we can ask, what is spirituality as a topic of conversation or study and then what is *my* or *our* spirituality as a personal or communal practice?

In a generic sense, I understand spirituality as *people's sense of relationality with a Transcendent Being and how this relationship shapes the way they live their daily lives.* Following on, a general understanding of Christian spirituality is *a people's sense of relationality with the one and triune God as the foundation of their being, and, empowered by the Holy Spirit, how they nurture this relationship to live as disciples of Jesus within a community of disciples for God's reign in the world.*

Then, when put to work by a particular person or community, their spirituality is *all of the stories and symbols, prayers and practices, patterns and perspectives that they draw upon to nurture their relationality with their Transcendent Being and to have this relationship shape their daily lives.* Following on, when practiced in the life of a Christian person or community, specifically Christian spirituality refers to all *the stories and symbols, perspectives and practices, prayers and patterns that, graced by the Holy Spirit, nurture them to live as disciples of Jesus.* Catholic Christian faith has a particularly rich treasury of such spiritual resources.

Of course, these meanings of *spirituality* are two sides of the same coin; since the specific implements the generic, their distinction often collapses—as they will here—into simply "spirituality." As I unpack them in what follows, I will distinguish when a distinction seems advised.

On another linguistic note, readers will already notice that I often use a plural pronoun to refer to a singular noun, as in "every Christian is to live their faith." This returns to the grammatical pattern of Elizabethan English and has been approved by the U.S. National Council of Teachers of English. My commitment is to promote gender inclusivity while avoiding the awkward "he/she" and "his/her" constructs.

On a similar note, I avoid using male images and pronouns for God, except when quoting the original scriptures. Because human language is never sufficient for God, we simply cannot be fully *inclusive* of all that should be said of the Divine. But surely we can be *expansive*, as the Bible is frequently, beyond male-only imagery for God. For some, this may be a new horizon; I respectfully invite you to consider it. And now, read on!

PART I

CHAPTER 1

God Is

Our Hunger for Life

Only in Tahiti?

I took a layover in Tahiti on my way to Australia to see a little of that lovely island and to break the long journey. Arriving late on Saturday evening, I took myself off to Sunday Mass the next morning. I was blessed to participate in a memorable celebration. The warm hospitality, the joy of the music and singing, the good preaching and prayerful presiding, all with a palpable sense of community, lent a moving experience of liturgy.

At the crowded coffee hour after, I struck up a conversation with a French woman who introduced herself simply as Françoise from Paris. As we chatted, she volunteered that she had been a believer once but is now an agnostic—at best. I gently offered that I was surprised, then, to meet her at Mass. She rejoined, "Oh, I came back to Tahiti hoping that God might find me again." She explained that she had grown up in Tahiti (part of French Polynesia) and remembered this parish for the quality of its liturgy, community spirit, and practice of compassion. She offered, "If God finds me anywhere again, it will likely be here." I'll wager that God did!

OUR ULTIMATE HUNGER?

Our hearts are ever hungry with a multiplicity of desires and needs. It would be daunting to name and address them all. Nor do we need to do so to make the case that Christian faith can be a rich spiritual resource to respond to the daily hungers; to attend to some central ones will make the point. And the authentic fulfillment of any one reverberates to help satisfy others, whereas false satisfaction of one will make the whole symphony sound off key.

In this opening chapter, we wonder if there might be an ultimate hunger beneath the rest, one that prompts and fulfills them all. Put another way, how can we name the source as well as the satisfaction experienced as we fulfill, however partially, our symphony of multiple desires? Aristotle of old proposed *happiness* as our ultimate quest and fulfillment, and many philosophers have agreed since then. One can readily recognize why happiness could name our desired "final end" (Aristotle's term); we focus on it in chapter 3.

The renowned social philosopher Charles Taylor proposes the term *fullness* as the sum total desire of all the hungers of the human heart; I'm taken with his proposal. *Fullness* is a word that *might* say it all, with a sense of being full to overflowing. Taylor goes on to recognize, realistically, that within historical time and by human efforts alone we must ever settle, at best, for "partial" fullness, and yet total fullness remains our ultimate allure.

The hunger for complete fullness can lend a spark of hope that ultimately it may be satisfied, if only in what Taylor well names "time out of time"—eternity. Further, he suggests that reaching for even partial fullness ever requires more than our own efforts; we need some transcendent help and the firm hope that such might be available. Meanwhile, without the possibility of at least partial fullness now, our human condition becomes a cruel joke of empty longings, constantly fooled and frustrated by mirages in a desert-like life.

Taylor recognizes that this question is being raised anew in our time, causing many postmodern people, even very "enlightened" ones, to consider the possibility that there might be some ultimate allure that both causes our hungers and empowers our efforts to satisfy them.

Might it be possible that the pivotal quest that turns all the longings of our hearts—amazingly universal across eras and cultures—is more than just a coincidence?

In this chapter, I propose that our quest for fullness is, in fact, a quest for God as our ultimate horizon, and that only God can completely satisfy the heart's symphony of hungers. In fact, they are implanted in us by divine design. Further, as we will develop in chapter 2, we need not depend on our own efforts alone to satisfy them; we always have the help of "Higher Power." Put more theologically, God is in covenant with us and works through our own hearts' strivings to bring us to partial fulfillment in our time, and this as a foretaste of the fullness that awaits when we finally rest with God in "time out of time."

As the great French philosopher Blaise Pascal (1623–62) said so wisely, "There is a God-shaped hollow in the human heart that nothing else can fill" (popular paraphrase from *Pensées*). Pascal intended "shaped" in both senses: that it is God who crafts the hollow and then fits it exactly for Godself. Pascal realistically recognized that his claim requires a great leap of faith. He proposed that our best "gamble" (his term) is to place the God revealed in Jesus at the center of our lives; even should there be no such God, such faith will help us to fulfill our hearts' desires and live more humanly.

The Psalmist clearly knew something of Pascal's "God-shaped hollow" when they prayed, "O God...I seek you, my soul thirsts for you; my flesh faints for you, as in a dry and weary land where there is no water" (Ps 63:1). So our need for God is dire. For now, let us recognize the reality of our deepest desire for fullness of life, and that much is riding on what we recognize as its source and goal. As alerted in the prelude, our heart longings can lead us aright or lead us astray.

What of Taylor's recognition that our fullness in this life will always be no more than partial? First, we can readily recognize this as true from our own life in the world. Humanly speaking, our hungers are insatiable. Even when some longing feels fulfilled, so many more remain, and moments of great satisfaction soon give way to the desire for more—of whatever. In the most complete of moments, the happiest of times, the greatest successes, the best of friendships, something is still missing or, more likely, remains beyond reach. If nothing else, we know that the passing of time and the coming of death makes every fulfillment relative—for now.

But think about it; if we could achieve complete fullness on this side of eternity, it would become our final end rather than a means to an end. And to make any satisfaction an end in itself can readily become an idol that leads to a "house of slavery" (see Exod 20:2). So fullness is necessarily partial on this side of eternity because, as the Psalmist sang often, only God possesses fullness (Pss 24:1, 50:12, etc.). Likewise, Paul recognized that in Jesus "all the fullness of God was pleased to dwell" (Col 1:19). This was because Jesus made flesh the Divine presence.

John's Gospel has Jesus declare, "I came that they may have life, and have it abundantly" (10:10); some translations have "to the full." Likewise, John the Baptist recognized of Jesus that "from his fullness we have all received, grace upon grace" (1:16). We return to this theme multiple times throughout, recognizing that grace—God's effective love at work in our lives—lends the help we need to strive toward fulfilling any and all of our hungers, and it is catalyzed in abundance by God's work of liberating salvation in Jesus Christ.

Yet, as the Baptist testified, we can receive *from* this fullness while not yet possessing it completely. To pursue as if we can possess it entirely now would lead us to worship a false god and the slavery that ensues. Meanwhile, our partial experiences, when realized as God desires for us, become a foretaste that gives hope along the way and helps us keep on toward our destiny of fullness of life with God.

I propose here, then, that God is the ultimate hunger of our hearts, the source and satisfaction of the fullness we desire. Further, our God takes the initiative, comes looking for us through our lives in the world—as Françoise knew well—inviting and gracing us toward partial fullness now with the promise of the *pleroma* hereafter. As 1 John 4:19 attests, "[God] first loved us"; in other words, God takes the initiative. Meanwhile, all our hungers of the heart can reflect what God desires for us, and when fulfilled according to God' s desire, will move us toward fullness of life, beginning now. For example, our hunger to love and be loved is precisely how God intends us to live, and the more we love as

God intends, the more we realize fullness as human beings. This is the divinely crafted nature of our human hearts.

But of course, this all presumes the conviction that God exists, or, as I prefer to say, that *God Is* (I explain later, this is more in keeping with the biblical way of affirming God's existence). It also presumes that the one true God is "merciful and gracious" and acts with "steadfast love" toward us (Exod 34:6–7), empowering our efforts to satisfy our hearts' desires in ways life-giving for ourselves, others, and the world (chapter 2).

To begin with, however, unless God Is, the hunger for fullness is surely hopeless, a great deception put upon our hearts by some malevolent genie. Ah, but can we be a people of faith that lends hope—even allowing for the doubts that make for faith—in our postmodern and secular world? Can we find sufficient resources to take the gamble, to make the necessary first leap that God Is? Or would this be to jump into the absurd?

PAUSE FOR REFLECTION

- Recall some recent experience that brought fulfillment of some heart's desire for you. What helped toward its satisfaction? Was it entirely by your own efforts or was there "gift" (grace) involved?

- What do *you* think? Would you be wise to settle for partial fullness now—as if there is no hereafter—and to rely entirely on your own efforts to achieve it? Why or why not?

A TOUGHER THAN USUAL TIME FOR FAITH

As I write, the news media are full of new reports about the sex abuse of children, adolescents, and young adults by Catholic clergy—priests and vowed religious. This began to be reported in the 1980s and broke into public awareness in 2002, catalyzed by investigative reporting by the *Boston Globe*. People became aware of the devastation caused by such dreadful abuse in the lives of victims/survivors and their families. Now, just when many thought the Catholic Church was turning a corner and implementing real reforms to punish perpetrators and prevent such crimes from happening, there is a fresh avalanche of tragic reports, many from legal tribunals established by civil authorities. Clearly this is still a dire emergency for the Church and throughout the world.

That some priests and vowed religious, albeit a small minority, have committed such horrendous crimes is a challenge for many people's faith. One can well argue that it need not be so, that the truths and wisdom, symbols and values of Catholic faith, far from being deficient, have simply been betrayed. And it is true that the hierarchical institution of the Church can be distinguished from the rich faith that it carries, and indeed, from the spiritual community of all the baptized disciples of Jesus who make up the Body of Christ in the world. Yet this scandal is a devastating blow to the faith of many Catholics, and especially among our youth and young adults. We will return in chapter 7 to this urgent issue and to strategies to assure that the Church can say "never again" to this tragedy. For now, I note sadly that the clergy sex abuse crisis is a stumbling block for many people's faith, and especially for Catholic Christians.

Here and for now, we focus on the challenges to faith in our contemporary cultural and historical context, one marked in general by a postmodern mentality and described as a secular age. Both postmodernity and secularization are complex realities with many varied facets; here we engage briefly the challenges they pose for knowing that God Is—that is, to faith. Not so long ago in Western cultures, everyone believed because everyone else was a believer, whereas now our culture pushes faith in God to the margins and often off the page. Yet while there are deep contextual challenges to faith—both personally and as a community—there may also be new opportunities, and perhaps for a more chosen and persuaded one. This should not surprise us.

An ancient Christian author named Justin Martyr (100–165) insisted wisely that every culture has "seeds of the word of God," aspects that resonate with and could encourage Christian faith. Conversely, every culture has "weeds" as well as "seeds," features that discourage faith and that faith should help to change. Ours is no exception for both seeds and weeds. This calls for a keen awareness of our cultural context and a give-and-take conversation (rather than one-way pronouncements) between Christian faith and our lives in the world. Indeed, Vatican II called precisely for "a living exchange" between Christian faith and its surrounding cultures (*Gaudium et Spes* 44), recognizing that they can both challenge and enhance each other.

Such exchange is needed because faith and especially Christian faith must always be contextualized—embraced and put to work as a *living* faith within its historical situation and circumstances. So let us briefly review these two contemporary sociocultural phenomena, postmodernity and secularization, and apropos faith in God. Though they work hand in hand, we can set them out separately to heighten awareness of how they both challenge and might encourage faith, albeit a different faith from what seemed inevitable in bygone days.

FROM MODERN TO POSTMODERN AND HOW WE KNOW

Modernity: A Mixed Bag for Faith. As the term implies, *postmodernity* follows on from an era named *modernity*, continuing much of the latter's legacy but reaching beyond it as well. From the interest of faith, we need a brief sense of each. At the outset, note the shift from modernity to postmodernity in daily life. For example, we can recognize the wall phone as modern and the cell phone as postmodern. Then note the myriad other shifts—from post office mail to e-mail, from road signs to GPS, from newspapers to social media, from typewriter to laptop, and so many more. What we are less aware of is that experiencing these developments causes a shift in human consciousness and can affect our mindset, pro and con, even for faith.

As a way of knowing (technically called epistemology) modernity might be dated from the writings of the great philosopher René Descartes (1596–1650) down to about 1970, with its legacy continuing and revising into postmodernity. Descartes's famous dictum, "I think, therefore I am," was a catalyst to place all emphasis on the power of critical reason for knowing—*the* hallmark of modernity. It was to be *critical* as in favoring self-initiated ideas based on reason alone rather than accepting traditional teachings and authorities (e.g., Christian faith and the Church). Modernity was determined to make us independent of any authority outside of the human mind.

This embrace of "free thinking" flowed on into the research methods of modern science, with truth and knowledge based on reasoning alone about empirical data, excluding the affect-laden wisdom that comes from one's own life experiences. As might be expected, many subsequent architects of modernity (Feuerbach, Nietzsche, Marx, Freud) saw critical reason and science as happily making religious faith obsolete, having no scientific warrant and being simply an old superstition, inimical to human progress.

But critical reason and modern science did not deliver the panacea as promised. While modernity was strong in rational knowing, it was weak in practical wisdom for life. Indeed, it deteriorated into a technical rationality, concerned only for production, with no consideration of the consequences. Many of its critics now argue that its lack of moral compass has brought us to the brink of nuclear Armageddon and to rampant environmental destruction. In part, this is because modernity's theoretical reasoning was incapable of providing a practical and compelling social ethic—having banned all spiritually grounded ones. And when free thinking combines with the limitless profit motive of modern capitalism, the common good is easily forgotten; this can be disastrous for all but a small minority.

Of course, modernity had its huge assets; just think of the benefits that have come from modern medical research, and then add the improvements in transportation, communication, technology, and just about every other feature of modern life. However, its championing of critical reason to the exclusion of the affective and experiential—always the prime sources of the spiritual—made it inimical to faith. Indeed, many "modern" people reject faith as incompatible with science as if needing to choose between them rather than embracing both as simply different ways of knowing.

Modernity also discouraged faith by intentionally avoiding the great ultimate questions of life that ever beset the human heart, like:

"Why is there anything rather than nothing?"; or "Why am I here?"; or "Does my life have any meaning and purpose?" Such "why" questions always remain pressing for us, though prompted more by our emotions and hungers of the heart than by reason alone. While the critical reasoning and science of modernity were brilliant at explaining *what* is in the world and *how* it works, they had no response to the ultimate questions of *why*.

This being said, there was an asset for Christian faith in the critical reasoning of modernity and that continues into postmodernity. Its emphasis on critical thinking actually encouraged more discerning believers—beyond "blind faith"—and strongly encouraged a deeper social consciousness. When one of its greatest philosophers, Immanuel Kant (1724–1804), issued the clarion call "dare to think," the critical reasoning that ensued reached into social structures and cultural practices as well, helping to unmask many of our worst oppressions and injustices. Indeed, modernity launched the whole quest for human rights. This new social consciousness prompted Christians to uncover what heretofore were like recessive genes in our scriptures and traditions, life-giving seeds for social justice that had been largely overlooked or left uncultivated. Catholic social teaching owes much to the critical reasoning of modernity.

Postmodernity: Atheists and Theists on Common Ground. Because of modernity's limited epistemology, many contemporary authors began to wonder if we need to broaden our ways of knowing beyond the purely rational and scientific, engaging the heart/soul and people's lived experience. Likewise, we need a higher motivation for social ethics than a purely reasoned one if we are to promote the common good of all—perhaps a spiritual grounding? Beginning with the 1970s, such hesitancies about modernity's overemphasis on critical reason began to gather under the broad umbrella of postmodernity.

Postmodernity inherits the assets of modernity, and yet, with a broadened epistemology, is far more open to "the spiritual." Many postmodern authors see social value in a "well-reasoned" religious faith, that is, not based simply on institutional authority or tradition but uniting affective and rational ways of knowing for faith that is embraced by personal conviction. Many postmodern voices see value in a spiritual perspective, even in the public realm, convinced that spirituality can lend higher grounding for a social ethic and deeper motivation to embrace it. The spiritual always encourages a more holistic way of knowing that includes but reaches beyond critical reasoning to engage people's emotions and lived experience; this can be more humanizing for all.

In sum, many postmodern authors show renewed interest in "the spiritual" for its potential to promote both our personal and common good. One popular expression of this sentiment is the oft heard claim, especially by millennials, "I'm spiritual," albeit often adding "but not religious." Yet this could be a new opportunity for Christian faith, and precisely because of the heart appeal of its spiritual resources. Let us focus, then, on the potential asset of postmodernity for faith, and maybe even for being religious as a way to grow spiritually. Here I will highlight one big asset (more to come throughout): postmodernity places atheists and theists on common ground. Let me explain!

First, remember that many of the great philosophers of the modern era assumed that faith and religion would disappear with the triumph of reason and science. As people became more "enlightened," they would dismiss religious faith as simply the superstition of their grandparents. But this "subtraction theory," as Charles Taylor calls it, with science and reason subtracting religion out of people's lives, has not transpired. According to the *Pew Research on Global Religion*, some 85 percent of the world's population still claims some kind of religious faith.

Following on, instead of thinking of atheism as an enlightened attitude and belief as based on ignorance or lack of critical reasoning, postmodernity is more aware that both positions are what Taylor calls "takes" on life in the world. In other words, both belief and unbelief are more chosen perspectives now, with neither one being any more reasonable or enlightened than the other. Indeed, while the great architects of modernity were avowed atheists (Feuerbach, Marx, Nietzsche, Freud, etc.), many leading voices of postmodernity (Gadamer, Ricœur, Levinas, Taylor, etc.) are critical believers.

So it seems that theists and atheists are on common ground now, making either stance a deliberate choice. Both are a reasoned and emotive gamble, and I wager that whichever people claim, they have their moments of doubt. For theists, the great stumbling block, as always, is all the *suffering* in the world (a topic we return to many times); for atheists, it is all the *gift* (grace) and *mystery* that we can encounter in daily life.

An older atheist friend of mine, who long ago claimed to have given up on finding true love, recently found himself totally enamored of a wonderful woman and, to his great surprise, she feels likewise for him. When he told me of his new love, I offered, "Oh, what a gift from God." Whereupon, he objected strongly, as I expected he would, to my God-talk. Pretending an apology, I offered faintly, "Yea, I'm sure 'tis only chemistry." There was a long pause and then my atheist friend said pensively, "No, I don't think so," and said no more—nor did I. I'll wager, however, that he was having doubts about his atheism.

For both belief and unbelief, postmodernity places atheists and theists on common ground.

CHALLENGES TO FAITH IN OUR SECULAR AGE

Secularization. The cumulative effect of the modern and postmodern mentality was to lead us into what social scientists now dub a *secular age*; as the title suggests, this era is far more *con* than *pro* faith.

Commentators use the terms *secular age* and *secularization* in varied ways. First, contemporary societies have become secularized with the typical separation of church and state. While this is a wise constitutional arrangement, it also makes religion less influential in the public square compared to traditional societies. Second, secularization is often used to describe the widespread falling off of religious practice, especially in the Western democracies. We must be cautious, however, not to presume that when people no longer attend church (or synagogue, etc.) that they have lost their faith. As the research of religion sociologist Grace Davie verifies, many contemporary people are "believers without belonging," meaning that many still believe in God, pray regularly, and have faith shape their daily lives and decisions—even though they don't go to church.

Then, as the great scholar and social commentator Charles Taylor elaborates, the most challenging aspect of secularization is that the conditions for faith have shifted from times and cultures that encouraged belief to what is now commonly agreed to be a secular age—at least in Western cultures. We have shifted from what legendary sociologist Max Weber (1864–1920) called an *enchanted* age when faith suffused the culture to a *disenchanted* one that makes belief an option—at best—and often against the cultural tide. Faith no longer comes by osmosis from the surrounding culture; indeed, it requires resistance to the secularizing influences of our age. This is a still relatively new phenomenon for us.

There was a time in Western culture—not so long ago, really—when everyone believed because the culture expected and mediated belief; faith was prompted and expected by the context. Atheism did not become an option for other than an intellectual elite until the mid-nineteenth century. So, in cultures suffused by faith, people embraced it as a taken-for-granted posture. While Taylor takes 1500 as a safe marker of an enculturated faith, I experienced it growing up in my Irish village of the 1950s.

There, God was at the center of village life. God-talk suffused our daily language patterns; among the frequent phrases were "thanks be to God" and "with the help of God." To miss Sunday Mass brought social opprobrium. Even the weather was attributed to God. A common remark was "'Tis a grand day, thank God." In that village, faith was expected, came by enculturation, and without much conscious choice. But such faith-encouraging cultures have all but disappeared in the West, even in that Irish village.

Now, Taylor argues credibly, our secular age proposes a viable alternative to faith, what he calls "exclusive humanism." It is *exclusive* in that it eschews any reference to the transcendent and *humanism* in that it intends human well-being but relies entirely on human agency. This is encouraged precisely by the achievements of modernity and postmodernity that can tempt us to think that we can fend fine for ourselves without any need for God. For Taylor, such humanism reflects an "immanent frame" or outlook on life—as if *this* is all there is and that all depends on *us*. This contrasts with a transcendent perspective that looks to an ultimate horizon for meaning and purpose, community and help—God.

Further, our secular culture and its immanent stance toward life encourages people to become what Taylor calls "buffered selves," living as if self-sufficient, while pursuing our own personal authenticity and flourishing as isolated automatons. Such conditions, of course, could encourage the most enslaving idol of all—a *selfie god*—resulting in its own "house of slavery." It is also antithetical to the Christian emphasis on community and our being responsible for and to our neighbor.

Yet, an *immanent frame* can appear to be a worthy alternative to a *transcendent* one, enabling people to live fulfilling lives as they might from a posture of faith. No more or less than believers, exclusive humanists settle for partial fulfillment of their hearts' desires. But instead of looking to some transcendent realm for meaning and help, people with an immanent outlook can appear to find as much from their own and the culture's resources.

Secularization, then, tends to push faith to the margins in contemporary culture. Instead of this being simply from antipathy to faith, however, the challenges can be occasioned by our technological and scientific advances, for example, in medicine, transportation, and communications. Such progress has simply changed *the cultural conditions of belief*, no longer favoring faith as they once did. I share a personal example to illustrate.

When I was about four years old, I developed pneumonia. My dad was away, my mom didn't drive—even if she had the car, we were seven miles from the nearest doctor, and, at that time in rural Ireland, without phone service. To take a sick child out on a cold winter's night in a horse and buggy was not an option. Nor was getting to a doctor the guarantee of a cure; my parents had lost a little girl to pneumonia some years prior, even with medical attention.

As she told the story so many times, my mom, in desperation, knelt down by my bedside and told God that she was not leaving her post until my fever broke. I fell asleep, she fell asleep, and when we awoke, my fever had broken. She declared it a miracle and told the story a thousand times thereafter—making it part of the canon of our family's faith story.

The point to highlight is that her grandchildren would be highly unlikely to do what their grandmother did and simply because *they would not need to*. Instead, they would pop their child in the SUV, be in the village in ten minutes, get a course of modern antibiotics, and the kid would be running about in a few days. In other words, we don't need God the way we used to, or so we can be lulled to presume. And think of all the myriad advances in medicine, communications, transportation, and so on, that have helped, intentionally or not, to push God and faith to the periphery of people's lives—and leaving families with no such faith story to tell.

By comparison and not so long ago, life was far more precarious than now, causing people to feel more keenly the need for God. There were rampant plagues and common diseases for which there were no cures, natural disasters with no social systems of rescue, and a constant fear of plunder and pillage by some marauding enemy.

That still "enchanted" world was suffused by otherworldly spirits, both friendly and malevolent. As Taylor elaborates, then the *self* was more "porous" than "buffered," meaning that people were more communal and open to the spiritual realm. Such conditions made the felt need for God's favor and protection all the more intense. Now, though we still have deep threats to our well-being, we presume upon our advanced sciences, social structures, and psychological therapies to alleviate them, while angels and devils are now fun costumes for Halloween. In fact, we need God as much as ever, but helplessness and fear have receded as disposing conditions for faith.

HOPE FOR FAITH IN A SECULAR AGE

Against the grain and admitting that they can be challenges as well, I can think of at least three *assets* for a contemporary faith in this secular age: (a) it encourages a personally chosen faith, (b) it invites us to expand our imaging of God, and (c) it highlights that faith must be free and freeing—an empowering choice as God intends.

(a) *A Chosen Faith*: As suggested already, faith during the enchanted age from which we have emerged was largely by enculturation and not much by personal choice. Integral to such cultural formation was the absolute authority invested in the Church, whose leaders employed generous measures of both fear and promise—hell and heaven—to encourage people in the ways of faith. This was largely a "blind" faith that entailed little critical discernment or personal choosing on the part of most believers. Such faith has a scarce future in our secular age.

Now faith must be and can be by personal choice that reaches conviction through critical reflection and from one's own experiences in the world. I use *critical* here not at all as negative but as a process of personal discernment that entails choice and encourages one's own conviction. As we will elaborate in chapter 9 (focused on faith), people need to come to faith by conviction that is persuaded by sound reasoning, by the affections of the heart, and that makes sense to their own life experiences.

And though rooted in personal conviction, faith for our time cannot be a choice in isolation as if by a "buffered self." Instead, it must always be located within some community of conversation and needs to be inspired and informed by the faith choices of companions on the journey. Christian faith, especially, is always communal.

Following on, such chosen faith must be contextualized in the sense of being located—incarnated—within its sociocultural context. Christian faith for sure must be a *living* faith that shapes how people engage in the world. For example, to love God by loving our neighbor as ourselves cannot be done in a vacuum but must be realized in the praxis of daily life. In putting Christian faith to work, then, we must critically discern what it asks of us in any particular time and place—in the historical contexts of our lives. Nothing less than such a chosen, discerned, and contextual faith is likely to flourish in our secular age. While the seeds of faith can be sown by family and community, our secular age can actually encourage our personal convictions and be all the more likely to promote a chosen and contextualized faith.

Undoubtedly, coming to and living such faith can also be a great challenge. Yet there is ample evidence that more and more people in our secular age are becoming disillusioned with a purely immanent frame, recognizing it as bankrupt by way of the longings of the human heart and the felt need to make meaning out of life. As Taylor summarizes, it can render "a terrible flatness in the everyday," with a felt loss of meaning, without effective symbols to mark the milestones, and taking little joy in the ordinary. Likewise, people increasingly experience the quest for individual fullness for oneself alone as both hollow and self-defeating. In spite of our secular age—or maybe because of it—there is a growing felt need for faith in God, and in a God of loving care who partners with us in seeking to fulfill all the hungers of our hearts.

(b) *Expanding our God Image*: This opportunity for contemporary faith is prompted by what Charles Taylor describes as a shift in human consciousness *from cosmos to universe*. The old cosmos perspective proposed a manageable worldview that we could imagine and even localize; we could think of heaven *up there*, earth *down here*, and the nether world *down below*. Sure, we could see the sun, the moon, and the stars, but meanwhile God presided *over all* this firmament, and the Psalmist could imagine that the Lord "looked down from his holy height, from heaven the Lord looked at the earth" (Ps 102:19).

By contrast, we now know that our own galaxy, the Milky Way, has billions of planets. Then beyond ours, scientists claim that there are millions more galaxies, with billions more planets, some whose light has been traveling toward us since the dawn of the universe (some 13.82 billion years ago is scientists' present estimate) and has yet to reach us. And what, we can well wonder, lies on the far side of the furthest planet of the last galaxy? We cannot even begin to imagine, much less comprehend!

Yet people of faith must try to imagine that our God—as if particularly *ours* who live on this little speck of a planet—is the originating Creator that causes this whole universe to come into being and maintains its continuing evolution across eons of ages, past and future, into eternal time. Challenged now to "think universe" in order to think God, it is understandable that many contemporary people try not to think about it at all.

Positively, faith for today helps us to recognize that our typical imaging of God is *always* too small. As the spiritual mystic Meister Eckhart (1260–1327) proposed long ago and is as true today, even as we try to conceive of God, we need a "God beyond God." In other words, it is imperative that we remember God's utter transcendence and that our human imaging of the Divine always falls infinitely short. Though daunting, this invites us to recognize that our word *God* is simply another name for Ultimate Mystery.

While the Bible says that we are made in the Divine likeness, even believers can be tempted to make God in *our* own likeness—with an image we can manage to imagine. An old favorite is of the puppeteer God who pulls strings if we ask nicely and behave well, and may send destruction if we don't. Another favored false image is of "God in a box," to be taken out for particular occasions (maybe weddings and wakes) but kept far from the everyday.

The most prevalent false image is of God as a benevolent old man with a white beard who wishes us well but generally leaves us alone; this is the dominant Divine image for some 75 percent of American adults. More dangerous by far, of course, are the angry and vindictive gods who demand that devotees kill or punish others in their name. We can say the same for gods that demean or diminish any person and for any reason; they are false to the one true God, even if proposed by faith communities or people who claim to be of faith. And most of our religious language and images for God are male; how limiting!

An asset, then, of our secular age that invites us to think universe beyond cosmos, is that it prompts us to imagine more expansively of God. Chapter 2 will address this issue directly, noting that the Bible offers multiple images of the Divine, implying that none can fully suffice. This encourages us to remember that God is always infinitely more than *our* images. Keeping this in mind makes it less likely that we will fashion our "God" in our own image and likeness and instead "let God be God."

(c) *Faith as Free and Freeing*: Our secular age that discourages more than encourages faith can be a challenge but also an asset that highlights our freedom before God, even in whether or not to believe in God. Dovetailing here is the mystery of our God-given power of choice and freedom to choose. For if God *Is*, and is as munificent as believers claim, then God is the One who makes us to be free agents in our lives. It would be a violation of our divinely granted dignity for God to simply program us for faith, *forcing* us to believe. Because we have intelligence, affections, and will, we must decide this matter for ourselves, albeit with the empowering but not overpowering promptings of God's grace.

33

So while God constantly searches us out and desires that we live with faith for our own good and the common good of all, there should be just enough warrant to believe. To make faith too patent and prompted would violate our human freedom, making us automatons rather than covenant partners with God. So faith in our secular age is far more of a free choice than it was in an *enchanted* world.

Following on and anticipating a little the God we will propose in this text, good faith is emancipatory for people, setting us free and empowering us to become the best people that we can be—for ourselves and others. Instead of a burden or a cross to carry, or a set of dos and don'ts that can spoil the fun of life, faith in the one true God can bring about our *liberating salvation*. Faith that is freely chosen and liberating is all the more likely to appeal in our secular age.

Françoise Was Right. Whether focusing on the assets or challenges to faith in our postmodern and secular age, our yearning for fullness and all the symphony of hungers it represents remains. We know in our gut that this cannot be simply an illusion or without purpose. Precisely because our hearts' desires cannot be satisfied by our own efforts—as in an immanent perspective—they still have the potential, proverbially, to bring us to our knees.

Even should we try to live within an immanent frame and by an exclusive humanism—as if *this* is all there is and all depends on *us*—signs of God's grace and presence continue to inbreak our daily lives (like my atheist friend who fell in love again). Likewise, the great *why* questions continue to press upon us, no matter how much we try to set them aside. This is as much true in our secular age as in any previous. To put it colloquially, God is always "up to something" in our lives. Likewise, and as my Tahiti friend Françoise knew in her heart, God ever continues to come looking for us. In a wise saying attributed to the Christian theologian Erasmus (1466–1536), "bidden and unbidden, God is present." And always remaining is Blaise Pascal's portrayal of that God-shaped hollow in the human heart that nothing else can fill.

And yet, even as we recognize the potential for faith in our postmodern and secular age, how demanding it is to be a person of Christian faith in our time and place; can we rise to the challenge? From all that has been said already, clearly our first and fundamental starting point is to embrace the conviction that *God Is*, opting for a transcendent rather than an immanent frame—the two clear choices now before people as never before. But do we have sufficient ground, good reasons of heart and mind, to make what Pascal well named "the leap of faith?" Let us see!

PAUSE FOR REFLECTION

- Name some personal experiences or sentiments that challenge your faith. What helps *you* to meet the challenge?

- Try to trace how you came by your own images and convictions regarding God. What aspects of your image of God seem true and life-giving? What might you need to reimagine?

REASONS AND FEELINGS ENOUGH TO SAY GOD IS

Some Old Arguments. Many of the "old atheists" at least saw some value in religious faith and as arising from the hungers of the heart. So, for Marx, religion reflected a cry of protest by an oppressed people; for Freud, it was our longing for a truly loving father. By contrast, for those now dubbed the "new atheists" (Dawkins, Hitchens, Harris, etc.), faith is simply stupid; plainly put, a reasonable and enlightened person cannot possibly believe. The God they reject, of course, is far too small, though belief in "him" allegedly causes all the wars, injustice, and suffering in the world. These new atheists continue to reflect the outdated attitude of modernity that education and enlightenment will put an end to such superstition.

By contrast, and as noted already, many postmodern authors are themselves believers and see renewed social as well as personal value in religious faith. My proposal here is that if life is to offer any possibility of even partial fullness and some fulfillment of the other desires within it, then the first foundation is to be able to say with conviction that God Is. Otherwise, we are faced with a dire emptiness rather than potential fullness. So let us sample some good reasons of *head* and *heart*, for faith that God Is.

First, why favor the phrase "God Is"? Simply put, it is a more adequate statement than saying "there is *a* God." The latter can give the impression that God is just one more thing among the many others that exist. Instead, God's "Is-ness" is the ultimate source and energy of all that is. Why there is anything rather than nothing is because God Is. God is not simply one being or the highest being but Being itself. Note the echo here with Moses's experience before the burning bush (check out Exod 3:1–15). He heard God declare the ultimate divine name as "I AM WHO I AM" (Exod 3:14). While scholars debate the translation of the Hebrew there, it reflects God's own bold statement of "I AM," inviting us to believe that God Is. Now, why might we so choose?

Since the dawn of history, people have had a heartfelt sense of Divine Presence and precisely because they experienced as much in their daily lives. Their felt sense of the Divine was expressed most often by belief in a pantheon of gods, usually associated with the powers of nature. Typically, too, there were good gods and bad ones, reflecting people's experiences of fortune and misfortune in life. And all the gods needed to be appeased in order to wring blessings from them. Recall the array of gods and goddesses that the ancient Greeks and Romans worshipped and tried to please as the transcendent ground of their existence.

It was, then, an amazing breakthrough in human consciousness when the ancient people of Israel began to insist that there is but one God: "You shall have no other gods before me," and "Hear, O Israel: The LORD is our God, the LORD alone" (Deut 5:7; 6:4). Second, the Israelites reached the core conviction that this one true God is "merciful and gracious" and acts with "steadfast love" (Exod 34:6–7) toward humankind within history, regardless of how pleasing we are or the sacrifices we offer. In other words, theirs is a personal God who shows unbounded care for people. And third, the God of the Israelites works in covenant partnership with humankind for our own well-being. These three convictions—God as One, as Personal Caregiver, and as Partner with us—were mega breakthroughs in the human conception of God and are foundational to imaging God as fully revealed in Jesus.

But revelation aside for now (our focus in chapter 2), for the first great instance of reasoned belief in God we turn to the ancient Greek philosophers. Aristotle is their best spokesperson for the conviction that God Is and as One. He based his rationale on what he saw as five self-evident principles from creation, all pointing to God's existence, oneness, and the source of all that is. Aristotle's reasoning was rearticulated by St. Thomas Aquinas (1225–74), perhaps the greatest Christian theologian of all time. Aquinas called them the *quinque viae*, the "five ways" to prove that God Is. At least for some, they can still be persuasive, and not by reason alone; they respond to our heart's hunger to make sense of all that exists and our lives within it.

Aristotle's (and Aquinas's) first and primary proof is from *causality*. The self-evident logic here is that all things that exist must have a *cause*; nothing can give itself existence. Therefore, there must be an uncaused first *Cause*—God. The second is from the amazing *design* that we find in creation. Even something as insignificant as a leaf reflects intelligent design, and this is magnified in the enormous complexity throughout creation. Therefore, all creation must have a purposeful *Designer*. Third, everything that exists is *contingent* in the sense that it does not need to exist. But then there must be something prior to all creation that is the necessary *Existent* and that brings to be all that is otherwise contingent. Fourth, all of creation is in constant *motion*, epitomized in the complex movement of those myriad planets. But nothing that is inherently static can place itself in motion, so there must be a prime *Mover*. Lastly, creation is full of different *grades* of beauty, truth, and goodness; this requires that there be some ultimate standard of *Perfection*.

As the reader will note, these five arguments for God's existence really come down to the two from causality and design. This chair I am sitting on could not possibly have fallen together by accident; it clearly needed a furniture maker who first designed and then made it—though it is not a very elegant chair. But how inestimably more complex is the working of the human eyes you use to see these words on the page, and then the functioning of your mind that can read and understand them, and cycle onward to make judgments and decisions about what you are reading. So we can well take our own very existence and complex design as proof positive of an ultimate Creator and Designer—whom we name God.

For many, this ancient reasoning can still be compelling for believing that God Is. However, many subsequent philosophers and great minds have offered what they consider to be even more persuasive reasons while appealing to the heart's hunger to make sense out of life. For example, the moral code that all normal human beings find within themselves lends evidence for some (e.g., the philosopher Immanuel Kant) that God exists as our internal Lawgiver. Indeed, they argue, good and evil, truth and falsehood have no foundation or measure without the existence of God.

Some say they experience God's existence just by the intuitive sense they have of a "presence" to their consciousness—that we are never entirely alone. It would seem that St. Paul was appealing to this argument when speaking to his more philosophical listeners in Athens. He suggested that God "is not far from each one of us. For 'In him we live and move and have our being'; as even some of your own poets have said, 'For we too are his offspring'" (Acts 17:27–28).

Reaching on with this line of persuasion, recall first that each person is unique; no one else has ever existed that is exactly like you or I. Yet every person has in varying degrees (we are differently abled) the functioning of the human mind, and typically with an ability not only to think but to think about our thinking—reviewing how well we are doing it. Such ability for reflective consciousness that is yet possessed uniquely by each one of us surely cannot be explained by the physical functioning of our brain tissues alone. So our very uniqueness as human beings and yet the potential of our thinking and our ability to reach into a limitless horizon of thought all suggest our common source in what theologian Paul Tillich called "the Ground of Being."

Indeed, such turning to our own consciousness, with its concomitant appeal to our hearts to find life meaningful and worthwhile, is perhaps my own favored way of recognizing—and it is as much recognition as cognition—that God Is. In sum: I know in the marrow bone of my being that my life *has* meaning and purpose, and that this is not just of my own making but a gift from Giftgiver. If God is not, then my life is absurd; but I know in my heart of hearts that I am not absurd, so it must be that God Is.

"Rumors of God" in Mystical Experiences. Following on, there is renewed recognition now that we come to know that God Is in heartfelt mystical encounters; these are through real life experiences of God's loving outreach to our lives. Note that the Israelites of old never set out to rationally *prove* the existence of God; they took this as a given from their experiences as a people of God's presence to them. Their conviction was not that they found God, but that God took the initiative and found them to become God's own chosen people. My Tahiti friend Françoise was in a long biblical tradition in hoping that God might find her again—and through her experience in a faith community.

Echoing this sentiment in recent times, the great Catholic theologian Karl Rahner (1904–84) proposed that postmodern people are more likely to come to faith in God by the mystical than the rational, in other words, by experiences of God's presence in the midst of life and how they move us emotionally. Addressing contemporary Christians, Rahner wrote, "In the days ahead, you will either be a mystic or nothing at all." Our side of the partnership requires us to open our hearts and be alert for the divine Presence, often encountered in the ordinary and everyday, though climatic moments surely have heightened potential.

So what might be the "rumors of God" heard through human experience? Well, they are myriad—like my atheist friend who was mystified by his falling in love again and finding it reciprocated. Such experiences can range from birth to death and everything in between. I've heard parents tell of the first time that they held their newborn child in their arms and having something of a mystical experience that they could not explain by reason alone. Likewise, I recall a dying friend, who was never famous for his piety, tell me, "I'm going home to God." He said it with such unshakeable confidence that I could not but believe him— and in God's love and mercy for us all.

Again, drawing on the work of Charles Taylor, I suggest three categories of the mystical in our lives. First, we all have experiences of times when we are keenly aware of *our own agency*. This is the sense of having a hand in our destiny, that we can consciously shape our lives in the world. This is unique to our human estate; we are the only ones in creation with the ability to be not simply the creatures of our circumstances but their reflective creators as well. We can assume, of course, that we do all by our own efforts alone. Yet in the midst of our chosen actions, we can have a mystical sense that our agency somehow participates in divine agency.

Then, echoing Kant above, experiences of *our ethical discernment* can be mystical, especially when it causes us to act boldly in a noble cause. The fact is that we *can* reach beyond our instincts or base drives or self-interests and make altruistic decisions on a higher plane and with generous motives. That we can do so lends a feeling that we are participating in a higher source of morality than what Kant called a philosophical "imperative." We can experience the sense that in doing good we are doing the will of God.

Third, our *aesthetic capacity* can also lend an experience of the mystical. This can be through the art we create or our experiencing the art of others. In exercising our own creativity and ability for beauty, or recognizing that of other artisans, we can experience a kind of partnership with an ultimate Creator—with beauty unlimited.

Likewise, our aesthetic experiences of nature and creation can be mystical, turning our hearts to God. This is surely what prompted Paul to write, "Ever since the creation of the world [God's] eternal power and divine nature, invisible though they are, have been understood and seen through the things he has made" (Rom 1:20). Or we hear the Psalmist constantly singing of God's self-evident presence in creation, with the whole created order attesting to God's handiwork (see Pss 19:1–6; 98:8, etc.).

You will likely add to these categories from your own mystical experiences. Like when we encounter great love and generosity, or mercy and forgiveness, or courage in difficult times, or moments of celebration and recreation, or of hope in the midst of suffering, and the list goes on. Indeed, there are myriad possibilities of mystical moments in our daily lives, and often in very subtle, barely noticeable (unless we are alert) ways. Check out the story of Elijah in 1 Kings 19:9–12. Notice that his experience of God's presence was not in the storm, nor in the earthquake, nor in the inferno, but in "a sound of sheer silence" (v. 12; the NAB translation has "a tiny whispering sound").

One of my most memorable mystical experiences came at a very unlikely moment—in disciplining my then three-year-old son, Teddy. The little guy looked so pitiful as he protested his innocence and my cruelty on what I had just designated the "time out" chair. Looming over him, I wondered if I was doing the right thing at all, and how I would love not to be meting out "consequences" to my precious three-year-old son.

I clung to the logic of the simple facts: Ted was acting up—and out. I gave him ample warning to cease or face consequences; he continued; his disobedience had to be offset. A quiet time-out seemed like good restorative justice for rambunctious behavior. Such reasoning, however, was of limited solace to my feelings. The trauma was heightened in that this was my first time to inflict such a consequence and Ted's first to receive one from me. That he now named me the meanest daddy in the whole wide world made me shudder—would he ever love me again? Then suddenly, like a bolt from the blue, I had this overwhelming sense of both *loving Ted* and of *being loved by God* myself.

I felt intensely the deepest love for my little son at a depth I'd rarely reached before. I was consumed with empathy and solidarity with him for having to suffer the consequences of his wrong actions— been there, done that. I dearly wished it did not have to be this way but also knew that my discipline was my love at work, even as I longed for the minute to be over and to take him in my arms.

Then, as I experienced my *loving Ted*, I had a sensation of *being loved* myself by God, and that God's love for me was so much more than mine for Ted. I had a bodily felt sense of God's love for both of us and, indeed, for all people. In that instant, I knew without a doubt that my feelings of love, empathy, compassion, forgiveness, solidarity, and more toward Ted were the same but infinitely amplified in God's sentiment toward me. My loving gaze upon Ted was only a faint flicker of how God was looking upon both of us.

At the end of Teddy's time out, I could not wait to pick him up in my arms for a great hug; to my surprise—and relief—he was longing for the same. We held each other in a deep embrace, his little head nestled beneath my chin and his arms wrapped around my neck. Well into my fifties (I got a late start in parenting), after many years as a theologian and religious educator, I knew as if for the first time, and in the marrow bone of my being, that God Is—and is in love with us all.

HOPE FOR OUR HEARTS

Since the beginning of time, people have had their deep hungers of the heart; they come with our human estate. At the outset of this chapter, I proposed *fullness* as subsuming all the human hungers that we experience and likewise their fulfillment. It is like the *table* of the diamond, that broadest facet at the top that is the main point of entrance and exit of light and enhances the radiance of all the other facets.

Similarly, down through history, people have looked to a transcendent realm of some kind for help with satisfying their hearts' desires. They seem to have known instinctively that we need more than our own efforts to satisfy them, that nothing short of the Divine can resource the fullness for which we long. And this is still true; for all of our self-sufficiency and claims to be postmodern, all of our hungers, singly or combined toward fullness, are a cruel joke—unless God Is.

Yet, as seen in this chapter, many people of postmodern mentality who embrace this secular age, for the first time in human history have shifted hope for fulfilling their desires away from a transcendent source. They look solely to human efforts and agency in negotiating the vicissitudes of life and satisfying their hearts' desires. Such an exclusive humanism can even enliven people's sense of responsibility for our personal and common well-being. It can fare fine—as long as everything is going well. However, it can also land us in the ultimate idolatry of the self as its own god and the slavery of self-sufficiency. And in difficult times, such functional atheism can come up empty, whereas faith in a God of kindness and mercy can hold out hope, even in the worst of circumstances, precisely because the outcome does not depend on our human efforts alone.

The intent of this chapter is to propose that even as the sense of a transcendent realm recedes in our sociocultural context, which often favors an immanent worldview instead, we can still find compelling reasons—of both mind and heart—to say that God Is. This is the first step in opening up the possibility that all the hungers within our quest for fullness might be fulfilled, partially for now and fully in God's eternal presence, and that we need not depend solely on our own efforts. What a hope for our hearts—in the high times, low times, and the everyday.

So being able to say that God Is offers seeds of hope that the hungers of the heart might not be self-delusional but instead be implanted by the God who Is, and in order to draw us to Godself. Perhaps, too, God is ever ready to lend us the help we need along the way—what we name by grace. And might the partial fulfillment of the hungers of our hearts now be a foretaste—an aperitif—of eternal fullness with God.

Note that I pose these conclusions as tentative for now. Being able to say that God Is, is only a first step toward the hope of fulfilling our human desire for fullness. So much depends on the question, "What kind of a God is this God who Is?"

For example, what if God is totally unconcerned about humankind and indifferent to the affairs of human history? Indeed, this was Aristotle's perspective. While his five "proofs" convinced him of God's existence and oneness, he conceived of God as totally removed from and uninvolved in human history. For Aristotle, God designed and made everything, got all the stars and planets moving (as Prime Mover), and then threw creation out into eternity, and "went home" to heaven, leaving us to our own devices. For Aristotle—and many philosophers after him, often named "Deists"—God exists, but is totally unconcerned with human history. Such a God has no interest in the desires of our hearts, much less of aiding their fulfillment.

So, while hope for the hungers of our hearts begins with being convinced that God Is, this is not enough; it all depends on the kind of a God who Is, and how and who this God is *for us*. Suggesting the theme of chapter 2, we need to now ask, *Who is this God who Is?* Does God actively love and favor us and empower our efforts to live into fullness as human persons?

This comes down to whether or not we can ascribe to God two crucial attributes we noted in the faith of the ancient Israelites—beyond their belief in God as One. First, is ours a personal God who is "merciful and gracious," acting with "steadfast love" toward us; second, does our God empower our efforts to fulfill our hearts' desires—or are we all on our own?

For if God is not *for us* and *with us* with loving favor, then, again, our hungers are self-deluded and will ever bring us toward emptiness rather than fullness. On the other hand, if we can trust that God is the loving Source of our desires and empowers their fulfillment, then we can engage all the hungers of the heart with hope. When pursued according to God's desires for us and with God's help to achieve them, all our heart-hungers can bring us toward the fullness that ultimately can be found only in God. And our hungers being even partially fulfilled here can lend hope that our restless hearts will, as St. Augustine longed, eventually rest forever in God.

PAUSE FOR REFLECTION

- Drawing upon both head and heart, reason and feelings, what might be *your* most convincing sources for believing that God Is?

- Pause and recall some mystical experiences that have come your way. Can you trust that God is their originating Source? What kind of God do those experiences suggest?

SPIRITUAL PRACTICE: REVIEW THE DAY WITH GOD

Every day has the potential for mystical experiences that can lend a sense of God's effective presence—grace—to our lives. Most often they are subtle: a kind word, a hug, a smile, a sunrise, an unearned insight, a too-big coincidence. Yet in the routine and busyness of the everyday, we can easily not notice and let such God-moments pass us by.

Even if we do, we can recall them at day's end, renewing our sense of God's presence throughout the day, which might make us a little more alert the following day (we are all slow learners). To this end, spiritual writers in the Ignatian tradition (from St. Ignatius of Loyola, 1491–1556) recommend the practice of an "examen of consciousness" and usually to be done at day's end. The intent is to look back over the day with God as partner, and to recognize how and where God's grace was at work, how God's Spirit was prompting, and how well we responded.

We can unfold an *examen* as five particular moments:

- Quiet down and get comfortable; breathe deeply; become aware of your breathing.
- Remind yourself that you are in God's presence; thank God for the gift of the day.
- Ask for the grace to see the day as God saw it.
- Review the day with God as conversation partner, recognizing the God-moments and also what was not of God. Discern how well or poorly you responded to the promptings of the Spirit.
- End with a prayer of thanksgiving and repentance— as needed. The Lord's Prayer well expresses both sentiments.

FOR FURTHER READING

Kreeft, Peter, and Ronald Tacelli. "Twenty Arguments for God's Existence." In *Handbook of Catholic Apologetics: Hundreds of Answers to Critical Questions*. San Francisco: Ignatius Press, 2009. See www.strange notions.com/god-exists/. A fine review of the standard arguments.

Phillips, J. B. *Your God Is Too Small: A Guide for Believers and Skeptics Alike*. New York: Touchstone, 2004. Considered a classic for "expanding" our imaging of God.

Smith, James K. A. *How (Not) to Be Secular: Reading Charles Taylor*. Grand Rapids, MI: Wm. B. Eerdmans, 2014. While the challenge of reading Charles Taylor's *A Secular Age* can be rewarding, Smith offers a friendly way to access Taylor's insights on secularization and postmodernity.

CHAPTER 2

God Is for Us

Our Hunger for Love

Emptying the Ocean

When my imagining of God bogs down, I'm still consoled by a tale I heard in high school religion class, allegedly of Thomas Aquinas. The story goes that the great theologian was walking the beach, contemplating the mystery of God. He came upon a child (afterward, he surmised, an angel) carrying water in a small bucket from the ocean to a hole she had dug in the sand.

The girl inquired what Thomas was doing, and he replied, "Trying to understand the mystery of God. And what are you doing?" She explained, "Trying to empty the ocean into this little hole in the sand." Aquinas protested, "But that is impossible." She rejoined, "Got a better shot than you do." Apocryphal or not, this is true!

A LOVING HUNGER BECAUSE OF WHO GOD IS

In chapter 1, I proposed the term *fullness*, having no better candidate, to describe the source and satisfaction of all the hungers of the human heart. Within our longing for fullness, which is ultimately for

God, there is surely no more heartfelt hunger than for *loving*—to love and to be loved. Indeed, the fullness we desire is a fullness-in-love.

We likely feel it first as a hunger *to be* loved. Our deepest desire is to be loved for ourselves alone, out of what Aristotle called "regard" for who we are. His ancient Greek colleagues distinguished *philia* as family love, *eros* as emotional love, and *agape* as altruistic love. All three are suffused with the longing to be loved for ourselves alone; for others to love us not from duty nor for their satisfaction but freely and out of regard for our own worth.

Even as we hunger to be loved, we have an equally deep desire to be lovers ourselves. Indeed, to be lovers is our greatest human potential, our highest calling in life. While we are terrifyingly capable of hatred, bitterness, and evil, we know deep down that these dehumanize us and can bring as much misery to ourselves as to our victims. To live toward fullness as human beings, and to have even partial success along the way, we must be lovers. If only for our own sakes, we are wisest to practice well familial and neighborly love, emotional love, and to reach for the altruistic love that is *agape*.

Now it is perfectly reasonable to wonder if this *loving* hunger is also well founded; might it simply be wishful on our part that we be lovers and beloved? Are we wise—or downright foolish—to let this love-hunger shape our lives, to define who we are? When we fall short, should we renew our efforts or give them up as futile and misguided? These questions prompt an even deeper one: Are we lovers by design or would we do better to live otherwise?

In chapter 1, we offered at least conducive reasons and feelings for the conviction that God Is, and *is* the grounding source and ultimate satisfaction of our longing for fullness of life. Now we propose that the nature and truth of ourselves to be lovers and beloved is shaped by *who* and *how* God Is *for us*.

The amazing good news is that God has revealed Godself and most completely in Jesus as unconditional Love for every person. Further, God crafts and invites *us* to at least approximate God's love by loving God and others as ourselves. In other words, God is the Tremendous Lover who designs and guides our loving hunger to reach toward its fullness-in-love. And the more convinced we become of God's love for us and for every person, the more likely we are to love others and embrace ourselves as eminently lovable—without a doubt.

Following on, it is imperative for us to recognize that God's love for us is at work within our lives and human history. It is not a love "off out there"—up in the heavens—but is effective here and now by what we call *grace*, from the Latin *gratia*, meaning free or gratis. Without us having to earn God's love—it is total gift—God personally outreaches to empower us to respond well and wisely to our loving hungers. Conversely, by living in right and loving relationships with ourselves, others, and God, we reflect *who* and *how* God Is for us and who and how we are to be as people of God.

Of course, responding to God's love is still our responsibility—our side of the divine/human covenant; yet God's love being effective in our lives as grace makes our responding all the more possible. We might well say that God's grace—effective love—comes to us for free *and* as a responsibility, or better still a response-*ability*.

Claiming that Love is who and how God Is for us, and thus the clue to who and how we are called to live our lives, surely adds to the mystery of both God and ourselves. In chapter 1, we recognized the awesome mystery that God is the Energy who creates and evolves the universe, reaching into infinity. Now, we augment the mystery by claiming that this Energy is the love of a Divine Person—God—who is "in love" with each of us personally. Like Aquinas's angel, we are more likely to empty the ocean into a hole on the beach than to fully comprehend the mystery that "God is love" (1 John 4:8) and *in love* with every one of us.

In chapter 1, we also suggested some conducive warrants of both head and heart to believe that God Is. However, we could not know that God is unconditional Love unless God so revealed Godself. And, indeed, this is the case. The three great religions that began with Abraham and Sarah (Judaism, Christianity, and Islam) are grounded in the conviction that God has explicitly and within human history—in certain times and places—reached out with primordial divine revelation to humankind. And God has done so out of infinite love. As the *Catechism of the Catholic Church* summarizes, "By love, God has revealed himself…and thus

48

provided the definitive, superabundant answer to the questions that people ask themselves about the meaning and purpose of life" (no. 68).

For Christian faith, this primordial revelation began with God's covenant with the ancient people of Israel, gradually unfolded, and then culminated in Jesus Christ, "the ultimate truth of God's revelation" (*CCC* 124). For our lives today, then, access to God's revelation of Godself begins with the Hebrew Scriptures and reaches fullness in Jesus as reflected in the New Testament. We continue to deepen our understanding of this primordial revelation throughout Christian tradition. We turn now to some depictions of God as divinely revealed, and ultimately as Love—both within Godself and always toward us.

PAUSE FOR REFLECTION

- What is your own image, understanding, or felt sense of *who* God Is for you. Do you imagine God empowering your heart to love and be loved? How and why?

- Name some of the sources for your image of *who* and *how* God Is for you—people, experiences, traditions. Try to discern between the positive and negative, true and false, what to embrace and what to set aside.

GOD'S SELF-REVELATION

Before we review the Bible's imaging of God, we need a brief parenthesis regarding the nature of divine revelation; this clarification will serve us well not only here but throughout the whole book. In Christian faith, the Bible is the revealed word of God for people's lives. This claim, however, needs nuance to offset portraying the Bible as if an *immediate* divine communication—like a text message from God. Instead, biblical revelation is historically *mediated* through human language and circumstances, and thus ever in need of interpretation.

Regarding the nature of the Bible as divine revelation, the Second Vatican Council summarized it well. First, it reiterated that "Sacred scripture is the word of God…consigned to writing under the inspiration of the divine Spirit" (*Dei Verbum* 9). So, the Bible is inspired by the Holy Spirit, thus making it divine revelation. Then, a little later, the same constitution adds that "the words of God" in scripture have been "expressed in human language…like human discourse" (no. 13). This is a key clarification. Being historically mediated through "human language" means that the Bible should not be read as if all is literally true—in a fundamentalist way. Instead, the sacred text must be interpreted to discern God's revelation for our time now. Such interpretation must take account of the genre of a particular text, its original context and what it was addressing, as well as our own context and the questions and consciousness we bring to it today.

Catholicism also emphasizes reading the Bible in conversation with the long-established faith tradition that has developed from its biblical source down through history. And both Scripture and Tradition are to be interpreted within and by the Christian faith community. *Dei Verbum* states, "Sacred Tradition and Sacred Scripture are bound closely together" as "one common source" of God's revelation (no. 9), and are to be interpreted by the whole Church (i.e., by all its members) "to whom the transmission and interpretation of Revelation is entrusted" (*CCC* 82).

It is also Christian faith that the Hebrew Scriptures (traditionally called the Old Testament) are integral to God's definitive revelation, in and of themselves. Though Christians read them in light of God's fullness of revelation in Jesus, the Hebrew Scriptures mediate God's word to our lives in their own right. Let us turn now to what God reveals explicitly of Godself in those most ancient Scriptures, with special interest in *who* and *how* God Is for us and shapes our heart's desire for love.

THE GOD OF HEBREW FAITH

A typical Christian caricature is that the God revealed through the Hebrew Scriptures is one of vengeance and wrath, whereas the God of the New Testament is one of love and kindness. Nothing could be further from the truth. Though both Testaments reveal that God holds humankind accountable to our covenant, which makes for judgment upon our lives (more below), the whole Bible's defining image is of God as loving and life-giving for all. And the characteristics revealed of God in the Hebrew Scriptures are constitutive to the New Testament climax that God is unconditional Love.

Here we must be very selective. Given the central role of Moses in the biblical revelation of who God Is, echoed in the Gospel portrayal of Jesus as "the new Moses," let us focus on the God revealed through him. Three foundational texts recounting Moses's mystical experiences make amply clear that God champions (a) *justice for all*; (b) *human freedom*; and (c) favors humankind with *steadfast love*—also translated as *loving-kindness*. All three reflect the operative nature of God's love and are constituents of human love; surely true love requires justice, freedom, and kindness.

For Moses's first encounter with God, take a read of Exodus 3, especially verses 1–15. Here we find Moses standing on "holy ground" before "the burning bush," which represents the very presence of God. Moses hears God say, "I have observed the misery of my people" in slavery, "I have heard their cry," and "I have come down to deliver them from the Egyptians" (3:7–8). This reveals God as aware of human suffering and willing to intervene within history to liberate people from injustice and oppression. What is even more amazing is that God takes the initiative, and not because of any petition or sacrifice made by Moses or his people. God, in and of Godself, recognizes and opposes every injustice and can intervene to liberate people from it.

And liberate them *for* what? Moses hears God say, "To bring them…to a good and broad land, a land flowing with milk and honey" (3:8). For an oppressed and wandering people, to come into their own land begins the possibility of a stable life, and one "flowing with milk and honey" is an added bonus. These were symbols of great fertility and blessing, akin to what the poet Yeats imagined as, "The land of heart's desire." And the rest of the story is that what God first promised was implemented in the miraculous escape of the Israelites from their slavery in Egypt, and some forty years later, their coming to possess their promised land. One who liberates *from* oppression and *for* the deep desires of people's hearts—this is who our God Is.

The second locus is at the beginning of Moses's experience of God at Sinai, a saga that begins in Exodus 19. In their long trek to the promised land, the Israelites arrive at Mount Sinai, previously named "the mountain of God" (3:1). Moses climbed up and heard God make an offer to the Israelites, "You shall be my treasured possession out of all the peoples....You shall be for me a priestly kingdom and a holy nation" (19:5–6). When Moses presents this offer of covenant to the Israelites, they enthusiastically agree to become God's own chosen people; they promise, "Everything that the LORD has spoken we will do" (19:8). Then God came down in a cloud around the mountain and delivered the Ten Commandments to Moses, beginning with, "I am the LORD your God, who brought you out of the land of Egypt, out of the house of slavery; you shall have no other gods before me" (20:2).

Thereafter followed the other nine commandments, and then the many laws of Torah, the Law of life by which the Israelites were to live as God's own people. Yet this first commandment held the summary of the other nine, and, indeed, of the whole Torah: to put God first in their lives. But why would God desire to be "first" in the lives of this small and up-to-this-time insignificant tribe of oppressed and now desert-wandering people?

Clearly it was not for God's sake; the least likely characteristic of God is an insatiable ego. The clue, of course, is in the prefatory line to the first commandment just cited. It is out of loving care for their ongoing *freedom*, from "the house of slavery," that God wants to be first in people's lives. Anything less than the God who liberated them from slavery in Egypt will be an idol that enslaves. The loving desire of God's heart for us is that we *live free* by putting "no other gods before me." Every idol leads into some "house of slavery."

My third text pertains to Moses's final encounter with God at Mount Sinai, climaxed in Exodus 34:6–7, and highlighting God's *loving-kindness* and mercy. Recall that Moses had already informed the Israelites of the Ten Commandments, and they had readily agreed to live them in covenant as God's own people. Then Moses returned to the mountain for further instruction. While he is above, however, the Israelites commit idolatry by making for themselves a golden calf. Moses descends with the Ten Commandments, now written on two stone tablets, and finds the people worshipping an idol. In angry disgust, he smashes the tablets. When he cools down a little, Moses tells the people, "You have sinned a great sin. But now I will go up to the Lord; perhaps I can make atonement for your sin" (32:30). Moses does not sound too hopeful!

At the mountaintop again, Moses hears God tell him to make new stone tablets of the commandments and to return once more to the mountain. He does so and ascends, surely in fear and trepidation, wondering if his people can earn God's forgiveness. But when God passes before Moses in a cloud, he hears God self-describe as "a God merciful and gracious, slow to anger, and abounding in steadfast love (*hesed*) and faithfulness, keeping steadfast love for the thousandth generation, forgiving iniquity and transgression and sin, yet by no means clearing the guilty" (Exod 34:6–7).

Here God reveals Godself to Moses as One of steadfast love toward all, of limitless mercy and unbounded compassion—and this forever. Out of *loving-kindness* (a common translation of *hesed*), God still holds the Israelites responsible to their covenant to live as a people of God; "by no means clearing the guilty."

To conclude this summary of God's identity as revealed to Moses in the Hebrew Scriptures, I note in passing here a theme that we return to many times, namely the responsibilities of a people of God and how they are to live—knowing for sure that God Is and then who and how God Is for us. One of the richest revelations of Hebrew faith is this notion of covenant, that God and humankind are in a partnership that calls us to be responsible to who our God Is and what God lovingly desires for all creation. Of course, God is the primary partner, takes the initiative, and ever sustains people's efforts to live as a people of God. And yet we remain responsible to our side of the covenant, toward God and each other. This means that what God desires for all people—freedom, liberation, justice, loving-kindness, compassion—becomes the law of God by which God's people are to live together.

With these sources from the Hebrew Scriptures, we are prepared well for the God revealed in Jesus. In him we encounter the Word of God that "became flesh and lived among us...full of grace and truth"

(John 1:14). Jesus embraces and heightens the image of God revealed throughout the Scriptures of his Jewish people, culminating in God as unconditional Love and the source that enables us to live toward fullness-in-love.

PAUSE FOR REFLECTION

- How does God as revealed to Moses in the Hebrew Scriptures echo with your own experience and imagining of God?

- A God of *justice for all, true freedom,* and *steadfast love;* what does your side of the covenant with God ask of *your* life now?

GOD'S SELF-REVELATION IN JESUS

The New Testament Letter to the Hebrews begins in this way: "Long ago God spoke to our ancestors in many and various ways by the prophets, but in these last days he has spoken to us by a Son" (1:1–2). A core conviction of Christian faith is that Jesus represented the completion of God's revelation, though it remains for humankind "gradually to grasp its full significance over the course of the centuries" (*CCC* 660). Jesus was "God is with us" (Matt 1:23), fully divine and fully human. The life of Jesus and God's work of liberating salvation through him that continues now by the Holy Spirit is the ultimate revelation of who and how God Is for us. Indeed, God was never more lovingly *with us* and *for us* than in Jesus. As John's Gospel has Jesus repeat in various ways, "If you know me, you will know my Father" (14:7).

We reflect on Jesus, the Christ, in detail over the next three chapters, who he was, in and of himself. In effect then, our discerning of who God Is for us continues in those later chapters. Anticipating our reflection on the blessed Trinity below, the traditional formula of faith is that God's Oneness is expressed in three Divine Persons—Father, Son, and Holy Spirit—who are "distinct and equal." It is imperative, then, to come to *know Jesus* as the revelation of God. Because he could say that "the Father and I are one" (John 10:30), he reveals not only himself but who and how God Is for us.

We must remember, too, that God revealed Godself not only in the divinity of Jesus, but also through his humanity—in that carpenter from Nazareth. So the truths and values the historical Jesus taught, lived, and died for also reveal who God Is for us. For example, the defining characteristic of Jesus's public ministry was *compassion toward all in need*, epitomized in his feeding the hungry, curing the sick, comforting the bereaved, and welcoming the marginalized. We can rightly conclude, then, that as Jesus was, our God is likewise—One of great compassion and mercy, especially for those who need it most. Again, as John has Jesus reiterate, "Whoever has seen me has seen the Father" (14:9).

For the same reason, Christians can look to Jesus's resurrection from the dead (we do at length in chapter 5) and what it means that the God "who raised the Lord Jesus will raise us also" (2 Cor 4:14). So in raising up Jesus we see clearly that our God favors life over death for us all, intending, as Jesus said, that we "may have life, and have it abundantly" (John 10:10)—forever. So who and how our God Is as revealed through Jesus will continue throughout the next three chapters; as we come to know Jesus better, we also come to know more deeply who and how God Is for us. Meanwhile, let us focus here on Jesus's personal understanding of God—the God that the human Jesus believed in. Being very selective again, I choose five texts that reveal Jesus's own faith in who and how God Is for us.

The first is at the beginning of Jesus's public ministry as recounted in Mark 1:14 15. There we read, "Jesus came to Galilee, proclaiming the good news of God, and saying, 'The time is fulfilled, and the kingdom of God has come near; repent, and believe in the good news.'" First, and beginning at the end, note well that Jesus's God is One of "good news"; the Greek word here (*evangelion*) is synonymous for Jesus's whole gospel. So whenever we or our churches make Christian faith sound like bad news *for anyone*—as sometimes we do—know that we are not reflecting the God of Jesus. Ours must always be a God of good news—of hope, of help, of compassion, of mercy, of welcome, of inclusion, all culminating as unconditional love for us.

Then, about Jesus's announcing "the kingdom of God," chapter 3 will elaborate on this as the central symbol that summarizes the heart of Jesus's Gospel and his mission in life. To give a foretaste, and here from the beginning of his public ministry, Jesus's sense of God's reign reflected his conviction that God wills to rule in people's lives *now*; "the time is fulfilled," we need wait no longer. And God wants to rule our lives not for God's sake but for our own—again, out of love. From his Jewish faith and knowledge of the Hebrew Scriptures, Jesus would have understood God's reign as the Divine Heart's best desires for humankind—all for our own good.

So the reign of God is to be one of *shalom*, a rule of justice and peace, mercy and compassion for all, with favor for those most in need, especially widows, orphans, and immigrants (Deut 10:18–19, etc.). Here, then, at the very beginning of his public ministry and continuing throughout, Jesus makes clear that his God wishes to reign in our lives in order that we might live into fullness-in-love. And rather than a far-ahead hope for some distant time or only for the hereafter, the God of Jesus intends this benevolent rule to begin within human history, to "come near" now and effect what God desires for us all—the very best.

My second text is likely the most cited summary of who and how God Is, namely John 3:16, with its capstone in 1 John 4:8–9. In 3:16, John has Jesus articulate his deep conviction of God's unbounded love for all people: "For God so loved the world that he gave his only Son, so that everyone who believes in him may not perish but may have eternal life." This summarizes what Jesus saw as self-evident in his being among us as God's own Son, namely God's limitless love for humankind and God's longing to draw all of us home to the fullness-in-love of eternal life. For John, Jesus recognized his own presence in the world as the ultimate proof of God's unconditional love for all people; God, then, is the Divine Source that empowers us to fulfill the hunger of our hearts to love and be loved.

Following on, 1 John 4:8–9 is like the climax of God's gradual self-disclosure that began with the call of Abraham and Sarah, continued with God's revelation to the Israelite people, and high points in

Jesus. In a three-word summary, the Letter proclaims, "God is love." It then adds, echoing John 3:16, that "God's love was revealed among us" precisely through the "only Son" sent "into the world" (1 John 4:9). A few verses later, the Letter repeats that "God is love" and adds, "those who abide in love abide in God, and God abides in them" (4:16). In other words, that God *is* love calls us to live in love, and this is how God "abide[s]" in us. So far from being led astray by the hunger of our hearts to love and be loved, Jesus convinced his disciples that God *is love* and that all our longings and efforts to love truly are somehow of God.

The third text is likely the prime locus in the Synoptic Gospels for Jesus's personal image of God—Luke 15. Here we find no less than three parables of a God who *seeks out* the lost to show them mercy. And mercy, to echo Pope Francis, is "the heart-beat of the Gospel" (*Gaudete et Exsultate* 97). To begin with (Luke 15:1–2), Jesus is challenged for welcoming and eating with sinners—a frequent accusation against him. His first response (Luke 15:3–7) is to echo a favorite biblical image of God as like a good shepherd, Psalm 23 being the classic. Though perhaps with a little hyperbole, Jesus makes it sound standard for a shepherd to risk leaving ninety-nine sheep unattended to go seek out a lost one. Upon finding the stray, the shepherd lovingly carries it home and throws a party, reflecting that there is "more joy in heaven [i.e., for God] over one sinner who repents" (15:7). Jesus's God is One of extravagant mercy, not only willing to pardon sinners but seeking us out to show forgiveness—amazing love at work.

The second and echoing parable of Luke 15 compares God to a woman who loses a coin, and though she still has nine left, lights a lamp, sweeps the house, and searches until she finds it. Thereupon, she, too, throws a party to rejoice with her friends. Jesus repeats that such celebrating reflects God's joy "over one sinner who repents" (15:10) and accepts God's unbounded mercy. Then Luke 15 follows with Jesus's crowning story of who and how God Is for us—the prodigal son, or is it the prodigal parent of limitless love? (Perhaps pause here and read Luke 15:11–32.)

We have heard this parable so often that the power of it can pass us by, and particularly around our imaging of God—clearly Jesus's purpose in telling it. To begin with, by asking for his inheritance, the son was treating the father as dead, showing total disrespect and breaking up the cohesion of the family unit, a deep cultural value in that time and context. Likewise, the father takes a huge risk in giving the youngest son half of his property. Jesus's first hearers would have wondered why the father does not impose his will on this rebellious son, which he had every right—even a duty—to do. God risks likewise with our human freedom.

Though he goes to a "distant country" and sins boldly, the prodigal son knows in his heart that he can return home to his kind of father; he must have experienced great love and forgiveness from him before. And think about it: his mother must have also practiced such loving kindness. Note, too, that the father is a person of both justice and compassion; the son remembers that "my father's hired hands have bread enough and to spare" (v. 17). The day laborers of the time lived in dire poverty, often without enough food for themselves and their families; the workers in Jesus's parable have food "to spare." Then, when the young man "came to himself" (v. 17) through his exile, he decides to return home. Note to us parents: some young people may need to go to a "far country" in order to find themselves.

The father sees the prodigal son returning "while he was still far off" (v. 20); in other words, he is on lookout toward the horizon, hoping the prodigal might return. Again, most likely the mother sent the father out to scan the skyline—hoping against hope. Upon seeing the prodigal, his heart "was filled with compassion" (v. 20, the Greek here refers a gut response). Then, most amazingly, the father runs, considered undignified for an older person in the culture, to meet the wayward child and, "put his arms around him and kissed him" (v. 20)—*before the son makes his apology*. Remember, he has one ready; he knows that he has lost the rights of a son and is not worthy to be so treated—but maybe as a day laborer? Instead, the father welcomes, embraces (ignoring the son's unclean state), and forgives him *first*, even before hearing his repentance. What a risk and a powerful image of God's unconditional love that permeates into mercy, always on offer, even when we are mired in sin.

When the son confesses his mistake and offers repentance, the father's response is not just to welcome and forgive but to restore and promote him within the family, as symbolized by giving him the "best" robe, and "a ring...and sandals" for his feet (v. 22). Then, to crown this excess of loving mercy, the father orders that they kill "the fatted calf" (v. 23); some scholars say that this implies one *he had been fattening*—with hope for the son's return. And why? Because "'this son of mine... was lost and is found!' And they began to celebrate" (v. 24).

As it has for two thousand years, the prodigal son story speaks powerfully to our hearts: the God of Jesus is One of unconditional love and everlasting mercy. Even when we stray, the desires of our hearts can lead us home to such limitless love, assured of a Divine celebration.

The fourth text I suggest as revealing Jesus's personal imaging of God is the Our Father. We find a shortened account in Luke 11:2–4 and the fuller version that Christians pray in Matthew 6:9–15. The words of this cherished Christian prayer, with deep echoes in Jewish prayer forms, are very revealing for how Jesus imaged God and proposed likewise to us. The opening address alone reflects Jesus's sense of God's intimacy with us; we can all call upon God as to a loving parent. And being God's children is not exclusive to any particular group; all are included in God's family as with parental love.

Note also that Jesus spoke Aramaic and the Gospels were written in Greek, so we cannot be certain what term Jesus actually used to address God here and elsewhere in the Gospels. However, if he regularly used "Abba," which some scholars think likely (encouraged by Mark 14:36), its etymology reflects both the heart of a father and the womb of a mother. The *Catechism* echoes this sentiment: "God's parental tenderness can also be expressed by the image of motherhood" (*CCC* 239). Jesus's intent for sure was not to pose a "graven image" of God as of male gender but to encourage all people, without exception, to approach God like a loving parent.

As the Lord's Prayer unfolds, the first three petitions are that God's name be kept holy, that God's reign begin now, and that God's will of fullness of life for all be done on earth as in heaven. The next four reflect Jesus's deep confidence in God's love and compassion so that we can request enough bread for the day, forgiveness of trespasses to the measure that we forgive others, help to avoid temptation, and to be protected from evil. Clearly the God of Jesus's prayer wishes us nothing but the best—fullness-in-love.

Note here a point that is easily missed, it being so obvious. I refer to the assumption beneath Jesus's own praying and his teaching disciples to pray, precisely that we *can* pray to God and get a hearing. The Gospels report Jesus as praying some thirty times; he went apart to pray and he prayed in community, he prayed before meals, before healings, in petition, praise, and thanksgiving; and he taught his disciples to pray likewise. So Jesus modeled the conviction that the infinite God who creates and holds the whole universe in existence actually "listens" to our prayers. We can talk to our infinite God, get a hearing, and sometimes, in the midst of life and often in the depths of our hearts, "hear" God's response. What an approachable and listening image of God; no one taught this better than Jesus.

My fifth selective text to appreciate Jesus's personal image of God may surprise a little at first—Mary's Magnificat prayer. Again, might you pause and read it in Luke 1:46–55, being particularly alert for the kind of God it presents as reflecting Mary's faith. Christians most revere Mary for her leap of faith in saying "let it be" to her august invitation to be mother to "the Son of God" (Luke 1:38 and 25). Following, Luke presents the Magnificat as reflecting Mary's personal image of God. The scholarly opinion, however, is that the Magnificat is not Mary's own original words; instead, Luke placed it on the lips of Mary and precisely to reflect the God revealed by her Jewish faith, reaching as far back as Abraham, now affirmed and amplified by her son, Jesus. But then, we can well wonder, *who originally shaped Jesus's image of God?* As fully human, Jesus had to be taught and to learn from experience (see *CCC* 472). Who else would have sown the first seeds of Jesus's God-image but his parents—as for us all.

So, the Magnificat reflects the God image that Jesus most likely first learned from Mary. It should not surprise, then, that Mary "rejoices in God my Savior" (Luke 1:47) who "look[s] with favor on the lowliness of his servant" (v. 48), can do "great things" (v. 49), and has "mercy... forever" (v. 54–55). Mary's God "has brought down the powerful from their thrones, and lifted up the lowly; he has filled the hungry with good things, and sent the rich away empty" (v. 52–53). Mary's God clearly favors the poor and downtrodden. She taught Jesus well!

PAUSE FOR REFLECTION

- To what extent do you share Jesus's convictions of who and how God Is for us? How does Jesus invite you to grow in your own God imaging?

- Might a God of love and mercy, rather than fearsome and vengeful, be more likely to encourage right and loving relationships in our own lives? Why and how?

THE ULTIMATE MYSTERY: GOD OF TRIUNE LOVE

After Jesus's resurrection, Matthew depicts the risen Christ assembling his remnant community on a hillside in Galilee. There he gave them the great commission to "Go therefore and make disciples of all nations," and to take people into Christian community through baptism "in the name of the Father and of the Son and of the Holy Spirit" (Matt 28:19). In other words, Christians are baptized into the very inner life of God, specifically named as triune.

Echoing such a trinitarian sense of who God Is for us, Paul, in an early New Testament text, could pray, "The grace of the Lord Jesus Christ, the love of God, and the communion of the Holy Spirit be with all of you" (2 Cor 13:13). Clearly this threefold depiction of who God Is was planted by Jesus in the faith of the first disciples.

The first Christians came to a deep faith in the God whom Jesus most often referred to as "Father," perhaps "Abba." They also came to realize that Jesus himself was God's presence in human history, God among us as one of ourselves. Likewise, they remembered Jesus to speak often of the Spirit as distinct from the Father and himself, and yet that the Spirit reflects divine presence and grace in the world. For example, John 3 has Jesus speak repeatedly of people needing to be "born of the Spirit" in order to "see the kingdom of God."

Later, John has Jesus promise that "the Advocate, the Holy Spirit, whom the Father will send in my name, will teach you everything, and remind you of all that I have said to you" (John 14:26). The first disciples experienced the coming of Jesus's promised Spirit at Pentecost, and thereafter continuing God's work of liberating salvation in Jesus.

But what a dilemma they must have had at first! As people raised in their rich Jewish faith, those early disciples were radical monotheists, knowing deeply that God is one and "you shall have no other gods" (Exod 20:3). How were they to make sense of experiencing God's saving love in three distinct ways, and yet hold to the oneness of God as demanded by their Jewish faith—deepened by Jesus?

Gradually, through much reflection and prayer, discussion and debate, and with carefully crafted language—often borrowed from Greek philosophy—the early Christian community came to recognize, believe, and embrace the doctrine of the Blessed Trinity. This reflects that God is one, and yet we can experience three equal and distinct expressions of the one Divine Essence, first named as "Father, Son, and Holy Spirit."

Highlight here that Christians do not confess three gods but one God in three personal realizations and missions to the world. Together they constitute what the Church has called "the consubstantial Trinity," meaning that all three persons are distinct and equal, and yet share the same divine substance that unites them as one. The *Catechism* quotes a summary from an ancient ecumenical council: "The Father is that which the Son is, the Son that which the Father is, and Father and the Son that which the Holy Spirit is, i.e. by nature one God" (*CCC* 253).

Now we must ask what the triune nature of God means for people who are made in God's "image" and "likeness" (Gen 1:26)? The *Catechism* claims, "The mystery of the Most Holy Trinity is the central mystery of Christian faith and life…the source of all the other mysteries of faith" (no. 234). But why is this so? Indeed, oftentimes throughout its history, the Church's catechesis and even its theologians simply presented the Trinity as *a mystery we cannot explain*—and said little more about the import of this doctrine for Christian living. Of late, however, we have come to realize that the Trinity is, in fact, the mystery of Christian faith that *explains everything*—about who and how our God Is for us, and likewise how we are to live in love as beings who image our triune God.

First, the Trinity reflects the revealed truth that our God, both within Godself and always toward us, is a triune community of infinite loving relationships. Taking seriously that "God is love" (1 John 4:8), an ancient formula proposed by St. Augustine images the Father as the Lover, the Son as the Beloved, and the Holy Spirit as the Loving between them. In other words, the circulating energy among the three Divine Persons, what Christian tradition has called *circumincession*, is unbounded Love. To image and grow in such likeness requires that we love and be loved.

Then as this inner life of divine Love flows out from God—as it must, by its very nature—we experience God's infinite love at work in our lives in three distinct ways or missions, traditionally named as Father, Son, and Holy Spirit and effective as our Creator, Liberator, and Sanctifier. Following on, as persons made in the divine image, humans are to reflect the inner love-life of God. In other words, our God of triune loving relationships calls us to live in right and loving relationships with God, ourselves, others, and creation.

So it is precisely the infinite love within Godself and toward us that makes it "natural' for us to love and be loved, and likewise sustains and guides our efforts to satisfy our loving hungers. So faith in God as one and triune Love holds out hope that the hunger of our hearts to love and be loved can be fulfilled—at least partially in this life, and with fullness in God's eternal presence.

IF GOD IS LOVE, WHAT ABOUT DIVINE JUDGMENT AND HUMAN SUFFERING?

The reader might still wonder about such an imaging of God—of liberation, freedom, and loving-kindness, of limitless compassion and mercy, and ultimately of unconditional Love, even for repentant sinners. Can we really believe it all, especially in light of the biblical portrayal of God punishing sinners, and, indeed, with suffering being often the lot of the innocent as well? Here we begin to address an ultimate mystery of Christian faith; we will return to it again in later chapters because human suffering keeps recurring. Indeed, as noted in chapter 1, human suffering may ever be the greatest deterrent to faith in God.

To begin with and regarding God's judgment, the Hebrew Scriptures make abundantly clear that God holds the Israelite people responsible to their side of the covenant. When they choose to disobey, this God of loving-kindness does not deem the guilty guiltless (Exod 34:7) or step in to save people from the consequences of poor choices. In failing to live their covenant, people bring judgment upon themselves and suffer whatever consequences may ensue.

The truth is that God's Torah or Law—summarized in the Hebrew Scriptures by the Ten Commandments—are wise guidelines for how to live. These are not arbitrary directives made by a whimsical God simply as a test for humankind. Instead they are pointers toward how best to live into true freedom, mandated for our own good by our God of loving-kindness. In the logic of life, people can bring suffering upon themselves by disobeying the Commandments—and especially Jesus's greatest commandment of love—but this is by our own doing rather than as God's punishment.

Yet the close correlation between sin and suffering in the Bible can make it sound as if God sends misery as punishment for sin. This must be understood within the worldview of biblical times. The Hebrew mentality was that God causes everything that happens. To an ancient Israelite, it is not that the apple falls from the tree, but rather that God drops the apple from the tree. So one tempting way to explain suffering was as a quid pro quo punishment for some wrongdoing.

But there is a whole book of the Bible, Job, that roundly rejects this explanation. It states unequivocally that Job's suffering is *not* a punishment for sin; in fact, he is innocent. Of his complaints to God, Job well lamented, "I have uttered what I did not understand, things too wonderful for me, which I did not know" (42:3). For Job—and for us—the mystery of suffering remains!

Though the gospel of Jesus is *good news* for people's lives, it also brings judgment on whether or not we live as disciples. Scholars attest that about a quarter of Jesus's sayings in the Synoptic Gospels are about judgment. He constantly called people to live their lives according to his teachings for the reign of God or to accept what could be negative consequences if they did not. Indeed, Jesus's central theme of the reign of God was a call to decision for or against the fullness-in-love that God wills for all people. As always with our divine/human covenant, there is no "cheap grace"; God holds us accountable and does not step in to save us from the consequences of bad judgments. In explaining the parable of the wedding feast, Jesus makes clear that those who were invited but declined will be shut out—respecting their choice (check out Luke 14:16–24).

What then can Christians say about human suffering if not sent by God to punish for sinful choices? As Job rightly insisted on his innocence, similarly much suffering in our world is experienced by innocent people. Lots of Christians presume (and are taught) that if we go to church and live good lives, then suffering will not come our way. The truth is that good, faithful Christians are just as likely to encounter suffering and tragedy as anyone else. Jesus himself implied as much when he said that "[God] makes [the] sun rise on the evil and on the good, and sends rain on the righteous and on the unrighteous" (Matt 5:45)—all alike. Meanwhile, in the face of the mystery of suffering and with faith in an all loving and merciful God, we can suggest some basic truths, though never amounting to an adequate explanation.

First, God never *causes* suffering, whether it comes by human choice or from nature. God laments all suffering but allows it out of respect for human freedom and the dynamics of creation. It is as if God chooses to limit the divine omnipotence, waiting upon human cooperation so that we might be free partners in the covenant. Likewise, suffering from illness or from natural disasters such as hurricanes and earthquakes happens because of the freedom granted to the dynamics of creation by its Creator. For God to be stepping in constantly to suspend nature would make God a puppeteer—ever pulling strings.

Second, and worth repeating, the overarching biblical revelation is that God does not use suffering as a quid pro quo punishment for sin. Indeed, sinful choices can bring suffering, for oneself and often for others. But this is from the sequence of cause and effect, not from a punitive God.

Third, even when humans make sinful choices, causing self or others to suffer, God may draw some good out of them. The *Catechism* summarizes, "God is in no way, directly or indirectly, the cause of moral evil. [God] permits it, however, because [God] respects the freedom of creatures and, mysteriously, knows how to derive good from it" (no. 311). Of course, this never justifies the evil done—always condemned by God.

Fourth, though Jesus offered no explanation for suffering, his image of God prompted him to make a mandate of his gospel that disciples help to alleviate it. Rather than acquiescing or being fatalistic before it, as if intended by God, Jesus makes clear that suffering is not what God wills for us at all. Indeed, Christians will be judged by our works of compassion and justice to *alleviate* human suffering (check out Matt 25:31–46).

Fifth, in his agony and death, Jesus symbolized God's solidarity with people who suffer, that God accompanies all who carry the crosses of life. So instead of a God who sends suffering, in Jesus we encounter what theologian Jürgen Moltmann well named "a crucified God," One who suffers with us. Following on, by raising Jesus from the dead, God defeated the powers of sin and offered enduring hope in the face of suffering. After God's saving work in Jesus, all evil, suffering, and even death have lost their ultimate "sting" (1 Cor 15:55).

HOPE FOR OUR HEARTS

Like faith, love is always a gamble. Of human love, there is never complete assurance that we are loved out of regard for ourselves alone (Aristotle) or that our own loving is totally altruistic, much less that it will be reciprocated. Like our quest for fullness, and humanly speaking, we love and are loved only partially on this side of eternity.

This partial nature of human love brings to mind Yeats's "Poem for Anne Gregory." Clearly, Anne had complained to the poet that men were falling in love with her just because she was a blond. The closing verse runs,

> I heard an old religious man
> But yesternight declare
> That he had found a text to prove

That only God, my dear,
Could love you for yourself alone
And not your yellow hair.

Yeats was correct in his counsel to the young woman: only God can love us fully and for ourselves alone. Yet the truth remains that God crafts us with a *loving* hunger, a deep desire to love and be loved, and precisely because we are to image our God. The only way to even begin to satisfy this desire, and to live toward the fullness-in-love of our humanity, is to take the risk of loving and being loved.

I have proposed in this chapter that we are encouraged in this love gamble by the deep conviction that we are unconditionally loved by God because God *is* Love and is *in* love with us. Our God is One of infinite love, with all that love implies—justice, mercy, kindness, compassion, and so on. Our God is a Trinity of loving relationships, both within Godself and always toward us. This conviction of who and how our God Is for us lends the foundation upon which our own life as lovers can rest assured, and from which we draw the confidence for loving and being loved. What extraordinary good news for our hearts!

Embracing the conviction that God so loves us and that we are to grow into fullness-in-love takes a lifetime to realize; at least it has taken me so long and I'm not quite "there" yet. Like fullness, our experience of God's love is ever partial in this life; we will not "know" it fully until we rest in God. Yet we can have glimpsing moments along the way.

I have a friend who tells of experiencing God's love—as so many of us do for the first time—in the love of a parent. When my friend was about twelve years old, he had a passion for playing baseball that could cause him to "forget the time" on a summer's evening and be late home for the family dinner. After many tardy arrivals, his parents warned him that "next time" he would have to go without his dinner.

Sure enough, there was a next time. Arriving home late, he was told to sit at the table with the family, but with an empty plate in front of him. After the family grace, there was an awkward silence. Then, his father took *his* full plate and exchanged it for the empty plate of his son. All proceeded to eat in silence, with the father going without instead. My friend attests that that was his first defining experience of God's unconditional love and mercy; thereafter, he was always home on time. With a bit of digging, might we all be able to recall some such experience of being loved unconditionally?

In chapter 1, we drew upon the human hunger for fullness as encouraging us toward the conviction that God Is. Now in chapter 2, in response to our love-hunger, we might come to believe that *how* our God Is for us is to love us unconditionally and craft us to live as lovers. We can afford to risk as much because God "first loved us" (1 John 4:19).

Faith in God's unconditional love should shape how we live and who we become. Thus, our next step is to figure out in more detail what it asks of us to live according to *how* God Is for us. In Christian faith, of course, this question turns us to the example and teaching of Jesus. He is our model and source for living in covenant with our God of triune Love as the only God of our lives.

PAUSE FOR REFLECTION

- Imagine some practical consequences that the doctrine of the Blessed Trinity has for your daily life. For example, what does God as Triune Loving Relationships recommend for your own relationships?

- What is your gut way of dealing with suffering and misfortune in life? How can faith in God as unconditional Love lend hope in times of suffering or setback?

SPIRITUAL PRACTICE: WATCH YOUR LANGUAGE, EVEN FOR GOD

From contemporary social science as well as the study of linguistics, we have become aware that words are our fundamental symbols and, as such, have a power of their own. So words not only express our thoughts, outlooks, and values, but shape them as well. This has prompted many to commit to "inclusive" language when speaking of humankind (note, not *man*kind), using "people" instead of "men" when women are included—usually other than when referring to bathrooms.

Then how about our language when we pray to or speak of God? First, our human language for God can never "include" all that should be said; human words always fall far short of the Divine. As Thomas Aquinas learned, we are far more likely to empty the oceans into a hole on the beach than find language enough to say all that should be said of God. But if not *inclusive*, might we consider being *expansive* in our God-language? It is true that the images for God in the Bible are predominantly male. This is not surprising since it emerged in patriarchal cultures. However, this need not limit our God-talk in very different contexts from biblical times.

Given its original cultural setting, it is amazing that there are, in fact, many female images of God in the Bible—though not as frequent. So God is like a comforting mother (Isa 66:10–13), a midwife (Ps 22:9), a womb (Isa 46:3), a nursing mother (Num 11:12), a mother hen (Luke 13:34), a woman who loses a coin (Luke 15:8–10), and more.

When God told Nicodemus that he must be "born again" of God (John 3), he was posing God as a woman; only women give birth. A favorite Old Testament title for God is *El Shaddai*. Though typically translated as "Almighty," its etymology suggests a mother's breasts. And as noted, Jesus's word *Abba*, which he may have used regularly in addressing God, etymologically is an inclusive term that connotes both father and mother.

The Bible uses umpteen different names and images for God, clearly trying to say what is ultimately unsayable. Just the first two verses of Psalm 18 have no less than ten different divine images. So why insist on male-only imagery? In Christian tradition as well, many saintly authors, especially women mystics like Hildegard of Bingen (1098–1179) and Julian of Norwich (1342–1416), regularly used female images for God. Given the possibilities reflected in both Scripture and Tradition, Christians are certainly not bound to exclusively male terms for God. To insist otherwise would disobey the first commandment and its prohibition against "graven images."

This is not a simple issue to solve, given the predominance of male imagery for God throughout the Bible and Christian tradition.

Yet we surely need not settle for all male imagery, either in our prayer or conversations of faith. Why not consider praying to God as Mother (or Grandmother—an old Shawnee Nation tradition) for a few weeks and see if it shifts you toward a more feminine sense of God. Might you consider adopting the good *spiritual* practice of this book and avoid referring to God with male pronouns—*he, him, himself*? It may help to move you a smidgen closer to knowing who God Is and how God Is for us, reflecting both maternal and paternal love, yet ever Mystery.

FOR FURTHER READING

Groome, Thomas. *Language for a "Catholic" Church*. Kansas City, MO: Sheed & Ward, 1991. A helpful resource for the spiritual practice recommended above. Might you embrace it yourself?

Himes, Michael. *Doing the Truth in Love: Conversations about God*. New York: Paulist Press, 1995. Everything that exists is because of God's love.

Johnson, Elizabeth. *She Who Is: The Mystery of God in Feminist Theological Discourse*. New York: Crossroad, 2017. A faith-expanding perspective on God, already a classic.

CHAPTER 3

Looking for Jesus
Our Hunger for Happiness

One Solitary Life

"Let us turn now to the story. A child is born in an obscure village. He is brought up in another obscure village. He works in a carpenter shop until he is thirty, and then for three brief years is an itinerant preacher, proclaiming a message and living a life. He never writes a book. He never holds an office. He never raises an army. He never has a family of his own. He never owns a home. He never goes to college. He never travels two hundred miles from the place where he was born. He gathers a little group of friends about him and teaches them his way of life. While still a young man, the tide of popular feeling turns against him. The band of followers forsakes him. One denies him; another betrays him. He is turned over to his enemies. He goes through the mockery of a trial; he is nailed on a cross between two thieves, and when dead is laid in a borrowed grave by the kindness of a friend.

Those are the facts of his human life. He rises from the dead. Today we look back across nineteen hundred years and ask, What kind of trail has he left across the centuries? When we try to sum up his influence, all the armies that ever marched, all the parliaments that ever sat, all the kings that ever reigned are absolutely picayune in their influence on humankind compared with this one solitary life."

—Dr. James Allan Francis, *The Real Jesus and Other Sermons* © 1926 by the Judson Press of Philadelphia, p. 123.

"AND THEY ALL LIVED…."

Rev. Judson's famous lines of 1926, reprinted since then on thousands of Christmas cards, lay out a few of the stark "facts" of Jesus's life. To put it mildly, they portray anything but a happy tale. And yet, might we consider the possibility that *the way* of life that Jesus taught disciples is the surest path to finding happiness—real happiness—in life? Might the love and compassion, peace and justice, mercy and forgiveness, respect and dignity for all—the core values that Jesus taught and modeled—be lived as their own reward? Might such living bring the greatest happiness here and now, flowing on into eternity?

Our favorite fairy tales end with "And they all lived happily ever after." This typically entails the good being rewarded and the bad being punished—or changed for the good (no longer a Grinch). The very image of *all* living happily ever after strikes a deep chord in our hearts, with a longing that this be so for every person. We want every story to be a redemption story. But is this only the stuff of fairy tales?

The hunger for happiness is as deep a longing as we find in the human heart. As noted in chapter 1, Aristotle named it the ultimate desire that subsumes all the others and their fulfillment. So happiness can be another name for our deepest hunger that we referred already as the desire for *fullness*; experientially, too, happiness might be a little more recognizable for us. For sure, fulfilling other hungers contributes to realizing this one, and our quest for happiness permeates all the rest.

Likewise, those of us of any vintage—beyond the fairy tales—know well that while the longing for full happiness never wanes, its fulfillment remains always, at best, partial. Even the happiest of moments soon become memories—and ever with a tinge of something still missing. Yet while we continue to long for complete happiness, we can enjoy at least its partial fulfillment *now*, and let our limited experiences become a foretaste of the ultimate possibility—with God.

The quest for happiness is existential for all people; as human beings we cannot decline its hunger. And at our best, such deep desire is not only for oneself but that all people might experience as much. To strive for happiness for oneself alone is to worship a selfie idol that brings its own slavery. No wonder, then, Jesus made the greatest commandment that we love God by loving *neighbors* as *ourselves*—intending their happiness as much as our own.

The most crucial decision for every person to make in life is what path to take and how to walk it in order to find happiness. Following on from the proposals of chapters 1 and 2, that God Is and that God Is for us as unconditional Love, we now propose—with Pope Francis—that *the way* taught and modeled by Jesus is the surest path to "the happiness for which we were created" (*Gaudete et Exsultate* 1).

There is an emphasis here that might be new to many Christians and thus deserves highlighting. So much of the Church's preaching and teaching throughout history has presented the demands of Christian faith as a kind of test that if lived faithfully will bring a later reward—in heaven. Christian living was a burden to be borne, a cross to be carried, in order to earn eternal happiness hereafter. What we often missed is that to live *the way* of Jesus is its own reward *now*. In fact, there is no surer path to happiness in our day-to-day living.

As the pages of history and our own lives attest, there is nothing inevitable about Christians following *the way* of Jesus. To live by his values and commitments is extraordinarily demanding, is achieved only gradually and never perfectly, needs to be deliberately chosen over and over again, and depends always on the help of God's grace. Meanwhile, there is no more consequential decision we can make in life than what path to follow as our habitual lifestyle.

And for sure, there are wrong paths that we can take, albeit in search of happiness. Likely the most favored of our time is wealth, and then the possessions, power, pleasure, and prestige that it can bring. Though not unique to our era, yet our unbridled capitalism that so idolizes money and possessions makes us all the more vulnerable to worshipping this idol.

Note, however, that the Bible portrays the Israelites of old as first breaking their covenant with God by making a *golden* calf to worship. Likewise, Jesus tells a story of a rich farmer who thought he could find happiness by building bigger barns to horde more grain (check out Luke 12:16–21). "Gold"—in whatever form—and possessions have always been most tempting idols.

Yet the avarice that seems native to the human heart across history is surely exacerbated in our time, if only by the advertising we encounter daily. It cons us to *want* and purchase what most often we do not *need*—always with the promise of a sure taste of happiness. Compared to previous times, we are now all the more bombarded by false idols, made all the more alluring.

And while money can buy some *things*, pause for a moment and think of what matters most for human happiness that, in the words of an old Charlie Pride song, "money *can't* buy." How about true love and faithful friendship, integrity of character, esteem and respect among peers, patience with oneself and others, enduring hope in the face of adversity, and the list goes on. To make the golden calf our idol is as false now as it was for the Israelites of old, though perhaps more seductive in our time.

In her book *The Myths of Happiness*, best-selling author Sonja Lyubomirsky proposes that many people think they will find happiness only when they have the perfect spouse, or the ideal job, or a model family—all fully realized. People can allow anything less than perfect achievement in marriage, work, and family to rob them of even partial happiness. She warns wisely that "believing in these happiness myths can have toxic consequences." For happiness is not found as an end point of success but how we live along the way, and especially in the present time and place.

We hear a similar sentiment from Jesus. He announced that "the kingdom of God is [already] among you" (Luke 17:21) and that "the time is fulfilled" (Mark 1:15) for God's reign—now. For Jesus, happiness is not just a future end but is realized by how we live the journey. And the best way to live is as disciples to *the way* he taught and modeled. When he said that he had come so that people "may have life, and have it abundantly" (John 10:10), he added no qualifier—like, "but later." In his final exhortation to the disciples, John's Gospel has Jesus say, "I have said these things to you so that my joy may be in you, and that your joy may be complete" (15:11). So while unending joy or full happiness will be hereafter, clearly Jesus intended it to begin here, with deep continuity between the two.

Pope Francis echoes well this sentiment throughout his Apostolic Exhortation entitled *Evangelii Gaudium* (The Joy of the Gospel). He wishes to mount an "apologetic of attraction" for Gospel-living (*EG* 14), in other words to entice people to Christian faith by persuasion rather than coercion, emphasizing especially God's "revolution of tenderness" (no. 88) in Jesus. Francis is convinced that in Jesus, "we have a treasure of life and love which cannot deceive, and a message which cannot mislead or disappoint" (no. 265).

As we noted in the prelude, the historical Jesus has taken on a fresh centrality for Catholic faith. Given this recentering onto Jesus of Nazareth, we will take the remainder of this and then another chapter to describe *the way* to happiness modeled and taught by that carpenter from Nazareth. First, we need to recognize that the heart of Jesus's gospel was a call to a *way* of life—to a *living* faith. Then, to appreciate the radical nature of *the way* he proposed, we will situate him in his historical context (here in chapter 3). Jesus's context will make all the more amazing the values and truths he modeled for us as the surest path to happiness (chapter 4).

PAUSE FOR REFLECTION

- On a scale of one to ten (very), how do you score your present happiness scale? What helps most to raise the score? What typically causes it to drop?

- How can you prevent your longing for happiness from being diverted to false idols? How might *the way* and wisdom of Jesus lend direction?

JESUS AND LIVING FAITH—FOR HAPPINESS

This chapter begins to make the case that a most promising path to true happiness is to live *the way* modeled and taught by the historical Jesus, that carpenter-turned-preacher who walked the roads of Galilee some two thousand years ago. In sum, when he said, "I am the way, and the truth, and the life" (John 14:6), he was not kidding. I propose that *living* Christian faith in discipleship to Jesus brings its own reward with the most happiness we can experience on this side of eternity.

The potential of Christian faith and its spirituality to help satisfy the hungers of the human heart is the overarching theme of this whole book. In chapter 9, we focus on the holistic nature of such faith and how it is to shape our beliefs and convictions, our prayers and relationships, our values and ethic, or, metaphorically, to engage our heads, hearts, and hands. Here I highlight that the wholeness of Christian faith must be incarnated by would-be Christians as a *living* faith. By this I mean a faith that is *alive* and *lived* as *life-giving* for self, others, and all creation. In sum, Christian spirituality both nurtures and is realized as a living faith.

First, an *alive* faith is fresh and vibrant rather than stale and listless. An alive faith is constantly renewing and deepening, reaching into new horizons of wholeness and holiness of life. Alive faith continues to grow and develop over a lifelong journey until we finally rest in God.

Developmental psychologists like James Fowler have done groundbreaking empirical research on the recognizable *stages* of faith that can unfold throughout the life journey. Fowler proposed that "faith" is a human universal; everyone lives by faith of some kind. However, instead of continuing to develop, research data shows that most people reach a middle stage of "conventional" faith and venture no further. As proposed in chapter 1, a purely conventional faith as shaped by a surrounding culture is less likely to survive—never mind to thrive—in this secular age. We need to own our faith with personal conviction and then nurture it regularly with spiritual practices, keeping it fresh and vibrant.

As Jesus promised the Samaritan woman at the well, and to Christians ever after, his Gospel is to be like "living water," "a spring of water gushing up to eternal life" (John 4:10, 14). We can take "eternal life" to refer to our final happiness—the ultimate end. The fresh waters of Jesus's gospel can encourage a *living* faith that is *alive* and vital, ever reaching into the horizon of God's reign. By contrast, we know that stagnant water kills. A faith that becomes dormant or, worse still, deadly for ourselves or others is surely not the *living* faith that Jesus proposed. The spiritual practice of returning regularly to the well of Gospels will always refresh our faith.

Following on, the very core of a living faith is that it be *lived* and be lived as *life-giving* for oneself, others, and the world. As God's Word was made flesh in Jesus, now his disciples are to embody his gospel. In John's great summary of the incarnation, we read, "the Word [of God] became flesh and lived among us" in Jesus whom the disciples came to recognize as "full of grace and truth" (John 1:14). In other words, Jesus incarnated God's love at work in the world (grace), embodying divine truth as *lived* within human history.

Throughout his public ministry, Jesus modeled and taught for a faith that is lived as *life-giving* for oneself, others, and for the life of the world. This is the life-in-faith to which he calls his disciples. And lived faith is demanded of Jesus's disciples precisely because they are to embrace *the way* that Jesus embodied for the reign of God.

To live Christian faith is an extraordinary challenge, even as sustained by God's grace and our failures consoled by God's boundless mercy. As Pope Francis likes to emphasize, we grow into it gradually, or better "progressively" (*Gaudete et Exsultate* 50). There is certainly no Pollyannaish promise here as if *the way* of Jesus is an easy street that banishes suffering and the challenges and crosses that come with life. Jesus never promised to take away our burdens; instead he urged us to take up our cross "daily" and follow him (Luke 9:23). With Jesus carrying alongside us, however, our crosses can be borne more hopefully and the graces of life bring all the more happiness.

According to Jesus himself, I am not overclaiming for lived Christian faith as a path to true happiness. John's Gospel has Jesus often portray himself as "light" and "life" and to promise, "Whoever follows me will never walk in darkness but will have the light of life" (John 8:12); note that "following" (imitating) is key to enjoying the "light of life." As the opposite of darkness and death, lived faith can bring great happiness even now. Then, making the claim, "I am the bread of life" and repeating, "I am the living bread that came down from heaven," Jesus went on to promise, "Whoever eats of this bread will live forever; and the bread that I will give for the life of the world is my flesh" (John 6:48, 51). In other words, to live Jesus's *way*, empowered by the "bread" of himself, will bring life here, transitioning into eternal life hereafter.

Then, all three Synoptic Gospels have Jesus declare that whoever follows him faithfully will "receive a hundredfold now in this age…and in the age to come eternal life" (see Mark 10:30). Jesus explicitly promised happiness to disciples who live faithful to his *way*. The Beatitudes are most often translated as "Blessed are…." However, the Greek word repeated there (Matt 5:3–12) is *makarioi*, which is equally well translated as "happy." So "happy are the poor in spirit…happy are those who hunger and thirst for justice…happy are the peacemakers," and so on.

I refer to discipleship to Jesus for happiness's sake as living *the way*. The first Christians were well named as those "who belonged to the Way" (Acts 9:2)—as if they were owned by *the way* of Jesus. There is an emphasis here that even Christians can miss—that our faith is primarily *a way of life* after *the way* of Jesus. It is practiced most by being *lived*, and as *life-giving* for self, others, and the common good of all.

Jesus repeatedly prioritized lived faith as the measure of discipleship. For example, "Not everyone who says to me, 'Lord, Lord,' will enter the kingdom of heaven, but only the one who does the will of my Father in heaven" (Matt 7:21). So, not the *confessing* but the *doing* of faith is the key to belonging to God's reign toward happiness. Jesus repeated often, in one way or another, "Blessed rather are those who hear the word of God and obey it" (Luke 11:28). In an amazing moment when his mother and family came looking for him, Jesus declared that his family now are "those who hear the word of God and do it" (8:21).

When John the Baptist sent messengers to ask Jesus, "Are you the one who is to come, or are we to wait for another?"—that is, are you the Messiah?—Jesus pointed to what he was *doing* as a response. He sent the messengers back to the Baptist to relate "what you hear and see: the blind receive their sight, the lame walk, the lepers are cleansed, the deaf hear, the dead are raised, and the poor have good news brought to them" (Matt 11:2–5). It was primarily the good *works* of Jesus that identified him as the Messiah. A living faith patterned on discipleship to Jesus must be lived as life-giving for oneself and others, and especially for those most in need.

Influenced by the rationalist emphasis of modernity, we tend to presume that *knowing* Christian faith comes first and then we may well try to live it. Jesus, however, saw *believing* and *doing* as essential rather than sequential to each other, with both being integral to Christian faith. And at times he reversed our presumed order, proposing that *doing* faith can come first, then shaping what we know and profess. We find this reversal most often in John. He has Jesus declare, "Those who *do* what is true come to the light" (John 3:21, my emphasis). So the doing of truth is what leads to spiritual wisdom. Again, Jesus explained that it is first by *living* his "word" as disciples that we can come to "*know* the truth"; his promise is that such lived truth "will make you free" (see John 8:31–32, my emphasis).

When Jesus summarized his *way* of *living* faith into the golden rule—as in "do to others as you would have them do to you"—he added, "for this is the law and the prophets" (Matt 7:12). So *living* the golden rule fulfills both the commandments and teachings, all the values and truths of the Hebrew Scriptures. Likewise, the greatest commandment of love that Jesus taught, summarizes "all the law and the prophets" (22:40). There is no more life-giving—and happy—way to live than to obey Jesus's radical law of love, even of enemies (5:44).

In sum, *living* faith that is *alive* and *lived* as *life-giving* according to *the way* of Jesus is the heart of his gospel and the surest path to happiness for disciples. This, then, begs the very practical question—how exactly did Jesus live? What was his *way*? What can we say reliably were the truths, values, and commitments that marked his life, and thus should mark the life of Christian disciples? These questions turn us to what scholars refer to as "the historical Jesus," the One who, "works in a carpenter shop until he is thirty, and then for three brief years is an itinerant preacher, proclaiming a message and living a life." Beyond this, can we know a little more now about "the facts" of Jesus's life than those portrayed by Rev. Francis's moving summary of 1926?

The answer is yes, we can, by drawing upon some two hundred years of New Testament scholarship in what is called "the quest for the historical Jesus." This research has passed through many "quests," each building on prior ones. The cumulative result is that now we can assemble a reliable portrayal of the values and truths taught by the historical Jesus—and thus accurately portray what is demanded of disciples as *living* faith.

Before proceeding, I make an important parenthetical point. Even as we quest for the historical Jesus, we must ever remember that the same person was also the Son of God, the Second Person of the Blessed Trinity, the risen Savior of all humankind—often referred to as "the Christ of faith" (our focus in chapter 5). To state the patently obvious, Jesus the Christ was one and the same person. As the dogmas of Christian faith insist, he embodied within his personhood two natures, fully human and fully divine. So at its core, Christian faith must be defined by both the historical Jesus and the risen Christ. The first is our model and teacher for *how* to live and the second enables us to *do so*. Jesus shows *the way* and we can respond because of God's "abundance of grace…through the one [person], Jesus Christ" (Rom 5:17).

Worth repeating here is the stirring summary statement of the core of Christian faith proposed by the *Catechism of the Catholic Church*: "At the heart…we find a Person, the Person of Jesus of Nazareth, the only Son from the Father" (no. 426). Note well the *CCC*'s insistence on both. So Christians must ground their *living* faith and their hope for happiness in both "Jesus of Nazareth" *and* in Christ, "the only Son from the Father."

As we embrace both the *Jesus of history* and the *Christ of faith* to live as disciples toward God's reign, we must let each *nature* shape our understanding of the other; again, he was only one person! So, how Jesus lived his human life reveals divine values by which God desires people to live. Yet he was not just a good person living an exemplary and heroic life. He was God's own Son present within human history. By being raised up by God, God affirmed Jesus's divinity and thus the model of *living* faith that he portrayed for disciples.

Their rock-solid faith in Jesus's resurrection and thus his divinity shaped how his first disciples remembered and interpreted the story of his earthly life as well. But rather than distorting their portrayal, Jesus's resurrection revealed who he really was when he walked the roads of

Galilee—God's own Son and our liberating Savior. In other words, his humanity and divinity illuminated each other for the first disciples and should for us as well.

So even as we look to the historical Jesus, we remember his rightful claim: "Whoever has seen me has seen the Father" (John 14:9). Yet the historical Jesus not only reveals God to us but us to ourselves as well. He reveals the potential we have as human persons to live as people of God—after *the way* he embodied. Then, through the paschal mystery of his death and resurrection, we have "the abundance of grace" needed to embrace our potential for such *living* faith.

For the remainder of this chapter, I outline a little of Jesus's cultural context and some broad strokes of his historical life. This will help us to appreciate all the more *the way* he taught and modeled (chapter 4) as living faith, and this as our surest path to happiness and to be a source of the same for others.

PAUSE FOR REFLECTION

- Reflect on the social and cultural influences that shape what you consider as "living the good life." What do you recognize as valid? As false?

- From what you know of the historical Jesus already, what are some distinguishing features of *the way* he modeled and taught? How might they bring you true happiness?

QUESTING FOR JESUS IN HIS TIME AND PLACE

Like any human person, to appreciate who Jesus was and *the way* he lived, it helps to situate him in his time and place. In fact, Jesus's historical situation makes his teaching and lifestyle all the more amazing and courageous; much of it was against the grain, and especially the politics (civil and religious) of his cultural context.

In the "quest for the historical Jesus," scholars employ scientific methods and criteria to establish what can be deemed historically reliable within the New Testament texts. They draw upon the findings of biblical archaeology and anthropology, analyze the literary forms of the scripture texts, make comparison with other ancient manuscripts, and employ a host of other scholarly methods. As a result, New Testament scholars have come to much consensus around who Jesus actually was, the time and place in which he carried on his ministry, and the values and truths he lived, taught, and died for.

No scholar claims that the Gospels are scientific history (if there be such a thing). They reflect the faith of the people closest to Jesus, of his original community that came to deeply believe that he was the promised Messiah, the risen Lord and liberating Savior of humankind. Yet we can be confident that the overall picture of the historical Jesus portrayed in the Gospels and other New Testament writings is reliable. The four Gospels, attributed to Matthew, Mark, Luke, and John, are our primary texts in this quest. Each puts its own spin on the historical Jesus, shaped by their context, intended audience, and the concerns of the community for which they were writing. Yet the Gospels are not just the *personal* memories of their four authors.

Scripture scholars agree that there were three recognizable phases in the construction of the Gospels. First, there was the public ministry of Jesus, what he actually said and did, the stories he told, and the stories about him, as remembered by his original community—those who had known and experienced him firsthand. The second phase came after Jesus's death and resurrection as various Christian communities formed in different centers to live as disciples. They handed on the oral traditions that came from Jesus's original community. In such an oral culture, those traditions were more reliable than they might be today, so dependent on written texts. The third phase emerged as the firsthand witnesses died off and there was need for written accounts to preserve the whole story of Jesus. So some forty to sixty years after his death and resurrection, the traditions, some oral and some by now in written fragments, began to be crafted into the four Gospels.

Of the three Synoptic Gospels, most scholars agree that Mark was written first and around AD 70. Some ten to fifteen years later, Matthew and Luke were constructed. Both borrowed from Mark, shared a common source other than Mark, and each had sources unique to them. Their shared source other than Mark was from a written collection of "sayings of Jesus" that scholars date from the AD 40s and 50s. John's Gospel was written last, probably in the AD 90s. John is from oral and written traditions independent of the Synoptics, and yet reaching back to the original community of Jesus. All four—as well as the other New Testament writings—were written in Greek.

Because the four Gospels are constructed from traditions that originated with those who personally encountered Jesus, they are reliable witnesses to *their* faith in his life and teachings. Many of those first disciples experienced Jesus as risen from the dead (Paul says as many as five hundred at one time, 1 Cor 15:6), helping them to understand better and be all the more committed to faithfully preserve his historical teachings. Many early disciples were persecuted for their commitment to Jesus, some giving their lives in testament to their faith. They must have been deeply convinced of its reliability to bear it such courageous witness.

From very early on, Christians became convinced that the overall Gospel handed down from Jesus was "the word of God," in other words, divinely inspired. St. Paul's First Letter to the Thessalonians is considered the earliest New Testament text, written in AD 52—long before any of the Gospels. Already, Paul invites the Thessalonians to accept the "gospel of God" that they heard "not as a human word but as what it really is, God's word" (1 Thess 2:9, 13). A little later, Paul, writing to his friend Timothy, referred to "the sacred writings that are able to instruct you for salvation though faith in Christ Jesus" and added that all such "scripture is inspired by God" (2 Tim 3:15–16). And the author of 2 Peter insisted that the emerging Scriptures were not simply of human origin; we have them because "men and women moved by the Holy Spirit spoke from God" (2 Pet 1:21). Within a relatively few years, then, Christians became convinced that all four Gospels and the other New Testament letters and writings were *inspired* by the Holy Spirit.

Yet, as noted in chapter 2, this does not make the Gospels a text message from God—a direct divine communication. Repeating what the Second Vatican Council's Constitution on Divine Revelation (*Dei Verbum*) stated concerning the whole Bible: "these words of God" were "expressed in human language…like human discourse" (no. 13). In other words, the Sacred Scriptures need interpretation for our time that takes account not only of the texts but of their historical context—and ours. Contemporary scripture scholarship is a huge asset in this regard, helping us to discover all the more reliably the *living* faith that the historical Jesus modeled and taught, and that is still our surest path to happiness.

A FEW MORE "FACTS" OF JESUS'S LIFE

We know that Jesus was raised in the small town of Nazareth in Galilee, a backwater village in a backwater province. He was the son of Joseph, a carpenter, and his mother's name was Mary. They gave him the name *Jeshua*, which in Hebrew literally means "God saves." People from Galilee were more dark skinned than those from Judea; most likely so was Jesus. They spoke with a heavy accent. Galileans experienced ethnic bias against them by both the Romans and their Jewish neighbors in Judea; they were viewed as country bumpkins when they went up to Jerusalem to celebrate holy days and pray in the temple.

Jesus spoke Aramaic as a child, a forerunner of Hebrew. Besides the home instruction and good example of his parents, he was likely tutored in his Jewish faith at the local synagogue. From his scripture quoting throughout the Gospels, it seems that he was well versed in both the Law and the prophets. He favored Isaiah and likewise the psalms and Wisdom literature; he is represented as quoting many passages from memory. By his home and synagogue, then, Jesus was well grounded in his Jewish faith. Apparently, he also learned how to read; in that home synagogue on a Sabbath day, Luke recounts that Jesus "stood up to read" from the Prophet Isaiah (4:16).

The Gospels attest that Jesus learned to be a carpenter from his father, Joseph; typically, male sons took on the trade of their father. Having a trade might seem like providing economic security but people in the Galilean villages would not have had the money for furniture except the very basics. Some scholars speculate that Jesus and Joseph likely sought work in Sephoris, the capital of Galilee, just five miles from Nazareth. The Romans had razed it to the ground to combat an uprising there around AD 6; they rebuilt it in Jesus's time. Needing carpenters, it seems likely that father and son found work there as day laborers—just a notch above the slaves. Knowing poverty from the inside was surely what gave Jesus his empathy for the poor and downtrodden.

During Jesus's lifetime, Galilee was a province within the Roman territory of Syria. From about 60 BC onward for two hundred years or so, the Romans ruled Galilee with an iron fist. They exacted exorbitant taxes, tributes, fees, and tithes from the people, who also had to pay a temple tax to the priests in Jerusalem. As a result of all the heavy taxation, most Galileans lived in dire poverty—and often in debt. Jesus's family would have been no exception.

The Galileans were brutalized by the Romans, who put down all forms of protest or resistance with terrifying cruelty. They regularly moved in and burnt down a whole village that was failing to pay its taxes. That Jesus would push back against the oppression of the "Empire," championing the reign of God instead, was likely to bring his own destruction—and he must have been aware of the danger. Even his insistence that God is our Father (not the emperor) and praying that God's reign (not the empire) might be realized now, were political positions likely to have dire consequences.

In the oppressive sociopolitical circumstances of Galilee, the family bond became all the more important as a means of survival. Family solidarity was an absolute, essential to the security as well as the identity of its members. Again, imagine the challenge that Jesus posed by encouraging disciples to leave mother and father to follow him (see Mark 10:29). Or his saying, "Whoever does the will of God is my brother and sister and mother" (Mark 3:35), making his *way* more of a priority than family bonds.

With grinding taxation by both civil and religious authorities, many people who once owned land lost it and went into debt, placing themselves in the hands of money lenders who would exploit them further. Jesus, by radical contrast, encouraged disciples to pray for the forgiveness of all debts—whether owning or being owed. This was surely popular with the debtors but not with the powerful creditors.

People who became poor day laborers not only lost their lands but their dignity as well, incurring social shame. Honor and shame were powerful forces in Jesus's culture. Anything that diminished a person, like sickness or poverty, also took away their status. Against the grain of his culture, in feeding the hungry, curing the sick, and including the marginalized, Jesus not only relieved their personal distress but erased their shame and restored their honor in society.

The Jewish people often rose in revolt against the cruelty of Roman rule, and the Romans literally stopped at nothing to put them down. Eventually, the Romans even destroyed their beloved Temple in Jerusalem (AD 70), the very center of Jewish faith and identity as a people. Quintillius Varus, the Roman ruler around 4 BC, put down a popular uprising in Jerusalem by crucifying some two thousand rebels and hanging them on a row of crosses that circled the city. And when they crucified rebels or protesters, the Romans liked to leave the dead bodies to hang for days for all to see—as a deterrent.

As a child growing up, Jesus must have heard the stories and personally experienced such cruelty and repression. So he would have known the risks he was taking when he declared, against all odds, that "the time is fulfilled" and called for the inbreaking "now" of God's reign of justice and peace (Mark 1:15). In fact, the previous verse in Mark's Gospel notes that Jesus made this first announcement of God's reign "after John was arrested" (1:14); Jesus surely knew that he, too, would be in danger. As he described the reign of God throughout his public ministry, it was the antithesis of the brutality of the Romans and the legalism of the religious leaders. And imagine the ire he caused in the latter when he called them "hypocrites" (Matt 23:27)—as he did often.

Imagine, too, how amazed his first listeners must have been to hear his utopian sentiments in the midst of their dire situation. No wonder that early on in Mark we read that his family "went out to restrain him, for people were saying, 'He has gone out of his mind.'" (3:21). One can understand their suspicion of his mental health. By proclaiming the inbreaking of God's reign in his historical context, Jesus was, in effect, proclaiming the end of all empires—beginning with the Roman one; to not recognize the risks involved *would* qualify him as crazy.

As we review the values and commitments reflected in Jesus's life (chapter 4), we will note many other instances of his preaching and praxis being in stark contrast with his cultural and religious context.

So prodigals get welcomed home, though this was contrary to Torah; a hated Samaritan becomes the neighbor to be imitated and a Samaritan woman is his first evangelizer in John's Gospel; repentant adulterers are forgiven when the law demanded that they be stoned to death; women are fully included in his inner circle of disciples; the beggar Lazarus goes home to heaven and the rich man to hell—contrary to the assumption that wealth was a blessing from God and poverty a punishment; workers who come at the eleventh hour get paid the same as those who had borne the heat of the day—not because they had earned it but as day laborers they needed it to feed their family; curing the sick and feeding the hungry are more important than keeping Sabbath; mercy is to be favored over punishment. And the list of his countercultural and politically dangerous stances goes on. Enough for now to say that Jesus was not likely to die in bed!

PAUSE FOR REFLECTION

- Respond to the proposal of a *living* faith. How might it challenge your own life in faith?

- How might Jesus's historical context deepen your appreciation of *the way* of life he modeled and taught? What can you learn from him for *living* faith in your context?

FROM HIDDEN TO PUBLIC LIFE

Concerning his thirty years or so of "hidden life" in Nazareth and what it was like for him growing up there, we can only imagine. As already noted, we can surmise that his deep formation in Jewish faith came primarily from his parents, Mary and Joseph, and from the local synagogue. Given the profound influence of home and parents on every person, we recognize that Mary and Joseph must have modeled the amazing values that marked the public life of Jesus. His foundational image of God as unconditional Love must have been mirrored in the love between Joseph and Mary, and then by their love for Jesus. Likewise, his compassion, mercy, respect, hospitality, inclusivity, and so on—that we will review in detail—must have been well practiced by Jesus's parental models.

There is one wonderful story that I like to think reveals great truths about Jesus and his parents; even if not literally true (as the scholars opine), it reflects an important faith memory in Luke's Christian community. I refer to the story of Jesus getting lost in Jerusalem as a twelve-year-old; treat yourself to it now in Luke 2:41–52. Remembering the full humanity of Jesus and likewise of Joseph and Mary, imagine how some event like this might have unfolded—really!

Just imagine his parents' panic about their only son being lost for three whole days in a dangerous city. And let us imagine how overjoyed Joseph and Mary were upon finding him. But then, might they give him a good scolding or at least a warning—as any parent would do—never to "wander off" like that again? How else might good parents respond to a twelve-year-old boy who strays from them in a big city? Might the text hint that Jesus learned his lesson when it says that thereafter he went down with them to Nazareth and "was obedient to them"? The story concludes that the adolescent Jesus "increased in wisdom and in years, and in divine and human favor" (Luke 2:51–52). And why wouldn't he—with the good parents he had!

In addition to reflecting the adolescent Jesus and the good parenting of Joseph and Mary, that last verse bespeaks the deepest faith aspect of the story, namely Luke's recognition of Jesus's full humanity. As the dogma of Christian faith in this regard summarizes, Jesus was "perfect in divinity and perfect in humanity" and yet "the character proper to each of the two natures was preserved as they came together in one person" (Council of Chalcedon, AD 451). In other words, Jesus's divinity did not suspend but enhanced his humanity. For this reason, and as the *Catechism of the Catholic Church* makes clear, Jesus had to be taught and to learn for himself "what one in the human condition can learn only from experience" (no. 472).

Humanly speaking, one must wonder why Jesus decided at about the age of thirty (senior years in his culture) to leave his home at Nazareth and travel some seventy miles (by foot) to where John the Baptist was baptizing at the river Jordan, just outside of Jerusalem. By then, Joseph was most likely dead, and Jesus would have been the main support of his mother, Mary. Why did he up and leave home?

Most scholars agree that as yet Jesus would not have had a clear sense of his identity as the promised Messiah; humanly speaking, this consciousness likely dawned gradually as his public ministry unfolded and people responded to him. Yet Jesus must at least have had a deep passion and sense of vocation to go and announce the inbreaking of God's reign. Nothing less would have driven him to leave his family and village and strike out into the unknown—to do what would most likely lead to his own destruction.

John was "proclaiming a baptism of repentance for the forgiveness of sins," and "Jesus came from Nazareth of Galilee and was baptized by John in the Jordan" (Mark 1:4, 9). Then, upon being baptized, there followed an amazing theophany around Jesus. All three Synoptics attest to "the Spirit descending like a dove on [Jesus]. And a voice came from heaven, 'You are my Son, the Beloved; with you I am well pleased'" (Mark 1:10–11). Might Jesus have been as surprised as the people there present by such an extraordinary affirmation—and "from heaven"?

Whatever we imagine, Jesus's baptism marked the beginning of his public ministry and perhaps of his own and other people's gradual recognition of him as the promised Messiah. Though John's Gospel has no explicit baptism of Jesus, it recounts John the Baptist pointing to Jesus as "the Lamb of God who takes away the sin of the world," and testifying "that this is the Son of God" (John 1:29, 34).

After his baptism by John, Jesus launched his public ministry, beginning, at least by Luke's account, at his hometown of Nazareth (Luke 4:16–30; Mark and Matthew simply say "in Galilee"). After the Baptist was arrested, it appears that Jesus relocated with his growing band of disciples to the house of the brothers Simon (later called Peter) and Andrew at Capernaum (Matt 4:12–13). His ministry of teaching, healing, feeding, consoling, forgiving, and driving out evil took him throughout Galilee and the surrounding areas, and eventually up to Jerusalem. If we accept John's chronology, Jesus's public ministry lasted for three years with at least four separate journeys to Jerusalem.

When the Romans put Jesus to death on a cross, they pinned to it "the charge against him" as "The King of the Jews" (Mark 15:26). This echoed Jesus's prior entrance into Jerusalem and the people hailing him as "the king who comes in the name of the Lord" (Luke 19:38); in Mark's account, the palm-waving people pin their hopes on him for "the coming kingdom of our ancestor David" (Mark 11:10). For the Romans' interest then, Jesus's crime or threat was a political one, explaining why they felt the need to crucify him. Note that crucifixion was the most painful form of execution imaginable and used particularly to punish or deter any political challenge to the empire's interests. It was so horrendous that in polite Roman circles, the word was not used; it was considered obscene to even speak of crucifixion.

The tradition is that Jesus was about thirty-three when Pontius Pilate, the Roman ruler of Judea (AD 26–36), had Jesus crucified on a small hill outside the city of Jerusalem. Luke calls it "Calvary" (23:33), whereas Matthew (27:33) and Mark (15:22) use its Aramaic name "Golgotha"; both meant "place of the skull." Pilate acted in cahoots with Herod Antipas, vassal Roman ruler of Jesus's home province of Galilee, with both refusing to take responsibility for his sentencing. But given the life he lived, the values he modeled and taught, and the causes he championed, it is no wonder that Jesus was crucified. He died for what he lived for—and will rise for the same cause, the reign of God!

With this brief overview of Jesus's historical background, we are in a better position to appreciate the heroic *living* faith he modeled for disciples (chapter 4). We can see more clearly why it might be the kind of life that brings true happiness for oneself and to contribute to the happiness of others and the well-being of creation.

HOPE FOR OUR HEARTS

Across my many years of teaching undergraduate theology at Boston College, I've been amazed at how students could much more readily believe in the divinity of Jesus than in his full humanity. Recognizing him as a real person was difficult for them (especially the Catholics!). I could cite that he got tired and thirsty (John 4:6), became hungry (Mark 11:12), cried when his friend Lazarus died (John 11:35), got ripping mad (Mark 11:15–18), was so afraid at the thought of his death that he sweated drops of blood (Luke 22:44), and, like every person, Jesus needed to eat, sleep, evacuate his system, and the list goes on. Yet they would hesitate to believe in his full humanity.

When I cited the Letter to the Hebrews (4:15), that Jesus was tempted in all the ways that we are, albeit "without sin," they became all the more skeptical (perhaps with doubts about the goodness of their own humanity?). Truth is that most Christians grew up with what author Ernest Larsen called "good old plastic Jesus," beginning with the kitsch baby Jesus in most Christmas mangers (certainly never in need of a diaper change).

This chapter proposes that Jesus was a real human being, located in a certain time and place, and with the same human hopes and needs as ourselves. Surely he shared all of our desires, and especially the longing to love and be loved. What good news for our hearts—if we can believe it!

The in-depth portrayal that there is no better way than *the way* of Jesus to find happiness in life will come in chapter 4, as we detail the central truths and wisdom, values and commitments that marked his public life. Already, however, we can detect that for Jesus the key to being happy is not about feeling good but about doing good, especially for others in need. This is the kind of *living* faith to which he called disciples, posing it as its own reward—now!

Clearly, for Jesus, happiness does not come from having possessions or being powerful or becoming famous, but from living one's own deepest truth with integrity and acting as if God reigns, regardless of cost or consequences. Our greatest happiness comes from living *the way* of Jesus now, and at every level of existence—personal, communal, and social/political.

Living faith after *the way* of Jesus brings happiness to every present moment and situation in life. When Jesus announced the inbreaking of God's reign, Mark 1:15 uses the Greek *kairos*, meaning the "right time." It is always the right time and place to live for the reign of God as Jesus

91

taught and modeled. It is not simply past, future, or elsewhere—or achieved only at an end point—but for here and now, wherever we find ourselves and however engaged in the world we are.

Beyond this, there are three related points to bring to our hearts that can lend hope to our quest for happiness. First, as for Jesus, following his *way* will often be countercultural, against the conventional grain. And this may well be at a price. Jesus himself forewarned that discipleship could cause others to "hate...exclude...revile...and defame [them] on account of the Son of Man" (Luke 6:22). Note: the latter was Jesus's favorite title for himself in all four Gospels. However, the Greek there, *huios tou anthropon*, is more accurately rendered as "Human One."

Second, and following on, to live Jesus's *way* as disciples often takes great courage. It calls disciples to risks that may get them into a lot of trouble with "the powers that be"—socially and sometimes ecclesially. As we elaborate in chapter 4, it was Jesus's running afoul of the political and religious leaders of his context that led to his death. Yet he still says to us, as he said to the first disciples in his final discourse on the night before he died, "Take courage; I have conquered the world" (John 16:33).

And third, being a disciple to Jesus will often demand resisting structures of social, cultural, political, and religious oppression. In other words, this *way* that he taught and modeled is to shape our politics as well as our prayers—indeed, every aspect of our lives. Instead of tolerating structures of injustice, we must actively oppose them; nothing less will walk *the way* of Jesus. Yet as challenging and demanding as Jesus's *way* can be, it is the surest path to finding happiness in life.

PAUSE FOR REFLECTION

- For a moment, imagine what the historical Jesus looked like—as if painting your own portrait of him. What features emerge (height, weight, hair, complexion, posture, smile, etc.)? Do you find him attractive as a person? Might he make a good friend for you?

- Compare a little your sociocultural world with that of Jesus. In spite of the differences, how might he still be a model for the way to experience happiness in life?

SPIRITUAL PRACTICE: GET TO KNOW JESUS THROUGH THE SCRIPTURES

The people who first knew Jesus had the extraordinary experience—and advantage—of encountering him directly, "in the flesh." Without such immediacy, we yet have the rich witness of their original faith, of being able to encounter him through the texts that emerged—inspired by the Holy Spirit—from his first community of witnesses. To turn us more intently toward the historical Jesus—as I propose throughout this book—requires first and foremost that we turn to the Gospels, and then to the other writings of the New Testament. By prayerful reflection upon them, we can come to know Jesus more personally and respond more faithfully as disciples.

A crucial spiritual practice for would-be Christians, then, is to read, study, and pray with the Scriptures. If you have not done so already, begin with the Gospels. Then move on to the rest of the New Testament: Acts, Letters, and the Book of Revelation. These texts, too, arose from the communities of faith that emerged from the original community around Jesus. Then ripple out into the texts that formed Jesus's own faith and whose messianic promises he fulfilled—the Hebrew Scriptures or Old Testament.

The Bible is not the easiest book to read, especially from cover to cover. One helpful way of selecting significant passages is to follow the official *Lectionary* of the Church, now shared by a number of main-line Christian denominations. These are the Scripture readings assigned for liturgy on each Sunday, holy day, and weekday. They unfold over a three-year cycle and many are selected to echo the seasons of the liturgical year—nativity readings at Christmas, resurrection accounts in the Easter season, and so on.

Over the three-year cycle, one can reflect on a fairly wide swath of Scripture, from both the Hebrew Scriptures and New Testament. Typically, the passages selected have real significance for *living* Christian faith. If not doing a daily reading, you can focus on the Sunday texts. Then, the key question becomes how best to approach a *prayerful study* (both) of a particular piece of Scripture.

It will help to have a commentary that is readable for nonspecialists and yet reliable in its scholarship. Though a bit big and nigh thirty years old, the *New Jerome Biblical Commentary* (1990) is still an excellent resource. The *Paulist Biblical Commentary* (2018) is more recent and more focused on the practice of faith. The *Catholic Study Bible* has helpful background reading for each book, with scholarly explanatory comments in footnotes throughout.

Then to read, study, and reflect prayerfully on the Bible, there are three good guidelines to follow; to be memorable, let's call them *context*, *canon*, and *community*. *Context* advises that we try to place a particular scripture text in its original context, both within its overall book of Scripture and in the cultural world of its time (this is where a good commentary will help). Likewise, consider your own context, what you are bringing to the particular text, and imagine what might be here as a potential "word of God" for your life now.

Canon first refers to the recognized "canon" of Scripture, in other words, the official books of the Bible. But beyond the list of canonical texts, it also helps to have "a canon within the canon," in other words, a general rule of thumb to guide your interpretation of any given text's meaning and application. For example, Jesus's own "canon within the canon" was surely the reign of God—the one great guideline of his life. To embrace and make Jesus's canon our own means that the interpretation we give to any particular text should be likely to promote the values of God's reign. So when we hear of Jesus allegedly saying, "I have not come to bring peace, but a sword" (Matt 10:34), we know not to take it literally as if Jesus favored violence; this would be totally contrary to *his* guiding canon—the *shalom* of God's reign.

And third, while we should read the Bible *for ourselves*, Catholic tradition emphasizes not to read it *by ourselves*. In other words, we need to read it within the faith *community*—the Church. So the third guideline is to take account of the truth and wisdom that has emerged from the Church's reading of any text of the Bible over the past two thousand years; this is gathered into Christian tradition and reflected in the Church's core teachings. Following on, the ideal way to study the Bible is in an actual community of conversation, where the communal dynamic can guide and add great spiritual richness to one's own study and prayer.

Keeping *context*, *canon*, and *community* in mind, what then might be an approach to Bible study that moves beyond learning *about* it to learning *from* it so as to learn *into* its spirituality for *living* faith? One effective approach, both scholarly and prayerful, is as follows. Having selected a text:

1. Place yourself in God's presence and consciously open your heart to the possibility that this text might reveal a "word of God" for your life.
2. Read the text through once to get an initial sense of what it is about, noticing how it might echo and be relevant to your own reality.
3. Pause and recognize what *you* are bringing to this text—a question, issue, concern, hope, or whatever—from your present context.
4. Read the text again, this time slowly and discerningly, listening for its potential "word of God" for your life and concerns. Consult a Bible commentary on the text to get a sense of its context and what it originally meant and might mean for now.
5. Discern how you might take it to heart, integrating its revelation into your daily life.
6. Pray for the grace you need to put its spiritual wisdom to work.

Again, the effectiveness of such an approach is enhanced when done within a faith community, with the conversation and discernment of participants helping to uncover the revelatory power of the text toward *living* faith.

FOR FURTHER READING:

Harrington, Daniel. *Jesus: A Historical Portrait*. Cincinnati: Franciscan
    Media, 2007. A summary portrayal of Jesus within his historical
    context, and by an outstanding New Testament scholar.
Pagola, Jose. *Jesus: An Historical Approximation*. Rev. ed. Miami:
    Convivium Press, 2014. Reads like a novel and summarizes much of
    contemporary research in the quest for the historical Jesus.
Pope Francis. *Evangelii Gaudium: The Joy of the Gospel*. Rome: Libreria
    Editrice Vaticana, 2013. Invites back to the heart of Jesus's teaching—
    for joy, mercy, and happiness.

CHAPTER 4

Following Jesus

The Way to True Happiness

Happiness Report

    Encouraged by the United Nations, the World Happiness Report has been published annually since 2012. It asks a representative sample of people from 160 different nations to rank their happiness on a scale of zero to ten (happiest). Researchers from various sciences then correlate the scores with data on what are considered six major sources of happiness in any given country, namely: the levels of government support for quality of life; the presence or absence of corruption; freedom in making life choices; quality of health care and life expectancy rate; care for the needy; and the gross domestic production (GDP) of the economy.

    The happiness rate of a country is taken as an indicator of how to move toward the United Nation's development objectives such as ending poverty and hunger, better health care, improving education for all, gender equality, and other humanitarian goals. The most recent report, issued March 2017, rated Norway the happiest country with Denmark and Switzerland following close behind (the United States was fourteenth). Burundi and the Central African Republic were at the bottom.

JESUS MIGHT SAY "I TOLD YOU SO" AND ADD...

Jesus would not be at all surprised that two thousand years later, much the same issues as in his own time are key to people's happiness today. This is why he had deep compassion and care for people in need, preached honesty in relationships and justice for all, promoted the freedom and dignity of every person, cared for the sick and suffering, fully included women in his community, and educated all he met in the personal and social values of God's reign—the most humanitarian horizon imaginable. Then, Jesus might add that while meeting such needs is essential for personal well-being, *helping* others to meet them brings happiness as well. And he would explain that such altruism is integral to fulfilling the hungers of our hearts because we are made in the likeness of our God.

Though we do not find it in the Gospels, the Book of Acts cites St. Paul as quoting Jesus, "It is more blessed to give than to receive" (Acts 20:35). Again, the word for blessed there is *makarios*, which, as noted, also means "happy." So the greater happiness may be found in helping to meet the needs of others rather than simply satisfying one's own. With echoing sentiment, Paul also taught that "God loves a cheerful giver" (2 Cor 9:7). The implication is that cheerfulness (the Greek *hilaron* there means "very happy") comes from providing for those in need and helping them to provide for themselves.

This note of altruism in caring for the needs of others as an essential source of happiness is not explicit in the criteria of the *Happiness Report*. Meanwhile, altruism and helping people in need defined Jesus's public life and his *way* to happiness. Nowhere was this more evident than in what he did on the night before he died. In John 13:1–20, we read an amazing account of Jesus washing the feet of his disciples at their Last Supper together.

Washing the feet of guests was a tradition of hospitality in a Jewish household of the time and performed by the house slaves. Long before modern means of sanitation, this was a repulsive and humbling task. Yet John recounts that Jesus "took off his outer robe, and tied a towel around himself. Then he poured water into a basin and began to wash the disciples' feet and to wipe them with the towel that was tied around him" (John 13:4–5). When he had washed all of their feet, he asked them rhetorically, "Do you know what I have done to you? You call me Teacher and Lord—and you are right, for that is what I am. So if I, your Lord and Teacher, have washed your feet, you also ought to wash one another's feet. For I have set you an example, that you also should do as I have done to you" (13:12–15).

Note that Jesus specifically claims for himself his role as their master and teacher. In the context, it was a cultural mandate for students to serve their teacher. Yet here was their revered master performing the most menial of services for them. And he said that he did so to give them "a model"—of generous service—to follow. A little later at the Last Supper, John has Jesus assure the disciples that he intends for them that their "joy may be complete" (15:11). So as Jesus taught and modeled throughout his public life, generous service to others is key to finding joy and happiness ourselves. Was Jesus onto something?

PAUSE FOR REFLECTION

- Remember an act of generous service you did in your own life. How and why might it have been a source of happiness for you?

- Why might Jesus have posed service and care for others as bringing happiness? How does this contrast with the perspective of postmodern culture that encourages a "buffered self"—living in our own cocoon?

THE VALUES OF JESUS

There are umpteen possible ways to review the values and commitments reflected in the public life of Jesus and thus the happiness *way* that he modeled for disciples. We already noted many of Jesus's values that he revealed in his imaging of God (chapter 2), and more commitments of Jesus will be echoed in every chapter of this book. Attempting a general summary here, I propose that Jesus's overarching commitment was to be an agent of the reign of God—posing God's desires for us as fulfilling all the hungers of the human heart. Then, within his passion for God's reign to be realized in every life, time, and place, I list three categories that help summarize the particular commitments of Jesus: to *compassion*, to *community*, and to *commission* of disciples, empowering them to participate in his work.

JESUS LIVED FOR THE REIGN OF GOD

Scholars agree that if we could ask Jesus the direct question, "What is your life purpose and passion?" he would summarize by saying "the reign of God." Traditionally, and in most translations of the New Testament, the Greek *basileia tou theou* is translated as "kingdom of God"; however, because it is more of an unfolding process than a geographic location—as kingdom implies—the term *reign of God* is more accurate. Also, Matthew's Gospel favors "kingdom of heaven." Rather than intending that God's reign is only for later—in heaven—scholars agree that Matthew, being an observant Jew, was simply reluctant to use the holy name and so inserted "heaven" as a synonym for *God*. Overall for Jesus, the *reign of God* refers to the full happiness and quality of life that God intends for all persons, societies, and creation, and this to begin "on earth" (Matt 6:10).

Luke gives an early summary of Jesus's description of his public ministry as, "I must proclaim the good news of the kingdom of God… for I was sent for this purpose" (4:43). Matthew's earliest summary runs, "Jesus went throughout Galilee, teaching in their synagogues and proclaiming the good news of the kingdom and curing every disease and every sickness among the people" (4:23). Note well that Jesus's good news also brings miracles of healing—of every kind.

Then, as noted before, Mark gives the earliest and classic summary. After Jesus's baptism by John the Baptist at the Jordan, he is submitted to a crucible of temptation "in the wilderness for forty days" (1:13). Mark continues, "After John was arrested, Jesus came to Galilee, proclaiming the good news of God, and saying, 'The time is fulfilled, and the kingdom of God has come near; repent, and believe in the good news'" (1:14–15). Surely Jesus must have known the dangers he would face; his cousin John had already been arrested for preaching a similar message. But Jesus is convinced that "the time is fulfilled"; the waiting is over and *now* is the right time for the inbreaking of God's reign. This calls people to change their minds and hearts (literal meaning of *metanoia*) and to "believe the good news"—the gospel.

Thereafter in the Synoptics, Jesus's favored pedagogy for teaching the reign of God was by parables. He most often began a parable with, "the reign of God is like…" and then cited something very familiar to people's lives. In addition to engaging their interests, Jesus was highlighting that the reign of God is to be realized in the ordinary and everyday of life now.

Though the notion that God is to rule all creation is a common theme in the Hebrew Scriptures, the term *reign of God* was just coming into vogue in the Jewish faith of Jesus's time. Its summary description is as *shalom*. Most often translated as "peace," *shalom* means the best of everything for everybody and for all creation—with all hearts' desires fully realized. Jesus embraced this utopian vision wholeheartedly to describe the central purpose of his life. So how did *he* personally understand this bountiful symbol?

For Jesus, God's reign means that God's best intentions for humankind will be completely realized eventually—in time-out-of-time—but are to begin *now*. Here we imagine fulfilling all the deepest and wisest longings of the human heart as being God's desire for us as well. So God's reign is realized through faith, hope, and love, by justice and peace realized, by compassion and mercy for all in need, by inclusion and hospitality in community, by fully recognizing the dignity and equality of all people, by putting an end to discrimination and prejudice, to injustice and oppression, to sickness and disease, to hunger and want. As God's reign is realized, we move toward full happiness and this for all people and the well-being of God's creation.

It is clear from Jesus's preaching that he understood the reign of God as a tensive symbol—ever a both/and hope. So it is for each person's spirit *and* yet a social challenge, reaching into all creation. It will be realized in its fullness at an end-time; indeed only God knows "that day

and hour" (Matt 24:36). Meanwhile *now* is the time for its inbreaking—
"the time (*kairos*) is fulfilled" (Mark 1:15). It is to shape people's prayers
as in "thy kingdom come" *and* likewise their politics as in committing
to doing God's will "on earth as in heaven."

Jesus told disciples that God must rule within their hearts (Luke
17:21) *and* that it demands outreach with compassion to people in
need. In fact, the works of compassion and justice are absolutely necessary for disciples to "inherit the kingdom" (Matt 25:34). And while
God's reign is realized only by God's grace, as always, grace comes as a
responsibility. Jesus's disciples are to be covenant partners in the realization of God's vision for all humanity and creation.

It is abundantly clear from how Jesus lived his life and taught his
gospel that the reign of God meant putting God at the center of his
life. Promoting the reign of God was his *way* of living the first commandment, itself the summary of Torah. Jesus's God, however, was not
as a ruling King but as a loving Parent, One he could call "Abba." As
noted in chapter 3, Jesus taught clearly God's unconditional love for all
people. Following on now, it is God's radical love for us that prompts
Jesus to make a radical *law of love* the rule of God's reign—love even for
enemies (Matt 5:44).

So when he is asked, "Which commandment is the first of all?"
Jesus responds by drawing together two classic texts from his Jewish
faith. These were the law to love God with all of one's "heart...soul,
and...might" (that is, with everything we've got) as in Deuteronomy
6:4–5, and then "you shall love your neighbor as yourself" as in Leviticus 19:18. Jesus was the first Hebrew prophet to bring together what
was in effect three laws—love of God, neighbor, and self (we often
forget that third leg).

In Mark's account (read 12:28–34), a scribe explicitly asked Jesus
for the greatest *commandment*—singular. At first blush, it would appear
that Jesus responded with threefold commands, and yet he concludes
by saying, "There is no other commandment [singular again] greater
than these." In other words, the three aspects are symbiotic; for Jesus,
our love for God is realized by loving neighbor as ourselves. When
the scribe agrees, essentially repeating what Jesus had said, the latter
responds, "You are not far from the kingdom of God." (12:34). For

Jesus, this radical law of love is the defining mode of our living into God's reign.

Observing the works and words of Jesus, we readily see that his putting God first was precisely what prompted him to favor with loving kindness and mercy the poor, the hungry, the sick, the bereaved, those in the powers of evil, the excluded, the beggars, the sinners, the downtrodden, the oppressed, the despised, the persecuted—the list can go on. Not only was Jesus helping people in need but erasing their social shame and lifting their exclusion from community as well. His very mode of helping people led to their social empowerment; now they were able to help themselves and be respected again by others.

Jesus's life lived for God's reign reflects a deep respect for the dignity of every person, treating all as made in the divine image and likeness (check Mark 12:17). For Jesus, God's rule actively opposes all injustice, exclusion, oppression, and inequality. God never approves abuse or discrimination for any reason but demands their opposites in every situation—respect for human dignity and justice for all. It is his commitment to God's reign that prompts Jesus to make what is often now referred to as his "preferential option for the poor." Simply stated, this means that he favored those who needed the favor most. Jesus believed that this reflects whom God favors, and so demands that a people of God must prioritize care for those most in need.

The Gospels make clear throughout that Jesus understood himself as the definitive agent of God's reign of liberating salvation in human history. John's great summary has Jesus say, "God so loved the world" as to send his "only Son" so that all might come to "eternal life" (John 3:16)—full happiness. Though John rarely uses the term *reign of God*, his sense of Jesus as the One who has come "for the life of the world" (6:51) is precisely what the symbol means in the Synoptic Gospels.

There is no better summary of how Jesus understood his life as agent of God's reign than Luke 4:16–21. Luke situates this text at the beginning of Jesus's public ministry in Galilee. Jesus comes into his hometown of Nazareth on a Sabbath day and goes "according to his custom" to the village synagogue for worship. He is chosen or volunteers to read the scripture text and is handed the "scroll of the prophet Isaiah"—his favorite. Jesus unrolls it and intentionally looks for and finds the text of Isaiah 61:1–2. When Jesus reads it, according to Luke's account, he mixes in a phrase from Isaiah 58:6, referring to freeing the oppressed. It would seem that Jesus was reciting from memory to expand a little upon Isaiah 61:1–2.

Jesus read as follows: "The Spirit of the Lord is upon me, because he has anointed me to bring good news to the poor. He has sent me to proclaim release to the captives and recovery of sight to the blind, to let the oppressed go free, to proclaim the year of the Lord's favor" (Luke 4:18–19). The last verse is the hope for a Jubilee Year, the fiftieth year after seven times seven years. The jubilee was the ultimate Sabbath time when everything was to be given over to God—who owns it all anyhow. So land was to be left fallow, debts forgiven, and all slaves and prisoners set free (see Lev 25:10–12).

In summary, then, this "anointed One" (in Hebrew, *messiah*) is to preach the good news of God's word to those who need it most—the poor; to liberate people held in captivity of any kind; to help all to see what should be seen; to lift the burdens of the downtrodden and exploited; and to live as if everything belongs to God and is to be used as God intends.

Luke says that after Jesus finished reading and sat down, "the eyes of all in the synagogue were fixed on him" (Luke 4:20). Then came the most dramatic moment: Jesus said, "Today this scripture has been fulfilled in your hearing" (4:21). With this as his "party platform," the remainder of Luke's Gospel unfolds how Jesus fulfilled his radical role as the Anointed One—Messiah—to effect God's reign of fullness of life and happiness for all.

Perhaps the most consoling—and confronting—aspect for disciples of Jesus is his witness to the generosity of God's mercy. Jesus was adamant that God prefers works of mercy over offering sacrifice (Matt 9:13). He said of himself that he had come "to call not the righteous but sinners" (Luke 5:32). Indeed a central aspect of his public ministry was his forgiving and welcoming sinners into his community of disciples. So radical was his forgiveness that he even forgave people who out of ignorance had not yet repented of their wrongdoing. He prayed on the cross, "Father, forgive them; for they do not know what they are doing"

(23:34). And he made forgiveness for disciples dependent upon our forgiving "those who trespass against us."

Another amazing instance of Jesus teaching the largess of God's reign is in the parable of the laborers in the vineyard (read it again in Matt 20:1–16). We can well ask, Why did the vineyard keeper pay those who came "at the eleventh hour" the same as those who had borne the heat of the day? The only possible answer is not that they had earned it but that they *needed* it—as day laborers to feed their family at day's end. So God gives us what we need even when we have not earned it. A people of God after *the way* of Jesus should be so generous as well.

Just as Jesus gave over his whole being to the reign of God, and was ultimately crucified for this commitment, disciples must give their all to what God intends. In two very brief parables, Jesus encourages this "go for broke" commitment to God's reign—holding nothing back. Thus, the reign of God is like a person who finds "treasure hidden in a field"; with "joy" they must sell *everything* to buy the field (Matt 13:44). Or God's reign is like a merchant who finds a "pearl of great value," and now must give *everything* to purchase the pearl (Matt 13:45–46).

The consoling aspect of this call to invest everything for the reign of God is that those two parables come immediately after two others that reveal that even small efforts toward God's reign can make a big difference. So the tiny mustard seed can become a big tree, and a little yeast can cause a huge pile of dough to rise (Matt 13:31–33). It is likewise regarding the reign of God. It is a partnership in which every human effort is magnified by God's grace—and so can bear fruit a hundredfold (Mark 4:20).

Which brings us back to the quest for happiness by *the way* that Jesus posed. Clearly for Jesus, to live for the reign of God—its peace and justice, love and compassion, dignity and respect, mercy and forgiveness—is its own reward. His best summary is likely the beatitudes, with each blessing being an instance of true happiness.

So, we could read "happy (*makarios*) are the poor in spirit, for theirs is the kingdom of heaven." Likewise, for happiness sake, the poor will inherit God's reign, those who mourn will be comforted, the humble rather than the haughty will inherit the earth, those who hunger and work for justice will get their fill, the merciful will receive mercy, the pure of heart will see God, the peacemakers will be considered children of God, and those who suffer for justice sake will be well rewarded (Matt 5:3–10). To live for all the values of God's reign as Jesus taught, realizing them for oneself and contributing to their realization for others and the world, is the Jesus *way* to true happiness—even now.

PAUSE FOR REFLECTION

- To be a disciple of Jesus is to commit to the reign of God as he embodied it. What are some particular *demands* that this places on your life now? The *happiness* it can bring?

- Living for God's reign as Jesus modeled is its own reward. Reflect upon and learn from a particular instance of experiencing this truth in your own life.

THE COMPASSION OF JESUS

The roots of the word *compassion* suggest a felt sense of "suffering with" others (the Latin is *com passio*). The Greek term in the Synoptic Gospels, and often attributed to Jesus, literally means to have a "gut feeling of empathy." We might say that compassion is the ultimate form of altruistic love, arising from felt solidarity with those in need and out of due regard for them—*agape*. New Testament scholars have long agreed that the most comprehensive description of Jesus's stance toward people was *compassion*, and especially for those in need. With the parable of the prodigal son, Jesus attributed the same disposition to God (check Luke 15:20).

We recognize the deep compassion of Jesus in his feeding the hungry. There are only two miracles recorded six times in the Gospels—the resurrection and Jesus's multiplying of loaves and fish to feed hungry people (in all four Gospels, then twice in Matthew and Mark). Being repeated so often, feeding hungry people must have been a central aspect of Jesus's public ministry. And beyond the service of alleviating

their hunger, Jesus empowered the poor by preaching his "good news…
to them" (Matt 11:5). The compassion of Jesus was to feed their souls
as well as their bodies.

Jesus's compassion is also evident in his curing people of various illnesses—physical, spiritual, and emotional. It would seem that
Jesus worked hundreds of miracles of healing throughout his public
ministry. So often we find a summary statement like, "And he cured
many who were sick with various diseases, and cast out many demons"
(Mark 1:34). And while scholars now think of his driving out demons
as responding to emotional illness or addictions, Jesus clearly intended
such miracles to free people from the grips of evil—of whatever kind—
and to empower them to resist every addictive lure.

A most amazing feature of many of Jesus's healing miracles is how
he affirmed the faith of the person being healed. He could have well
claimed credit for interceding with his heavenly Father on their behalf,
but never; instead, so many times he says, "*Your* faith has made you
well" (Mark 5:34; 10:52, etc.; emphasis added). What an affirmation of
the agency of the person being cured, honoring *them* rather than taking
credit for himself.

Note, too, that in many of his healings, Jesus reached out to touch
the sick, even a leper (Matt 8:2–3) or was touched by them, like a
woman with a hemorrhage (Luke 8:43–48). That kind of touching
would have made Jesus ritually unclean. He clearly rejected such sham-
ing, socially liberating as well as healing those who touched him.

Jesus's compassion is also evident in his healing people spiritually by saying, "Your sins are forgiven you" (Luke 5:20). He portrayed
God's mercy for the repentant sinner as being like a good shepherd
who leaves the ninety-nine to go searching for one lost sheep. Finding
it, the shepherd (God) throws a party, rejoicing "for I have found my
sheep that was lost" (15:4–6). Jesus embodied God's boundless mercy
for sinners—again, an act of deep compassion.

We see the compassion of Jesus, too, in his sympathy for the
bereaved. Three times and again moved with compassion, Jesus is cred-
ited with restoring people from death to life. He did so for the poor
widow of Nain who had lost her only son and thus her sole means
of support (Luke 7:11–16). He did likewise for the synagogue official

Jairus who had lost his only daughter (8:40–56). Indeed, Jesus himself experienced the pain of loss of a loved one with the death of his friend Lazarus (John 11:1–44). We read first that "Jesus began to weep"—the shortest verse in the Bible (11:35). He then raised Lazarus from the dead and gave him back to his sisters, Mary and Martha (11:34–44).

For the gospel writers, Jesus's raising of the dead surely anticipated his victory over death for all people, promising, as Paul would explain, our own rising with him into "newness of life" (Rom 6:4).

Being compassionate toward people was such a priority in his ministry that Jesus even placed it ahead of keeping Sabbath. There are at least seven gospel accounts of healings that Jesus worked on the Sabbath—often to much protest from literalists of the law. For sure, Jesus was not abolishing the Sabbath. He was simply saying that there is a hierarchy of values in God's reign, and some good deeds are more important to do than others—like healing the sick over keeping Sabbath. Christians need to practice the same kind of discernment in implementing the laws of Christian faith to their lives now.

PAUSE FOR REFLECTION

- Think of those in your personal life and social context who are most in need of compassion at this time. How might Jesus inspire you to reach out to them?

- Why might showing compassion to others be key to happiness for yourself?

JESUS'S *COMMUNITY OF TOTAL INCLUSION*

As previously noted, many of Jesus's acts of compassion were also acts of inclusion, of bringing back into community with respect and dignity those who were excluded—the poor, the sick, sinners, the ritually unclean. However, his whole public ministry was an explicit outreach toward every kind of people—men, women, and children;

fisher-folk and farmers; merchants and homemakers; rich and poor; tax payers and tax collectors; the righteous and sinners—to welcome all into his community of disciples to live for God's reign.

Further, Jesus went out into the highways and byways, the villages and market places, seeking out and inviting people to join his community for the reign of God. This was unusual for a teacher in his time and place; typically, students sought out their teacher rather than the other way around. Jesus happily went looking for people to join him, with all being welcome.

Then there are multiple examples of Jesus reaching out in particular to the marginalized and excluded, giving them an added welcome—because they would need it—into his community of disciples. This is reflected powerfully in his table fellowship that welcomed all to the table. Again, to invite to the table and share food together was a potent symbol of inclusion, meaning much more in his culture than in ours. Very early in Mark's Gospel we read that the scribes and Pharisees objected that Jesus was "eating with sinners and tax collectors." Jesus rejoined that he had "come to call not the righteous but sinners" (Mark 2:15–17). Just a few verses later, "the Pharisees…conspired…to destroy him" (3:6). To welcome the marginalized into table fellowship was a revolt against cultural norms that could have dire consequences.

We can also see the radical inclusivity of Jesus in his welcome for children. Children had the lowest status of all in Jesus's historical context, considered the property of their parents, alongside of slaves. They were among the poorest of the poor and, of course, the most defenseless. Jesus's special outreach to them was typical of his favor for the weakest and poorest. No one would remotely expect children to be privileged in the reign of God, yet Jesus insisted many times that they are.

Read the story in Mark 10:13–16 (repeated almost verbatim in Matthew and Luke) of when the disciples tried to keep children away from Jesus. Given their lack of social status, one can understand why the disciples rebuked parents for bringing their children to meet Jesus. By now he was attracting large crowds of people (Mark 10:1) and was an important public person. But Jesus was "indignant" with his disciples, as if they should know better. He told them "let the little children come to me; do not stop them; for it is to such as these that the kingdom of God belongs." And he explained that they—the adults—must become more trusting like children in order to "receive the kingdom of God" (10:14–15). In an amazing gesture, "he took them (the children) up in his arms, laid his hands on them, and blessed them" (10:16). This would have stunned the people who first witnessed such inclusion of children.

The most amazing aspect of the inclusivity—we might say the "catholicity"—of Jesus's community was his outreach and invitation to women into his core group of disciples. Again, his was a world where women were at best second-class citizens, considered the property of their fathers and then husbands (Exod 20:17). They were seen as ever at risk of being ritually unclean because of their monthly bleeding; this was one reason why they were excluded from priestly functions in the temple. Women had no official status and were not required to recite the daily *Shema* prayer (which begins with Deut 6:4–5) as mandated for Jewish men. This makes Jesus's outreach and full inclusion of women in his core community of disciples all the more extraordinary.

Jesus's respectful interaction with women throughout the Gospels, his outreach and inclusion of them, his allowing them to touch him, are nothing short of revolutionary for his time. A prime example was his encounter with the Samaritan woman at the well. John's Gospel (chapter 4) has Jesus explain the core of his gospel to her. The text well notes that when his disciples appeared on the scene, "they were astonished that he was speaking with a woman" (John 4:27). Indeed they should have been; in the world of the time, teachers rarely spoke to women and never in public. And having heard his gospel message, the Samaritan woman became Jesus's first evangelist. She went to her own people and said suggestively, "He cannot be the Messiah, can he?" (John 4:29).

This was only the first instance in John's Gospel of Jesus rejecting the sexist—and racist—mores of his culture; many more followed. For example, note the theological discussion he had with Martha upon the death of her brother Lazarus (read the story in John 11:17–27). She and Jesus must have been good friends; she begins with something of a reprimand, asking why he did not get there before Lazarus had died. Jesus reveals his true identity to Martha by saying, "I am the resurrection and the life" and explaining that people who believe in him will never *really* die (11:25–26)—what a claim to make!

110

Jesus then invited Martha's own confession of faith in him with, "Do you believe this?" Without hesitation, she proclaimed, "I believe that you are the Messiah, the Son of God, the one coming into the world" (11:26–27), Martha's amazing witness to Jesus as Messiah is on a par with Peter's classic confession likewise (compare at Matt 16:16), though hers has never garnered as much attention or acclaim. I wonder why!

Note, too, Jesus's mercy, respect, and extraordinary gentleness for the woman caught committing adultery, literally saving her from death (John 8:1–11). Add the story in Luke of "a sinful woman" who came to Jesus while having dinner in a Pharisee's house; she anointed his feet with oil, bathed them with her tears, and dried them with her hair. Jesus takes the opportunity to teach the Pharisee that those to whom much is forgiven are likely to love all the more. He says to the woman, "Your sins are forgiven" and, as typical, adds an affirmation of her dignity and own agency: "*Your* faith has saved you; go in peace" (see Luke 7:36–50; emphasis added).

Beyond showing such respect for the dignity of women, Jesus insisted on their full inclusion in his community of disciples. The Gospels explicitly reflect that women were included within his inner circle. This would not have been so unless invited by Jesus. Luke recounts the names of some of the women who were traveling with Jesus in his public ministry: Mary Magdalene, Joanna, Susanna, and then adds "and many others" (see Luke 8:1–3). Some of those other women close to Jesus were Mary "the mother of James the younger" (Mark 15:40), Salome (Mark 15:49–41), and "the mother of the sons of Zebedee" (Matt 27:56).

As Jesus's end drew nigh, it is difficult to imagine that he excluded the women disciples from his Last Supper, given their membership in his inner circle and the inclusivity that marked his table fellowship throughout his public ministry. For sure, all four Gospels record that a group of Jesus's women disciples accompanied him to the cross, though because men were crucified naked, women were required to stand "at a distance" (Luke 23:49). So the women disciples got as close to the foot of his cross as permitted. Meanwhile, all the male disciples "deserted him and fled" (Mark 14:50); Judas betrayed him and Peter, their leader, denied that he even knew Jesus (14:66–72). What a contrast to the courage and faithfulness of the women disciples!

All three of the Synoptic accounts say that the women at the foot of the cross "had followed him from Galilee" (Luke 23:49). In other words, they had been with Jesus from the beginning in Galilee and throughout his public ministry. If one takes John's chronology, this means for three years. In the world of the time, such inclusion of women in the inner circle of a teacher would have been extraordinary.

The most amazing instance of Jesus's inclusion of women is surely the role the risen Christ gave to Mary Magdalene in witnessing and announcing his resurrection from the dead. Note, too, that this was in a world where women were not allowed to bear witness in a court of law.

For Christians to appreciate the role of Mary Magdalene in the life of Jesus, we need first to debunk the false portrayal of her as "the prostitute." This scurrilous stereotype of Magdalene in later Church history, especially in its art, is absolutely false. Luke 8:1–3 reports that Mary Magdalene traveled with Jesus in his public ministry throughout Galilee and, as an aside, notes that Jesus had cured her of "seven demons" (echoed in Mark 16:9). The later Church assumed that this meant she was a prostitute, with no warrant for this other than stereotyping.

As if to hammer home the point, for Mary Magdalene's feast day (July 22) the Church long assigned the gospel reading of Matthew 7:36–50, the story of that "sinful woman" who washed and anointed Jesus's feet. Though changed in 1974 to John 20:1–8 (her finding Jesus's tomb empty), this still stopped short of recounting the risen Christ's appearance *first* to Mary Magdalene in the follow-on text of John 20:11–18. Only very recently has the Church begun to reclaim and honor the *true* Mary Magdalene.

Besides being a member of Jesus's inner circle and accompanying him to the cross, the three Synoptics record Mary Magdalene as witnessing where Jesus was buried, staying with him until the bitter end. Thereafter, all four Gospels have her going to Jesus's tomb on Easter morning with other women. Then, Mark 16:9 summarizes what the other three Gospels also attest: "He appeared first to Mary Magdalene." John's Gospel goes further and says that the risen Christ commissioned Magdalene as the first witness of the resurrection to the other disciples. And as instructed, "Mary Magdalene went and announced to the disciples, 'I have seen the Lord'" (John 20:17–18)—the risen Christ.

For this reason, and for the first six centuries of Church history, Mary Magdalene's title was *apostola apostolorum*—"apostle to the Apostles"—and rightly so. Thereafter, her good name was maligned as "the prostitute," portrayed in Church art as a sexy temptress. To reclaim the inclusivity of Jesus's original community, the Church needs to undo the damage of such bias, and come to treat all, and particularly women, with total equality. Nothing less will be faithful to the Gospels and example of Jesus.

A small step in the right direction was when Pope Francis recently (July 2016) had Mary Magdalene restored to her proper title of *apostola apostolorum*, "apostle to the apostles." Likewise, he raised her feast day in the liturgical calendar, July 22, from the status of a "memorial" to a major feast; this means that there are now appropriate Scripture readings and prayers that mention Mary Magdalene by name and seek her intercession. Hopeful signs!

PAUSE FOR REFLECTION

- Think of real people in your social context who suffer from exclusion of one kind or another. What might being a disciple of Jesus encourage of you in their regard?

- Imagine ways that the Church can witness to the full equality of women. How can you encourage that along?

COMMISSION OF DISCIPLES TO SHARE THE GOSPEL

As well noted already, Jesus had an unwavering sense of his own calling in life—to be a catalyst of God's reign in human history. Within this overarching vocation, he stated his mission at times with slightly differing emphases, so: "to seek out and to save the lost" (Luke 19:10); to call "sinners" to repentance (Mark 2:17); "to testify to the truth" (John 18:37); that all might have life "abundantly" (John 10:10); to bring "light" to the world (John 12:46); that all "may have eternal life" (John 3:16); and more.

Then, from the very beginning of his public ministry, Jesus made clear that he was empowering disciples to become active participants in his mission for God's reign. Discipleship for Jesus is not simply a personal choice and for one's own benefit; it also brings a mandate to outreach with his gospel to others. So a deep value of Jesus was to empower disciples to be proactive participants rather than passive recipients; disciples are to be agents of their faith. In a lovely phrase popularized by Pope Francis in our time, Jesus called and empowered people to be "missionary disciples."

From the very beginning of Mark's Gospel, we find Jesus calling *helpers*—not just followers; the first were two fishermen, Simon (later named Peter) and his brother Andrew. His invitation was "Follow me and I will make you fish for people" (1:17). So besides following him, Jesus invited them to be coparticipants in his mission to the world. Note that the verb for "come" there is the Greek *deute*, which is an invitation more than a command. Jesus calls into a community of mission by invitation, to be accepted freely *or* rejected (check out John 6:66–69; Mark 10:22 for instances of rejection).

Early in his ministry, Jesus began to send out disciples—without him being present—to explicitly participate in his mission, and not only "the twelve" (Luke 9:1–6) but some "seventy others" besides (10:1–12). Their commission echoes throughout all three Synoptics; they were to cure the sick, have power to cast out evil, and to proclaim his gospel of God's reign (see Matt 10:7–8). John summarizes Jesus's commissioning disciples with "As the Father has sent me, so I send you" (20:21). However, the classic calling and commissioning of disciples to carry forward Jesus's mission is found in Matthew 28:16–20. (See Mark 16:15–16 and Luke 24:47–48 for their shorter versions.)

Note first that this is a meeting of the community of disciples with the risen Christ Jesus. Matthew's Gospel says that Jesus had given them prior instruction to meet him on a hillside in Galilee. In Matthew, this was the remnant community's first encounter with the risen Christ and the text notes that "some doubted" (28:17). Then claiming "all authority in heaven and on earth," the risen Christ Jesus gives them the Great Commission (28:18–20).

They are to "go and make disciples of all nations," carrying his good news to the ends of the earth. They are to incorporate people into a community of faith that is bonded into the very triune life of God: "baptizing them in the name of the Father and of the Son and of the Holy Spirit" (v. 19). They are to teach people to embrace and *live* the commitments and values that marked the life of Jesus; "teaching them to obey everything that I have commanded you" (v. 20), so proposing a *living* faith. He concludes with the promise of his own abiding presence; "Remember, I am with you always, to the end of the age" (v. 20).

A few points are worth highlighting. First, note that Jesus gave this great commission to all disciples there present; all Christians are called to collaborate in Jesus's mission to the world. Second, the work of evangelizing—sharing the good news (*evangelion*)—demands teaching a lifestyle as well, the one modeled by Jesus himself. Third, surely these two commissions—to evangelize and teach a *way* of life—are two sides of the same coin. The most effective way for Christians to evangelize is by their own *living* faith. By baptism, every Christian is so called and commissioned to actively participate in the mission of Jesus to the world. We are all to be "missionary disciples."

With all the promises that *the way* of Jesus brings happiness, is there not a stark reality to face if we truly participate in Jesus's mission? As it did for him, might commitment to his *way* also bring *us* to the *cross*? We address "why the cross" for Jesus in chapter 5 and propose that his execution was the result of the values by which he lived. If we live likewise, can we yet pose happiness as the promised outcome, while the cross of Jesus stares us in the face?

Jesus repeated often that he brought good news ("gospel"), which was both to cause and be shared with joy (John 15:11). Yet all three Synoptics have him state clearly, "If any want to become my followers, let them deny themselves and take up their cross and follow me" (Mark 8:34). What are we to make of this commission to "the cross"—and what of the happiness promised to disciples?

First, note well that Jesus never said, "I will carry your cross for you," but instead charged would-be disciples to "take up their cross and follow me" (Matt 16:24). Second, Jesus never urged people to take on extra crosses beyond those that come with the territory of life. In the Garden of Gethsemane on the night before he died, Jesus himself prayed to God that his impending cross might pass him by (check Luke 22:39–46). When faced with crosses in life, we can surely say a similar prayer.

Third, while Jesus does not promise to take away whatever suffering comes with life, Christian faith is that Jesus, Son of God, suffered in solidarity with humankind and that this helps us to carry our own crosses. Recall the beautiful passage in Matthew's Gospel (11:28–29), when Jesus invites all who "are weary and are carrying heavy burdens" to come to him and "I will give you rest." Then he adds, "Take my yoke upon you, and learn from me…and you will find rest for your souls" (v. 29). He concluded with, "For my yoke is easy, and my burden is light."

A key point in interpreting this text is to remember that the yoke used as a farm implement in Jesus's world was always a double, a pair. So, when Jesus says "take *my yoke* upon you" he is really promising to walk alongside, to pull the load with us. Our faith that Jesus is pulling with us can lend hope, even with the heaviest of crosses. And God's reversal of Jesus's death by raising him up, lends the ultimate hope in the face of all suffering.

HOPE FOR OUR HEARTS

The summation of this chapter's proposal of how to find happiness in life is well stated by a verse in the Letter to the Hebrews. It advises that we "keep our eyes fixed on Jesus" (12:2, NAB). To fulfill our heart's desire for happiness, disciples must "fix" on Jesus. Indeed, this can be well posed as the central theme in the papacy of Pope Francis—to center on Jesus first and foremost, and to let everything else of Christian faith follow on from there.

As noted in the prelude but worth repeating here, centering on Jesus may still be a stretch for many raised in a traditional Catholic faith. For various historical reasons, we are more prone to "fix our eyes" on the Church, or on the Mass and sacraments, or on the dogmas and doctrines, or on Mary or a favorite saint, or on the papacy, and so on—as if these are the defining aspects of Catholic Christian faith. Instead and as for all Christians, our "canon within the canon"—that by which we interpret every other feature of our faith—must be Jesus, the Christ. Of course, all the other aspects are important and integral to Christian discipleship, but it is Jesus who defines the heart of it all, to animate and permeate everything else.

The prelude also well warned against "Christomonism," an ancient heresy that reduced *everything* to faith in Jesus. Though it began in the early Church, you can find its contemporary version in Sunday morning TV sermons. So often they pose Christian faith as no more than "just me and Jesus" in a warm, fuzzy relationship, promising great prosperity as our award for simply accepting him as Lord and Savior, and with little about following in his footsteps. What a scam! Instead, to grow in living the demanding life of discipleship, we need all the features and resources of Christian faith, its whole story and vision. So we put our "fix" on Jesus to understand who our God is, the role of the Holy Spirit, the nature and mission of the Church, the meaning and celebration of the sacraments, the Creeds that summarize our faith, and so on for all its constitutive aspects. While Jesus is like the key to the door, we need the whole house!

For sure, growing as a disciple of Jesus is demanding, and its horizon of holiness ever calls us to what St. Ignatius of Loyola called "the more." Yet, paradoxically, it is also the path to happiness of life. Was there a bit of hyperbole when Jesus concluded his "come to me" invitation with, "For my yoke is easy, and my burden is light"? Given the demands of following Jesus, it is hard to think of his *way* as a light load, much less of being its own reward. And yet, think about it: love is a joy to carry whereas hate burdens our own hearts the most; being at peace brings contentment that is destroyed by enmity and conflict; being truthful reflects our genuine selves whereas falsehood betrays us; living justly and working for justice is far more life-giving than complicity with injustice and indifference to social oppressions; compassion is its own reward whereas being mean sours our souls; belonging to a faith community is more humanizing than spiritually going it alone; and the list goes on.

Embracing *the way* of Jesus may well lend the "lightest load" to carry and be the surest path to fulfill our human longings for happiness in life. Of course, the crosses come our way. But in Christian faith, the cross never has the last word—as it didn't in the life of Jesus. Here we anticipate the resurrection story and the rock-solid hope for happiness it brings to our hearts (next chapter).

Having said as much, I must honestly confess that to believe what I have written here and to "fix my eyes on Jesus" remains an ongoing challenge to my own heart. The Catholicism of my childhood, so imbued with its Irish cultural flavor, encouraged me to see discipleship to Jesus as solely a great demand upon my life. It was most often presented as a listing of rules and regulations, all to be strictly observed or there literally would be "hell to pay." Oh, if its heavy load would be carried well, it brought the promise of eternal life hereafter. Meanwhile, life in faith was mostly a burden to be borne, a cross to be carried, with a tinge that the most difficult path is always the most meritorious one for us.

To defend a little that old Irish Catholicism and its focus on the cross, it did lend hope to a poor and downtrodden people for whom even a modicum of happiness in this life seemed beyond reach. Such a Catholicism did as much for many oppressed peoples, with the promise, if well lived, that their faith would bring eternal happiness hereafter. Meanwhile, it is still a challenge for me to see that *the way* of Jesus is its own reward *now*. Yet it is surely so; and its promise remains that as we live, so shall we die, and find full happiness hereafter.

I recognize from my own life, too, that even at my best of times, I never fully follow *the way*. Yet to echo a theme that runs throughout this work—we always have the abundance of God's grace to so live, and of God's mercy when we fall short. God's grace ever both prompts and sustains our efforts to follow *the way* of Jesus.

Assured of God's help—for free, *gratia*—just imagine what extraordinary people we can become and what happy lives we can live the more we grow in imitating Jesus. How faith filled, how loving, how hopeful we can be; how honest, truthful, and just in all our dealings; how compassionate toward people in need; how committed to justice and an end to all oppressions; how merciful and forgiving; how reconciling and peacemaking; how resilient in times of trouble, failure, or addiction; how inclusive in our care and community; how committed to the equality of all people; how respectful of the dignity of every person; how confident of God's mercy when we sin; and the list goes on. Indeed, echoing Jesus's Beatitudes, how blessed/happy we can be by following *the way* of Jesus. What a gift to our hearts!

And, as said earlier about happiness in general, finding it by *the way* of Jesus is not by achieving certain distant goals (the perfect spouse, career, kids) nor need we be robbed of happiness by our failures in life, past or present. We can be happy along the way, both by embracing the gifts of life and by contributing to the well-being of others as God's reign intends. This is Jesus's promise to our hearts; we can trust him!

PAUSE FOR REFLECTION

- To what might Jesus be calling and commissioning you personally at this time? What does it ask of you to respond?

- Think of some cross you are carrying in your life. How might Jesus help you to carry it with hope, with him sharing "the yoke"?

SPIRITUAL PRACTICE: BEFRIENDING JESUS

At the Last Supper, John's Gospel has Jesus say that living his love command, instead of a burden, is to bring joy to disciples (15:11). He then added, "I have called you friends" (15:15). Becoming a friend of Jesus can surely bring joy and happiness to our lives. But how can we become friends of Jesus? Let me suggest one simple spiritual practice that can help deepen the Jesus friendship in our hearts.

There is an old tradition that Christians call "centering prayer"; some version of it is common in many of the great world religions. It usually begins by focusing on one's breath, becoming aware of breathing in and out, doing so slowly and deliberately. Close your eyes if this makes you less distracted. Then, as you breathe, begin to focus on the two words, *Jesus* and *friend*, repeating the holy name of "Jesus" as you breathe in, and "friend" as you breathe out. When distractions come, refocus on your two words, *Jesus/friend*. Continue for at least some minutes, perhaps gradually building up the length of time.

Besides growing our friendship with Jesus, such centering prayer is medically verified to be a health practice that slows down the heart rate and relaxes bodily tensions. Spiritually, over time it will help you to inhale friendship with Jesus into your heart.

FOR FURTHER READING

Harrington, Daniel J. *Following Jesus: What the New Testament Teaches Us*. Huntington, IN: Our Sunday Visitor, 2012. A readable and scholarly summary of what the Gospels portray as following Jesus.

Johnson, Elizabeth. *Consider Jesus: Waves of Renewal in Christology*. Crossroad: New York, 1990. A beautiful introduction to Christology focusing on Jesus as "the heart" of Christian faith.

Lohfink, Gerhard. *Jesus of Nazareth: What He Wanted, Who He Was*. Collegeville, MN: Michael Glazier, 2015. An excellent review of the best contemporary scholarship on the life and teaching of the historical Jesus.

CHAPTER 5

The Risen Christ Jesus

Our Hunger for Freedom

"All Changed, Changed Utterly"

No line better captures the meaning of Easter than the refrain of William Butler Yeats's poem "Easter 1916." It runs, "All changed, changed utterly: A terrible beauty is born."

On Easter Monday, 1916, a handful of Irish patriots, with little popular support, launched a rebellion against British rule in Ireland and for the freedom of the Irish people. They called it "The Rising," with the name and timing deliberately chosen to echo the resurrection of Jesus from the dead. The Rising was swiftly and brutally put down by the British army and sixteen of its leaders were summarily executed by firing squad.

At first, Yeats was ambivalent toward the Easter Rising. He still wonders in the poem why its leaders, some of them distinguished poets like himself, would step out of "the casual comedy" of everyday life, full of its "polite meaningless words," and the ready diversions offered "where motley is worn"—the circus of life. However, as for disciples and the resurrection of Jesus, Yeats and the Irish people gradually came to realize that something extraordinary had come to pass in their nation's Rising up for freedom. Yeats's immortal refrain well captures the meaning of the first and every Easter since, "All changed, changed utterly: A terrible beauty is born."

GOD'S FAVOR THAT SETS FREE

The first Christian communities would readily agree that Yeats hit the nail on the head. For them, the Easter event redirected the whole course of human history. After that, everything was changed, changed utterly. But can we reasonably believe such a lavish claim? If so, then we must wonder what new possibilities it poses for humankind in every age, and indeed, for all of creation. If Easter be true, then what was the "terrible beauty" (Yeats meant *astonishing*) that it birthed, the watershed change it brought about?

First, let us recognize it as a foundational truth claim of Christian faith, that "God raised [Jesus] from the dead" (Acts 13:30). Paul rightly recognized this as a make-or-break condition for Christian faith; as he reminded the Corinthians, "If Christ has not been raised," then "your faith has been in vain" (1 Cor 15:14). Against his negative hypothesis, however, Paul and those first Christians came to a rock-solid faith, repeated often and from the beginning, "This Jesus God raised up" (Acts 2:32).

Almost equally amazing, the early Christians became fully convinced that by bonding with the risen Christ through baptism, all disciples are raised up with him and can "walk in newness of life" (Rom 6:4). For "the one who raised the Lord Jesus will raise us also" (2 Cor 4:14). Now even death has lost its "sting" (1 Cor 15:55–57). Oh for sure, within historical time we will all die, but just as surely "all will be made alive in Christ" again (1 Cor 15:22). After Jesus's victory of rising from it, those first Christians viewed death as no more than a change of life—into time out of time with God.

We will elaborate further on such fantastic truth claims after we have assessed their credibility and what might have actually happened in Jesus's rising. But first, and turning to the hungers of our heart, we can well wonder what deep human desire might find the resurrection story particularly appealing, and especially in this secular age and postmodern world. As we will see, Christians from the beginning used many metaphors to express God's purpose in raising Jesus, all with appeal to people's hearts; what might have compelling appeal in our time?

I will propose *freedom* as a defining hunger of our age that can find hope for fulfillment—however partial—with the resurrection of Jesus.

Our desire for freedom or liberation is another facet that permeates all the other hungers of our diamond heart. Might God's raising up of Jesus be a catalyst for us toward such terrible beauty?

To appreciate the freedom that results for us from the resurrection of Jesus, we need to understand the *means* that Christians believe he made possible to this end. What helps us to live into true freedom? From the beginning, the Christian response has been God's *grace* that is now, as Paul repeats often, made all the more abundant in Jesus Christ (see Rom 5:17, etc.).

Of the four Gospels, only John uses the term "grace," and specifically of Jesus. So he recognizes Jesus as "full of grace and truth" (1:14), and as effecting for us "grace upon grace" (1:16). The rest of the New Testament, however, repeats the term some one hundred and fifty times and precisely as naming the *means* to the *end* of *living* Christian faith that sets free.

No Christian theological term has been more contested than *grace*. Differing understandings and emphases, especially regarding how grace "works" in our lives, is still debated among Christians. A great battle cry of the original Reformers (Luther, Calvin, etc.) was *sola gratia*, meaning "grace alone" saves. They were trying to offset the exaggerated Catholic emphasis of the time on the need for our own good works as if God's saving grace must be earned. As a recent declaration of agreement between the Catholic Church and many mainline Protestant denominations recognizes (elaborated in chapter 9), both sides had an important point to make. Both grace and our own good works are essential, or better still, we need God's help to empower our own good works.

Looking to grace's etymological roots, the Greek *charis* and the Latin *gratia* suggest a variety of meanings. However, their dominant reference is to an *unearned favor*—help that is gratis (hear the echo), or for free. Reflecting the best of both Catholic and Protestant perspectives, I understand grace as *God's free and effective love at work in our lives that empowers us to respond to God's initiative to set us free.* In other words, though God's grace is free, its effect is not to suspend our agency but to empower it all the more toward true freedom. As said before, God's grace is free and yet comes as a responsibility, or better a *response-ability*.

So, with the help of God's abundant grace in Jesus Christ, we *can* live as his disciples and into true freedom. As an old Celtic wisdom saying has it, "there is an ebb to every tide, except the tide of God's grace"; God's effective love is always at high tide for us now.

As with the human condition in general, help can be given in ways that empower and free people or that make recipients dependent or codependent. God's grace does the former "in spades," because it is not only free but freeing as well; grace empowers our own efforts and agency. And we receive God's help not because we earn it but because we need it. Rather than lessening our human responsibilities, grace heightens them, both prompting and sustaining our efforts to live into the freedom of God's reign as disciples of Jesus.

As the great Lutheran theologian Dietrich Bonhoffer insisted, God's grace is never "cheap" as if to make our side of the divine/human covenant unnecessary. Instead, God's grace makes us all the more responsible and precisely to do good and live well. As Paul explained, through Jesus, God gives every grace "in abundance, so that [we]…may share abundantly in every good work" (2 Cor 9:8). Note well: grace is given precisely to empower our good works. And here I propose that by so responding to God's grace, we can be agents who live into our heart's desire for true freedom.

As human beings, we are ever faced with more than we can handle by our own efforts alone. We literally *need help*. All people experience a deep precariousness to life and multiple threats to our well-being. The influential philosopher Martin Heidegger (1889–1976) captured well this feeling of being existentially threatened, describing it as "thrownness." It is as if we are flung into life, whether we like it or not, and find ourselves in the midst of tremendous hazards to our well-being. Daily we experience the threat of illness, danger, misfortune, accidents, loss of family and friends, injustices and oppressions of many kinds, and the list goes on. The ultimate threat, of course, is that the human mortality rate is 100 percent.

Heidegger also named *freedom*—over against the existential threats of life—as the defining quest of people in our postmodern age. He argued further that it is only by facing into our thrownness, rather than trying to escape from it, that we can find a modicum of freedom.

However, he made it sound as if we must set ourselves free by dint of our own efforts. Indeed, Heidegger's position reflects the self-sufficient assumption of our postmodern world in general and how it quests for freedom as an individualized and self-reliant project. It assumes that we must "go it alone," that we can and should be self-sufficient, becoming our own liberators—as the "buffered selves" of postmodernity that Taylor described (chapter 1). As warned before, trying to be our own god becomes a slavery.

Christian faith has a more realistic proposal to make: because of Jesus's dying and rising, we *can* live into true freedom by drawing upon the help of God's grace to prompt and sustain our best efforts to do what should be done. And given the claim by Heidegger and other philosophers that freedom is a distinguishing hunger of our era, then speaking of the Easter event as setting free can have deep appeal to contemporary hearts.

In fact, the first Christians imagined multiple metaphors to express what Jesus's dying and rising caused in human history—trying to name what cannot be said completely. Since then, different metaphors have appealed variously according to the time and context. A particular favorite is *salvation*, with Jesus as our *Savior*. The term has a sense of being made safe, secure, whole, of being delivered from danger, of being kept from disaster, of enjoying good health (Latin: *salus*). While *salvation* has perennial appeal (and I settle below for *liberating salvation*), we can imagine it being even more engaging to the heart when people's well-being and health were severely threatened by plagues, epidemics, incurable diseases, and threats to well-being on all fronts.

Likewise, *redemption* from sin has been a favorite Christian metaphor from the beginning, portraying Jesus as our *Redeemer*. Again, redemption will always have its appeal as we recognize our own sins, our need for forgiveness and mercy, and for help to counteract human sinfulness. However, it likely spoke more powerfully at a time when warring tribes took hostages and demanded payment for their release (*redemeo*—to buy back). Note, too, if taken too literally, *redemption*, like all metaphors, can become misleading. So that "Christ died for our sins" (1 Cor 15:3) cannot be taken literally to mean that God needed God's own Son to die a terrible death in order to "pay" a debt of ours

125

before forgiving and loving us again. What a terrifying image of God! As theologian Elizabeth Johnson summarizes, "The mercy of God does not need the death of Jesus" (*Creation and the Cross*, 27).

Given these examples from Christian history, we can well ask, What might be an appealing metaphor for the effect of God's grace that would find ready resonance in our postmodern context? To pose God's work in Jesus and continuing now by the Holy Spirit as *liberating* and Jesus as our *Liberator* can have particular appeal to the *freedom* hunger of our time.

Throughout history there has been extraordinary witness to the human hunger for freedom. The American Declaration of Independence well named humankind's "unalienable rights" as "life, *liberty*, and the pursuit of happiness." The quest for *life* and *happiness* are already well reflected in previous chapters; here we focus on the desire for *liberty*. And this postmodern era has brought an unprecedented rising up by subjugated peoples, demanding to have voice and agency to craft their own lives in the world. While freedom is not a new hunger to our time, the raised consciousness regarding human agency and its increased possibilities in our postmodern age intensifies our hunger for it.

In chapter 2, we reflected on God as revealed in the exodus event. In freeing the Israelites from slavery in Egypt, we recognize a liberating God who intervenes in human history to set free an oppressed people. St. Paul recognized a similar divine intervention in Jesus: "The Spirit of life in Christ Jesus has set you free from the law of sin and of death" (Rom 8:2). Likewise, Paul taught that in Jesus, "creation itself will be set free from its bondage to decay and will obtain the freedom of the glory of the children of God" (Rom 8:21). Not only people but creation itself is set free by Jesus's dying and rising.

Though a heart's desire in every age, the freedom catalyzed in the exodus event and by Jesus's paschal mystery was brought forcefully into Christian consciousness by a contemporary movement often referred to as *liberation* theology. It arose especially from among people suffering oppression and injustices of various kinds from the underside of history—always a privileged locus of God's grace at work. The convictions of this liberation movement are now considered mainstream in Christian theology and well reflected in Church teachings.

Following a central theme of liberation theology, the freedom won by Jesus's death and resurrection is both *personal* and *social*. Indeed this is imperative because sin is *both* personal and social—so our liberation from it must be likewise. Our personal sins contribute to sinful social structures, and vice versa; contexts and structures of sinfulness dispose us to personal sin. The liberation by Jesus, then, must help set free from both.

So Jesus our Liberator delivers us from being overpowered by our own sinfulness and addictions, and likewise empowers our struggle against sinful social structures and oppressive cultural mores. As such, it is a liberation *from* sin, both personal and social, empowering us not to be held bound by either. Not only as freedom *from*, Jesus's paschal mystery empowers freedom *for* living into liberation as God's people, and this for ourselves, for others, for the public realm, and for all of God's creation.

Let us be keenly aware that freedom through Jesus is the antithesis of *license*—as if "free to do whatever we please." Such license readily becomes its own enslavement. Note the many enduring addictions in our society (alcohol, drugs, etc.) and the emerging one around social media. License readily becomes a slavery and, as any recovering AA member will attest, is overcome only with the help of a "Higher Power"—God's grace. The freedom that Jesus won is the empowerment to do what we *should* do in order to live free for ourselves and for the true freedom of all.

Let us bring with us this human hunger for freedom, forefront all the more in our time, as we elaborate on the meaning for us of Jesus's death and resurrection, and the "terrible beauty" that it birthed. Does Jesus's paschal mystery catalyze the grace we need to live as free and freeing disciples; does it empower us to work for liberation for all people and for God's creation? Of course, before interpreting the meaning for us, so much depends on "what really happened" in Jesus's death and resurrection, to which we now turn.

PAUSE FOR REFLECTION

- Is there a social oppression or personal obsession that besets your own life at this time? How might God's grace empower you to live into greater realization of freedom?

- What are some assets and then limitations of posing God's work in Jesus as setting us free? Name some characteristics of such grace-empowered liberation.

THE CRUCIFIXION OF JESUS

The story of Jesus's resurrection and the emancipatory grace that it catalyzes within human history must begin with his crucifixion; Jesus's cross and resurrection are inextricably intertwined. I lay out the narrative briefly, relying mainly on Mark's account—collaborated by the other three. As the first Gospel written, Mark likely narrates closest to the actual events. I review the crucifixion story under three headings: (1) why was Jesus condemned; (2) the events of his passion and death; (3) the account of his burial—as a prelude to his resurrection.

Why Kill Jesus? Historically speaking, Jesus was crucified *because of the life he lived*. Think of his compassion and kindness to all in need, regardless of their social status, his siding with the poor, downtrodden, and excluded, his pushing back against so many of the political and religious oppressions of his culture, the inclusivity of his community and table fellowship, his confidence in God's love and boundless mercy for sinners, his priorities that put meeting human needs ahead of keeping Sabbath, his threat to the economic structures by expelling the money changers from the temple and praying that all debts be forgiven. Add, too, his announcing in the midst of an oppressive empire the inbreaking of God's reign of justice, peace, and unconditional love for all, demanding radical love by disciples—even for enemies (i.e., the Romans in particular). As reviewed in previous chapters, in any context, but especially in the Roman empire of his day, such a good life and person was bound to engender great animosity.

Caiaphas was the high priest of the time, and Pontius Pilate the Roman governor of Judea. The Gospels give the impression that for both of them, Jesus's preaching of God's reign posed a political threat. Remember that his favored term *basilea*—kingdom—could well be translated as "empire," as Pilate likely heard it. Then John's Gospel has the chief priests worry that if people keep gathering around Jesus, "the Romans will come and destroy both our holy place and our nation" (11:48). For all those in power, religious or political, Jesus was just too dangerous to let go on living and teaching his revolutionary *way*.

Mark has it very early that upon Jesus's healing a man with a "withered hand" on the Sabbath, the Pharisees and Herodians "conspired...how to destroy him" (3:1–6). Though this initial animosity is attributed to his breach of Sabbath law, the story comes just ten verses after the same people objected to him eating with "tax collectors and sinners" (2:15–18). So the inclusivity of his table fellowship may have been what first sparked the ire of the authorities and the beginning of the end for Jesus.

Perhaps the final trigger for his death was in his cleansing of the temple, an event recounted in all four Gospels. With this, Jesus was interfering in the economy of his religious context; people can become very angry when their purses are threatened. Thereafter, "the chief priests and the scribes...kept looking for a way to kill him" (Mark 11:12–19). They soon got their opportunity.

"Two days before the Passover" as "the chief priests and the scribes were looking for a way to arrest Jesus by stealth and kill him" (Mark 14:1–3), Judas came to them with an offer. He would "betray [Jesus] to them When they heard it, they were greatly pleased, and promised to give him money" (14:10–11). Matthew names the price of Jesus as "thirty pieces of silver" (26:15).

Later, at his trial before the high priest and his Council (*Sanhedrin*), the ultimate charge against Jesus is blasphemy, as evident in his claiming to be "the Messiah, the Son of the Blessed One" (Mark 14:53–65). This blasphemy charge is echoed in John: "Because you [Jesus], though only a human being, are making yourself God" (10:33). For the Romans, however, Jesus's crime as they would nail to his cross in mockery was that the people were hailing him (Luke 19:38) and he was aspiring to be "*King* of the Jews" (Mark 15:26)—a political threat and claim.

The Passion and Crucifixion of Jesus: As the clouds are gathering, Mark places Jesus in Bethany, a village near Jerusalem, at the house of "Simon the Leper" (had Jesus cured him?). There, over dinner, a woman came and anointed Jesus's feet with some very costly ointment (though the details vary, all four Gospels have some version of this story). Some protested that this was a waste, but Jesus said, "She has anointed my body beforehand for its burial....Wherever the good news is proclaimed in the whole world, what she has done will be told in remembrance of her" (Mark 14:3–9). By Jesus's directive, I include it here! Thereafter, things moved quickly.

On the night before he died, Jesus had a Last Supper with his friends. In John's account he washed their feet. In Mark, echoed in Matthew and Luke, Jesus uttered the immortal words over some bread, "Take; this is my body" and then, over a cup of wine, "This is my blood" and gave to them to eat and drink (14:22–25). Luke's account adds that Jesus directed the disciples: "Do this in remembrance of me" (22:19). Following on, Jesus foretold that Peter would betray him (Mark 14:26–31); and sure enough, he did (14:66–72).

After this Last Supper, Jesus went with his disciples to the garden of Gethsemane. There, being "deeply grieved" at the thought of the death he was about to die, he prayed to God to be spared the ordeal (Mark 14:32–42). This soon became the site of Judas's betrayal; he identified Jesus with a kiss and Jesus was arrested. With that, "all of them [Jesus's male disciples] deserted him and fled" (Mark 14:43–51).

Jesus was brought first to the high priest and his council. Matthew and John name him Caiaphas. There, as noted already, the charge against Jesus is blasphemy (Mark 14:53–65), punishable by being stoned to death according to Torah (Lev 24:10–16). The Sanhedrin sent Jesus to Pilate; he could be executed only by Roman authority. Pilate asked Jesus, "Are you the King of the Jews"? (note again his political concern). But Jesus refused to defend himself and "Pilate was amazed" at his silence (Mark 15:1–5). Luke also has Pilate send Jesus to Herod, who was the vassal ruler of Galilee; "even Herod with his soldiers treated him with contempt and mocked him." Then Herod sent Jesus back to Pilate (Luke 23:6–12).

All four Gospels have Pilate offer the option of releasing Jesus or a criminal named Barabbas. The gathered crowd chose Barabbas and of Jesus cried, "Crucify him!" With that, "after flogging Jesus" (a painful torture), Pilate "handed him over to be crucified" by his Roman soldiers (Mark 15:6–15). This was a most ignominious death, meant to humiliate the crucified and terrorize the onlookers. First, the soldiers mocked Jesus, crowning him with thorns, and "they began saluting him, 'Hail, King of the Jews!'" (15:16–20). Even the common soldiers resented his alleged political ambitions.

Then, "they brought Jesus to the place called Golgotha," outside the walls of Jerusalem. There "they crucified him....It was nine o'clock in the morning....And with him they crucified two bandits, one on his right and one on his left." The chief priests and scribes mocked Jesus saying, "He saved others; he cannot save himself"—surely reflecting his full humanity (Mark 15:21–32). Luke has Jesus say, "Father, forgive them; for they do not know what they are doing" (23:34).

On the cross, Jesus cried out, "My God, my God, why have you forsaken me?" and soon after "breathed his last." A Roman centurion who had helped crucify him now confessed, "Truly this man was God's Son!" (Mark 15:33–41). John has the soldiers pierce Jesus's side with a spear (19:34). As all four Gospels attest, the women disciples remained close by the cross of Jesus while the men all ran away.

The Burial of Jesus: I make a point of Jesus's burial and its location because of a later claim—contesting his resurrection—that the tomb found empty was not the one where he was buried. All four Gospels record his burial, though each has its own description. The three Synoptics have it witnessed by the women disciples who had remained by Jesus's cross.

Mark tells how "Joseph of Arimathea, a respected member of the council...went boldly to Pilate and asked for the body of Jesus" (15:43). Pilate verifies with the centurion in charge that Jesus was already dead. Because crucifixion could be a very slow death, lasting for days, families or friends would sometimes steal the crucified and try to revive them.

Being satisfied that Jesus was dead, Pilate gave over to Joseph the body of Jesus.

Joseph took Jesus's body from the cross, "wrapped it in the linen cloth, and laid it in a tomb that had been hewn out of the rock. He then rolled a stone against the door of the tomb." So it was left secure, countering another later claim that Jesus's tomb was robbed. However, "Mary Magdalene and Mary the mother of Joses saw where the body was laid" (Mark 15:42–47). So there were at least two witnesses—as required by law—to its location.

Matthew agrees almost verbatim with Mark; he emphasizes that Joseph of Arimathea "rolled a great stone to the door of the tomb" (27:60)—thus one not easily removed. Only Matthew adds the detail that soldiers were stationed at the tomb to prevent the disciples from stealing Jesus's body (27:62–66). This offsets the later claim by the chief priests that Jesus's body had indeed been stolen rather than resurrected (28:11–15).

Luke follows Mark's account, adding that Jesus was the first to be buried in this particular tomb. He does not name the women witnesses but says that "the women who had come with him [Jesus] from Galilee followed, and they saw the tomb and how his body was laid." Because it was the Sabbath-eve, the women could not anoint Jesus's body as was the custom. Instead, they went home and "prepared spices and ointments" to do so later (Luke 23:50–56). John's account essentially agrees; however, he has Nicodemus (who previously had come to Jesus, "by night" [see John 3]) join Joseph of Arimathea in anointing and burying Jesus's body (19:38–42). If this had been the end of the story, as Paul noted, Christian faith would be in vain.

PAUSE FOR REFLECTION

- What stands out most for you in this narrative of Jesus's crucifixion?

- Why do you think he was crucified? How might Jesus crucified become the Liberator of humankind? What kind of freedom might he make possible?

THE RESURRECTION OF JESUS

Stop to think about it: from a human perspective at least, it would seem imperative that God raise Jesus from the dead. Jesus was the very presence of God in human history and the best person who had ever lived. If left "for dead," then death, evil, sin, and oppression would have triumphed; goodness and God would have been defeated. Jesus was what theologian Jürgen Moltman well names our "Crucified God." But how could God allow Jesus's crucifixion to have the last word? This would be to let his body, which embodied the very presence of God, rot away in a tomb—decayed and defeated by death.

And how else was God to affirm *the way* that Jesus modeled and taught? If God had not raised him from the dead, the historical Jesus and his Gospel would have been soon forgotten. So there is a deep logic to Jesus's resurrection. Yet we can still well ask what happened, and why can we believe it?

What Resurrection?: First, let us recognize a great mystery here, something deeply of God and beyond human experience. Jesus's rising was *not* a resuscitation of his earthly body as if he returned to daily life. Nor was it a reanimation or reincarnation as if a soul rejoins its body or takes on a different one—as believed in some religions. And yet it was "real" for Jesus's earthly body.

So he could eat breakfast with his disciples (John 21:1–14), and invite "doubting Thomas" to put his hand into Jesus's bodily wounds (20:24–29). However, the risen Christ could also pass through locked doors (20:19) and could appear to disciples at will. So while the earthly body of Jesus was not left to decay—the tomb was found empty—yet his risen body is of the divine realm that we have yet to experience ourselves.

So what happened? Favoring Mark again, he recounts, "When the sabbath was over, Mary Magdalene, and Mary the mother of James, and Salome bought spices, so that they might go" to Jesus's tomb to anoint his body. They were wondering, "Who will roll away the stone" at the entrance, yet when they got there, "they saw that the stone, which was very large, had already been rolled back." Within the tomb "they saw a young man, dressed in a white robe" and "they were alarmed" (Mark 16:1–5).

He tells them, "Do not be alarmed; you are looking for Jesus of Nazareth, who was crucified. He has been raised." He added, "But go, tell his disciples and Peter that he is going ahead of you to Galilee; there you will see him, just as he told you." Mark ends with, "So they went out and fled from the tomb, for terror and amazement had seized them, and they said nothing to anyone, for they were afraid" (16:6–8).

Then, in "the longer ending" to Mark's Gospel, we find three more resurrection snippets. The first states boldly that Jesus rose on the first day of the week and "appeared first to Mary Magdalene" (16:9). She went and told the other disciples "that [Jesus] was alive and had been seen by her" but "they would not believe it" (16:10–11). The second says that Jesus appeared to two other disciples while walking in the country; "they went back and told the rest, but they did not believe them" (16:13). Last, Mark says that the risen Christ Jesus "appeared to the eleven" and "upbraided them for their lack of faith and stubbornness, because they had not believed those [i.e., the women] who saw him after he had risen." Then he gave them a commission to "go into all the world and proclaim the good news to the whole creation" (16:14–15).

Mark concludes with a brief account of Jesus's ascension; it receives much more detail in Luke 24:50–53 and Acts 1:6–11. Mark simply states, "So then the Lord Jesus, after he had spoken to them, was taken up into heaven and sat down at the right hand of God. And they went out and proclaimed the good news everywhere" (16:19–20).

The other three Gospels echo much of Mark and yet add their own accounts of disciples encountering the risen Jesus; we note some of their details below. For now, the Gospels clearly claim that Jesus rose from the dead and that he was seen repeatedly by disciples, beginning with Mary Magdalene and other women. Indeed, Paul, in his First Letter to the Corinthians, written as early as AD 53, states that Jesus "appeared to more than five hundred brothers and sisters at one time, most of whom are still alive, though some have died" (15:6).

Can We Believe It? Imagine for a moment that Jesus's resurrection was just a concocted story as some have claimed from the beginning (Matt 28:11–15), or as if he rose only in the wishful hearts of disciples. This would have required a massive conspiracy and deep delusion among a huge number of people, many of whom would suffer persecution and even give their lives in witness to Jesus's resurrection (check Acts 7:54—8:3). Taking such a proposal as ridiculous, we can note at least three compelling reasons why it is credible to believe in the realness of Jesus's resurrection.

First, rather than conspiring to fabricate the story or being overly credulous, it is abundantly clear that the disciples were not expecting Jesus to rise and could not believe it at first. Second, if it was a fabricated or make-believe story, the male disciples would surely have represented themselves better and, given their culture, never would have cast the women as the primary witnesses. And third, it transformed the male disciples from being a bunch of chickens who had "deserted him and fled" (Mark 14:50), into being fearless witnesses of Jesus's life, death, and resurrection. Let me amplify each good reason.

First, we already noted in Mark's account that the male disciples "would not believe" the women's testimony, nor the two who encountered the risen Christ Jesus while "walking in the country." Remember, when he appeared to "the eleven," he "upbraided them for their lack of faith." This same incredulity and lack of expectation is repeated in the other Synoptic accounts.

For example, Luke says that when the women told the apostles of Jesus's resurrection, they considered it "an idle tale [by women?], and they did not believe them" (24:11). Then, Luke tells of two disciples on the road to Emmaus who encounter the risen Christ but do not recognize him (24:13–35). They confessed that they had lost hope (24:21), even though they had already heard "some" women's testimony to Jesus's resurrection (24:23). They spend a whole day with the risen Christ without realizing who is present to them. Eventually, at an evening meal, when Jesus "took bread, blessed and broke it, and gave it to them," echoing what he had done in feeding the five thousand (24:30; cf. 9:16) and at the Last Supper (22:19), they finally "recognized him" (24:31). Blinded to who he was for a whole day in his presence, they were surely not expecting a risen Jesus.

Then those two travelers returned with their resurrection testimony to the others in Jerusalem and heard that Jesus had also appeared to Simon (Peter). Yet at an appearance of the risen Christ immediately thereafter, those present again "were startled and terrified, and thought that they were seeing a ghost" (24:37). Clearly this was not an overly credulous community, imagining and expecting Jesus's resurrection.

Second, if this was a made-up or wistful story, surely the male disciples would have made themselves look a bit better. All of them were, in effect, "doubting Thomases," totally incredulous about Jesus's rising. Then, to crown it all, the women disciples are the first to see, believe in, and bear witness to the risen Christ. In a world where women were not allowed to bear witness, a contrived story would not have given them the starring role. The disciples literally could not have made this up.

Third, those disciples who had abandoned Jesus and ran away now became fearless witnesses to his gospel and resurrection. Mark says that "they went out and proclaimed the good news everywhere, while the Lord worked with them and confirmed the message by the signs that accompanied it" (16:20). This was because "he presented himself alive to them by many convincing proofs, appearing to them during forty days and speaking about the kingdom of God" (Acts 1:3). Later, the same Peter who had denied Jesus, gave a mighty speech in which he boldly proclaimed that "God raised him [Jesus] up" (2:24). Thereafter, "with great power the apostles gave their testimony to the resurrection of the Lord Jesus" (4:33).

All of this lends credibility to the realness of Jesus's resurrection!

PAUSE FOR REFLECTION

- What are convincing reasons for you to believe that God raised Jesus from the dead?

- What do you imagine Jesus's resurrection means for your own life in faith?

- What might it mean now for the life of the world?

JESUS ROSE FOR US AND FOR ALL CREATION

We already reviewed how the historical Jesus called disciples to live *the way* he modeled, and that following is the surest path toward happiness (chapters 3 and 4). In embracing Jesus as the risen Christ, we return to the possibilities that his paschal mystery mediates to our contemporary lives. In particular, does Jesus's rising from the dead empower the heart's hunger for freedom—personal, social, and cosmic—a desire that has intensified in our time?

As suggested already, we *can* embrace the conviction that Jesus's rising is a catalyst that makes abundant God's liberating grace. It empowers us to do what needs to be done to realize freedom in our own lives and help bring about God's liberating reign for all people and creation. Indeed, St. Paul proposes that by Jesus's paschal mystery, "creation itself will be set free from its bondage to decay" (Rom 8:21). As renowned theologian Elizabeth Johnson summarizes well, "Easter is nothing less than a new creative activity of God that pledges a blessed future of the whole cosmos" (*Creation and the Cross*, 101).

First, let us situate this contemporary proposal of freedom/ liberation within how the first Christians named the purpose of Jesus's resurrection.

Having here a mystery beyond human ken, no wonder the first Christians used many metaphors to try to capture the transformation wrought within human history by Jesus's dying and rising. They were struggling to name the "terrible beauty" that it wrought. All the metaphors have an echo of freedom and liberation. First, let us note well the bedrock conviction of those early Christians regarding what God had done in raising Jesus. Here we turn again to Paul, interpreter par excellence of Jesus's resurrection.

Verifies Jesus and Frees All from Power of Death and Sin: As noted at the beginning of this chapter, Paul understood the resurrection as verifying the divinity of Jesus. So, Jesus "was declared to be Son of God... by resurrection from the dead" (Rom 1:4). Then, by being bonded with the risen Christ through baptism, Christians are also empowered to live into newness of life. "All of us who have been baptized into Christ Jesus were baptized into his death....so that, just as Christ was raised from the dead…we too might walk in newness of life" (6:3–4). Jesus has set us free, even from death—what an extraordinary claim to make. Of course, we will all die out to this life but only to be born into eternal life with God.

Paul was also convinced that Jesus's paschal mystery frees us from the power of sin. There is no worse enslavement in life than to patterns and structures of sin—personal and social. By God's grace in Jesus, we can resist sin's allure and not be enslaved to it. Paul wrote to the Romans, " The Spirit of life in Christ Jesus has set you free from the law of sin and of death" (Rom 8:2). We are no longer held bound by "a spirit of slavery" but have received a "spirit of adoption" enabling us, like Jesus, to call God "Abba" (8:15). Because of Jesus's dying and rising, we can all live into "the freedom of the glory of the children of God" (8:21).

Another classic text where Paul portrays how the resurrection confirmed Jesus and raised up humankind toward freedom is in 1 Corinthians 15. Again here, Paul reiterates that God verified Jesus by raising him from the dead, and made possible *our* rising when united with Jesus. For Paul, this conviction is the make-or-break of Christian faith, for "if there is no resurrection of the dead, then Christ has not been raised; and if Christ has not been raised, then our proclamation has been in vain and your faith has been in vain" (1 Cor 15:13–14). But rather than being in vain, Paul sees Jesus as the "new Adam," and "as all die in Adam, so all will be made alive in Christ" (15:22). In effect, then, the last enemy Jesus has "destroyed is death" (15:26) (our ultimate fear) lending us "victory through our Lord Jesus Christ" (15:57).

Many More Metaphors: At the outset we noted *salvation* and *redemption* as two favored metaphors that Paul and other New Testament writers used to express the meaning of what God had worked for humankind and all creation in Jesus; they have been favored down through history, and rightly so. Paul wrote often of "the *salvation* that is in Christ Jesus" (2 Tim 2:10; emphasis added) and named him "our Savior" (Titus 1:4). Likewise, disciples can find "*redemption*…in Christ Jesus" (Rom 3:24; emphasis added), making him our Redeemer who mediates "forgiveness of our trespasses" (Eph 1:7).

The challenge for the first disciples was to make sense out of the paradox of Jesus's horrible death and then the extraordinary reversal that God wrought by his resurrection. Why and to what end was this for us? In their efforts to express the mystery, small wonder that Paul and other New Testament writers used multiple metaphors—beyond salvation and redemption. Let us sample a few more.

Paul writes that Jesus "was raised for our *justification*" (Rom 4:25), that those "in Christ" are "a *new creation*" (2 Cor 5:17). Likewise, Christ has won for us *adoption* as children of God (Gal 4:5–6). Paul frequently speaks of the *peace* that God's grace brings to our hearts: "we have *peace with God* through our Lord Jesus Christ, through whom we have obtained access to this grace in which we stand" (Rom 5:1–2). And having been *reconciled* with God through Jesus, disciples now have "the ministry of *reconciliation*" to the world (2 Cor 5:18).

Sometimes Paul uses multiple metaphors in the same verse. So Jesus "became for us *wisdom* from God, and *righteousness* and *sanctification* and *redemption*" (1 Cor 1:30). Likewise, Jesus is the One "in whom we have *redemption*, the *forgiveness* of sins" (Col 1:14). As if summarizing all the metaphors, Paul says that we "have come to *fullness* in [Jesus]" (Col 2:10).

And lest Paul be thought the only metaphor maker, consider an inspiring summary text from 1 Peter: "Blessed be the God and Father of our Lord Jesus Christ! By his great *mercy* he has given us a *new birth* into a *living hope* through the resurrection of Jesus Christ from the dead, and into an *inheritance* that is imperishable, undefiled, and unfading, kept in *heaven* for you" (1:3–4). And though many metaphors were used to express what the risen Christ means for here and hereafter, they inevitably fell short of this inexhaustible mystery.

A LIBERATING SALVATION

It would seem that each era and context needs to find the metaphor that most effectively conveys the meaning of Jesus's death and resurrection for its time and place. For example, an emerging contemporary metaphor is to see God's work in Jesus as empowering *human flourishing* and Jesus as the model *Human One*. In all four Gospels and echoing the messianic prophecy of Daniel 7:13–14, the Greek *huios ton anthropon* is Jesus's own favored title for himself. As noted before, rather than "son of man," it is more accurately rendered as "Human One." In the New Testament and from Christian tradition, there is ample ground for seeing the paschal mystery as God's work of humanization, empowering our vocation to become "fully alive to the glory of God" (St. Irenaeus, writing ca. AD 200).

Consistent with Scripture and Tradition, I reiterate that an engaging metaphor for the consciousness and needs of our time is to see Jesus's dying and rising as liberating us toward true freedom. The paschal mystery can liberate *from* all that holds us bound, personally and socially, and empower us to live freely *for* God's reign in our own lives and for the life of the world. As Paul wrote to the Galatians, "For freedom Christ has set us free. Stand firm, therefore, and do not submit again to a yoke of slavery" (5:1). Theologian Elizabeth Johnson reviews multiple metaphors from New Testament texts and summarizes, "All have the theme of liberation running through them" (*Creation and the Cross*, 131).

The liberation wrought by Jesus's paschal mystery—death and resurrection—frees us from being enslaved by our own proclivity to sin and its alluring power. Instead of being held bound by the grip of sin—of whatever kind—God's liberating work in Jesus means that we have the *help* we need to choose and act with freedom. Likewise, we need not be held bound by the effects of the sins of others and of humankind, gathered into sinful social structures and cultural oppressions. By God's emancipatory grace in Jesus Christ, we are always free to do the good and to work to change the social structures and cultural mores that enslave people and destroy creation.

This being said, the time-honored and holistic term *salvation* will always have broad appeal as well. Indeed, *salvation* is used some four hundred times in the Bible to express God's intentions and hopes for humankind. Going forward in this text, I will oftentimes use *liberating salvation* to catch the richness of both metaphors. Here I am following the pattern of a papal exhortation *Evangelii Nuntiandi* (On the Evangelization of Peoples) (1975) of Pope Paul VI. He wrote prophetically, "The Church links human liberation and salvation in Jesus Christ" (no. 35). And so well it should!

HOPE FOR OUR HEARTS

Surely no hunger of the human heart has inspired more people to heroism than the struggle for freedom. Across the course of history, the record for dictatorships is that all have fallen—eventually—precisely because of people rising up and joining the struggle to be free. Clearly God constituted the human heart to resist slavery and insist on living in freedom. So we can readily embrace that God's "abundant grace" through Jesus's dying and rising empowers our liberation. God's grace sets us free to do what we need to do to live in freedom—for ourselves, for all people, and for God's creation. What a gift to our hearts!

Disciples of Jesus must face the reality that there remain so many instances of slavery and oppression in our time, personal and then social, political, and cultural. On the personal level, the intensity and variety of addictions have exploded in this postmodern era. Likewise, the instances of injustice, oppression, and discrimination continue to abound in our various cultures and societies.

Even in democracies where constitutional freedom seems well established, demagogues can emerge who encourage racism and sexism, anti-Semitism and xenophobia, favoring the privileged and threatening the most vulnerable—which the Bible repeatedly names as widowed women, orphaned children, and immigrants to the land (see Exod 21:21–22). Then our ability to destroy the environment and its natural resources is unprecedented and now at a crisis point; it would seem that "creation itself" is in greater "bondage to decay" than ever before, with it, too, needing to "obtain the freedom…of the children of God" (Rom 8:21).

There is an anomaly, too, around freedom. For while human hearts long to be free, we can find the struggle for freedom daunting to the point of settling for far less, even acquiescing in some form of slavery. Or we can fear the obligations that freedom brings; unlike license, it places great responsibilities. Indeed, we can recognize a deep hesitancy about freedom even among the Israelites of old.

Soon after their miraculous liberation from the slavery of Egypt, the Israelites complained and even rebelled against Moses's leadership. In their defense, Moses had neglected to mention that big desert they would have to cross on their way to living free. They rose up and told Moses, "It would have been better for us to serve the Egyptians than to die in the wilderness" (Exod 14:12). A little later they lamented that at least in Egypt they had "fleshpots and ate our fill of bread"; they seemed ready to give up and return to their slavery (16:3).

We can find a resonant note in our own ambivalence about freedom. Its struggle can be demanding, long, and daunting (the Israelites spent forty years wandering in that desert). Small wonder, then, that we can balk at its demands or be intimidated by the journey. But after Jesus's dying and rising, our confidence can be that God's grace sustains every struggle for freedom and can lead—eventually—to its "promised land."

God's liberating and abundant grace in Jesus can empower us to resist and live free of our own bad habits, sins, and addictions. Likewise, it empowers us to engage the struggle for freedom for all peoples and for God's creation, resisting every kind of oppression, injustice, enslavement, and destruction. By God's liberating grace we can be agents of freedom for ourselves and for the life of the world.

Because of Jesus's dying and rising, we can be confident that no falsehood can become true, no tyranny can endure, no oppression triumph, no injustice prevail, no slavery remain unchallenged, no discrimination be deemed just, no cross be too heavy, no addiction be beyond recovery, no bad habit be unbreakable, and the list goes on. And as Jesus is the catalyst of God's abundant grace, we access the help we need by "abiding" in him as a branch to a tree. This is how the Gospel of John portrays the needed relationship between disciples and Christ Jesus (15:4–7), and suggests the spiritual practice recommended below.

Like all the longings of the heart, realizing freedom is always partial on this side of eternity. Yet Jesus's dying and rising empowers us to embrace *la lucha*—the struggle—in order to realize something of God's reign of freedom now. And rather than a "rule over" people—as in human kingdoms and empires—God's reign means the opposite. God rules *with* and *for* people, empowering us with grace to do what needs to be done for ourselves and for all to live in freedom. So Yeats got it right. By Jesus's Easter Rising, all is "changed, changed utterly, a terrible beauty is born."

PAUSE FOR REFLECTION

- How does the metaphor of freedom and Jesus as Liberator echo in your heart?

- For what works of liberation is God empowering you at this time? What decision does this invite for your life?

SPIRITUAL PRACTICE: CONSCIOUSLY ABIDE IN JESUS

In many ways, the Christian spiritual path can be summarized as "to abide in Jesus." John's Gospel uses the word *meno* more than twenty times; it seems that the best translation is to *abide*, though some texts favor *remain*. To abide implies to make one's home and to dwell within it. To abide in Jesus means to consciously ground oneself in relationship with him, to intentionally make him the anchor and the lodestar of one's life.

John's climactic text about abiding in Jesus comes in chapter 15:4–7, where we encounter the beautiful image of the vine and the branches. Jesus first exhorts, "Abide in me as I abide in you." So our bond with Jesus through baptism and discipleship means that he lives within us, and his abiding is the model for ours. Then, this co-abiding is like the vine and its branches. "Just as the branch cannot bear fruit by itself unless it abides in the vine, neither can you unless you abide in me. I am the vine, you are the branches." Indeed, the branch that does not abide in the vine, "withers." So how are we to develop our abiding in Jesus in order to flourish?

To begin with, it requires us to become friends. Forging a friendship with anyone requires spending time together and being often in conversation. Likewise, we need to spend time with Jesus and talk to him as we might a best friend. While we can talk to him at any time—the high times, the low times, and the everyday—it is wise to set aside a set time for checking in. And instead of having to construct our own prayer to Jesus every time, there are many formula-type prayers that one can say, even if half asleep or super busy. An old favorite, especially among Eastern Catholics, is known as "The Jesus Prayer." It runs: "Lord Jesus Christ, Son of God, have mercy on me, a sinner." So we need to talk to him regularly, confident, as he promised, "I am with you always" (Matt 28:20).

As we might consult a good friend at times of decision, our abiding in Jesus means that we bring our issues for discernment into conversation with him. Likewise, to abide in Jesus calls us to strive always to follow his example, *the way* that he modeled. While it may sound a little simplistic, abiding disciples must ask in every situation, "What would Jesus do?" (WWJD), and then ask him for the grace to act accordingly.

FOR FURTHER READING

Habermas, Gary, and Michael Licona. *The Case for the Resurrection of Jesus*. Grand Rapids, MI: Kregel, 2004. Summarizes the key arguments in favor.

Johnson, Elizabeth. *Creation and the Cross: The Mercy of God for a Planet in Peril*. Maryknoll, NY: Orbis Books, 2018. An inspiring and learned summary of what the paschal mystery means for our lives and for the whole cosmos.

Kelly, Anthony. *The Resurrection Effect: Transforming Christian Life and Thought*. Maryknoll, NY: Orbis Books, 2008. Explains why and how Jesus's resurrection is the lynchpin of Christian faith.

CHAPTER 6

The Holy Spirit

Our Hunger for Holiness

Does Spirituality Need to Be Religious?

    "I'm spiritual but not religious" has become a mantra of our age, at least among young adults and millennials. When I ask such people, respectfully, how they keep their spirituality alive and flourishing, I've heard about time spent in nature, listening to music and concerts, art and aesthetic experiences, deep personal conversations, walks by the ocean, gardening, hanging out with good friends—often on social media—and practices like yoga, deep breathing, and mindfulness. Though amorphous, I'm not surprised that people can encounter the Holy in what the poet Paddy Kavanagh called "the bits and pieces of Everyday" (Catholics call this sacramentality).

    But then I wonder! Would their spirituality be more likely to flourish if they recognized that the spirit in their spirituality is the Spirit of God who reaches out to them with effective love; that their spiritual nurture is by gift (grace) as well as their own efforts? Might their spiritual journey be more life-giving by also being religious, drawing upon particular stories and symbols, prayers and practices, patterns and perspectives as found in a spiritually well-tested religious tradition? For what else are the great religions—at their best—than spiritual resources inspired by the Divine Spirit?

Might it be wisest of all to be both spiritual and religious? Let's see!

HOLINESS AND AUTHENTICITY AS ONE

The twofold proposal of this chapter is: (a) that the human heart has a deep hunger for holiness as authenticity; and (b) that Christian holiness as modeled by Jesus is now empowered by the Holy Spirit to make it all the more possible to become holy and authentic people. Having reflected on God the Creator (chapters 1 and 2), and on Jesus the Christ (chapters 3—5), here we reflect explicitly on the role of the Third Person of our one and triune God, the Holy Spirit.

All three Divine Persons participate in each other's functions. Yet the distinguishing role of the Holy Spirit is as Sanctifier. From the Latin *sanctificare* meaning "to make holy," the Spirit's particular role is to help people grow in holiness of life—in response to a deep hunger. This begs the question, what do we mean by *holiness* of life and then what is the hunger that prompts it? This chapter poses a possible response for disciples of Jesus and as empowered by the Holy Spirit, who now continues God's work of liberating salvation. First, let us recognize a serious *image* issue by way of holiness.

There are at least two uphill battles in getting contemporary people to be excited about becoming holy, much less to recognize it as a great hunger of their hearts. First, holiness has generally had a bad press. Ask a group of undergraduate students (as I have) their image of being holy and you get a cascade of negative stereotypes. They think of it as "running to church all the time," as saying a lot of prayers, as always being "nice" (but boring), as pretending to be a holy Joe or Jane in front of grandparents, and certainly as no fun at all. They imagine that trying to be holy would greatly cramp their present lifestyles and lose them many friends.

Some of the negativity is because the Christian Church has done a poor sales job for holiness. For example, most of the official saints chosen to be models of holiness—their primary function—have little attraction to postmodern people. At least in Catholicism, so often the canonized saints were vowed religious who founded some religious order, living a unique rather than a typical lifestyle—with a spouse, family, and kids.

The old Roman missal (used until after Vatican II), when celebrating the feast days of great saints, recognized them within a list of categories. Favored groupings were as martyr, or virgin, or virgin martyr (real achievement), and then *neither virgin nor martyr*. This was the designation for the rare canonized saints who had spouses and raised families, like Bridget of Sweden or Elizabeth of Hungary. It was as if identifying them explicitly as *married* and *parents* would detract from their witness to sanctity. Things have improved a little with the canonizations made by recent popes, but the Church has a long way to go in proposing attractive models of holiness.

Second, many Catholic Christians have little conscious sense of the effective presence of the Holy Spirit to their lives, as constantly prompting their journey into a wholesome holiness of life. While Catholics need remedial work in embracing the historical Jesus, we might say the same in spades about the role of the Holy Spirit to nurture our spirituality. As I elaborate below, our sense of the Holy Spirit is also far *too small*.

So often, Western Christians advert to the Spirit as an afterthought in naming the three Divine Persons of the Trinity, but with little relevance to daily life. In practice, we are more like binitarians—two persons—than trinitarians (Eastern Catholics and Pentecostal Christians do a little better). The truth is that God's Spirit *is* the very presence of God to our lives now as grace, continuing God's liberating work in Jesus, empowering us to follow his *way* into a wholesome holiness of life.

One promising possibility for rebranding holiness is to understand it as arising from our hunger to become *authentic* human beings, in other words, to become *true* to all that God intends us to be. As we elaborate below, such authenticity demands our own *integrity* as persons and our *mutuality* with others. And as noted previously, St. Irenaeus summarized an ancient conviction of Christian faith that the more we become "fully alive" as human beings, the more we give glory to God. Might authenticity be an attractive way for contemporary people to understand the Christian call to holiness of life?

Charles Taylor poses authenticity as a defining quest of people in our postmodern age, as more intensely felt than ever before. In premodern times (and in traditional cultures still), people understood themselves exclusively as members of their tribe, as totally communal beings, with little sense of individuality. Now it seems that things are reversed, with all emphasis on individuality and little on communality. Recognizing a positive potential first, this postmodern sentiment could offer the opportunity for persons to quest for authenticity like never before. If powered by an appropriate spirituality, it could encourage people to become authentic to who we can be to the greater glory of God.

On the other hand, there is great danger if the quest for authenticity is purely individualized and serves only the self. Taylor cautions, as previously noted, that contemporary culture encourages authenticity as "buffered selves." This means to quest only our individual preferences, to focus on personal satisfaction, and to depend on self-effort alone. It means acting as if an isolated individual, shaped entirely by one's own ideas and choices, and exclusively to one's own satisfaction. Taylor warns that such individualized authenticity has no real ethic and no "horizon of significance" other than the self. So a self-centered authenticity becomes a false god that enslaves; indeed its solipsism is antithetical to Christian faith.

Of course, so much depends on how we understand the human person—as individual, as communal, or both. Anticipating what will be the central theme of chapter 7, Christian faith emphasizes both the *personal* (a more relational term than *individual*) and *communal*, that we live most authentically as persons-in-community and as a community-of-persons. Such authenticity, then, calls us to both *personal integrity* and *communal mutuality*. It invites us to flourish by living in right and loving relationships with God, self, others, and creation. The quest for such authenticity is also well named as the hunger for holiness of life.

Bernard Lonergan (1904–84), a great Catholic theologian and philosopher, also posed authenticity as central to the contemporary human quest and understood it as an eminently spiritual hunger, arising from the human soul. By contrast to the *self*-centered approach, he was adamant that "authenticity is achieved only by self-transcendence." So for

Lonergan and somewhat ironically, we find the true self only by rising above self-centeredness. He well described the growth into authenticity as a *lifelong* process of "conversion" that is intellectual, moral, and spiritual, engaging the whole person. Such self-transcending conversion is well named as growth into authenticity of life—ever striving to live up to who we are and can become with the help of God's grace.

Christian spirituality, then, encourages an authenticity that reflects both personal *integrity* and a *mutuality* of right and loving relationships—with self, God, other people, and creation. That our personal integrity can only be achieved through right and loving mutuality is because of the triune nature of our God—whose personhood we reflect. The Trinity affirms each person as integrally divine, and likewise the triune mutuality of love within the Godhead. So we cannot be authentic to who we are—and to who our God Is—by living as buffered selves.

Here we can obviously echo Jesus's preaching of his greatest commandment, that we are to love God by loving our neighbor as ourselves. As Karl Rahner well argued, for Christians, love of self and love of neighbor—calling to integrity and mutuality—go hand in hand with our love for God.

From a Christian perspective, then, authenticity means coming to embody the holiness of life that Jesus modeled and proposed for disciples. To find such holiness attractive, we need to set aside its pious-piffle stereotypes and see it as a totally wholesome way of life. Josef Godlbrunner (1910–2003), an eminent twentieth-century theologian, wrote a short but classic book entitled *Holiness is Wholeness*, and made his argument on biblical grounds. In many ways, the title said it all: Christian holiness of life moves us toward wholeness as human beings. It invites us to become authentic persons, fully alive to the glory of God; what could be more wholesome!

In sum and from the perspective of Christian spirualty, becoming authentic—and thus whole and holy—means to grow in personal integrity and communal mutuality, and doing so according to *the way* that Jesus modeled. Then, rather than becoming authentic by our own efforts alone (which is impossible), we have the grace of God's Spirit who works through our spirits, from within and without and especially through faith community, empowering us to live into personal integrity and communal mutuality. Because we have this august potential as persons akin to our God, it becomes a deep spiritual hunger of our hearts.

Christian Spirituality as Intentional Care of Soul: All the deep hungers of the heart are spiritual in that they arise from the human spirit—the soul; likewise they can be satisfied only by spiritual means and resources. As posed in the prelude to this work, we can think of spirituality, Christian or otherwise, in a generic way or as specific personal/communal practices. There we described Christian spirituality in general as people's sense of relationality with the one and triune God as the foundation of their being, and, empowered by the Holy Spirit, *how* they nurture this relationship to live as disciples of Jesus within a community of disciples toward God's reign in the world. Now that we are focusing on the Holy Spirit as the source of people becoming holy, we need to imagine the *how*, the means through which the Spirit *works*. In other words, what constitutes a Christian spirituality in *practice*?

Spirituality in practice amounts to all of our intentional efforts to care for the soul itself and to satisfy its distinctive hunger for holiness as authenticity. Christians need to craft a spirituality that enables them to grow into holy authenticity after *the way* of Jesus. To neglect care of soul is to diminish our personhood, whereas to practice a life-giving spirituality is the surest path into the authenticity and holiness that God intends for us all.

Talk of spirituality is much in vogue. Not so long ago, a financial report in the *New York Times* declared spiritualty to be a "growth industry." This reflects the increased number of people who, most often claiming to be spiritual but not religious, yet invest in resources and paraphernalia to nurture their spiritual lives. The practice of Christian spirituality, however, is in marked contrast to much of what "the market" now offers.

Browse the spiritualty section of any bookstore or the spiritual offerings online and they are almost invariably self-help strategies, focused on finding an individual kind of peace and harmony. It tends to encourage the rugged individualism that marks our late capitalist societies. What, by contrast, might distinguish the practice of a Christian spirituality?

To begin with, the fruit of Christian spirituality is the authenticity that can be realized by living as disciples of Jesus. The intent of all the spiritual efforts of Christians is to nurture their *living* faith as disciples.

If this be the intended outcome, what more specifically is the practice of Christian spirituality for a person or community. Here we echo again the prelude, and now add the kind of spirituality proposed in this chapter. So, the practice of Christian spirituality amounts to *all the symbols and stories, perspectives and practices, prayers and patterns that Christians engage and through which the Spirit works to nurture them to live with integrity and mutuality as disciples of Jesus and thus into authenticity as human beings.* In more colloquial terms, the practice of Christian spirituality is the fuel in the tank of discipleship to Jesus.

Rather than having one defining spirituality, Catholicism is blest with multiple spiritual "schools" and charisms, with varied emphases for how to live into holiness of life—Benedictine, Ignatian, Franciscan, Mercy, Carmelite, Catholic Worker, and so on. What we propose here is that all instances of Christian spirituality, regardless of distinguishing charism, must help to nurture people in the *living* faith modeled by Jesus. Thus Christian spirituality in practice is to nurture personal integrity and communal mutuality toward authenticity of life after *the way* of Jesus. And the Holy Spirit "works" through our practiced spiritualty to this good purpose.

The Spirit's mode of nurturing people to holy authenticity is to work from within our own hearts and spiritual resources, and from the outside through other people, through a Christian faith community, and through our experiences of life in the world. Christian spirituality and the holiness it nurtures are always personal and communal, with the Spirit working from within and without to satisfy our hunger for authenticity of life.

PAUSE FOR REFLECTION

- What is your own understanding of holiness? Of authenticity? Of Christian spirituality? Has anything shifted in light of the above reflections?

- What would it mean for you to be authentic to your own personhood? Name some characteristics.

- How does your spiritualty encourage you toward personal integrity? Toward mutuality with others?

THE HOLY SPIRIT AT WORK

The Spirit Calls to Be Holy Like Our God

Fantastic as it may seem, the Holy Spirit calls people to be holy like our God is holy, and thus to reflect the integrity and mutuality of God's oneness *and* triune nature.

Recall that St. Augustine imagined this central mystery of Christian faith by portraying the Father as the Lover, the Son as the Beloved, and the Spirit as the Loving between them. Among other things, this highlights that God's very nature is as triune loving relationships. The Trinity's circulating love between the three Divine Persons reflects the dynamic within Godself (what theologians call the "immanent" Trinity) *and* prompts God's three-way outpouring of love for humankind (the "economic" Trinity). As well elaborated in chapter 2, God's very nature is to love—both within Godself and outward to all humankind.

What then might our One God as triune loving relationships mean for the holiness and authenticity of persons made in the divine image and likeness? Logically it calls to a practiced spiritualty that nurtures toward the ideal of unconditional love, a love for *one*self just as God is one, and then unconditional loving outreach to others to reflect God's nature as triune loving relationships. To grace us toward such holiness of life, the Holy Spirit, in concert with the whole Godhead, is constantly reaching into our hearts/souls, drawing us toward personal integrity—the true expression of self-love—and to mutuality with others, epitomized by love of neighbor.

As if putting icing on the cake of his greatest commandment, in John's Gospel Jesus says, "I give you a new commandment, that you love one another" (13:34a) But what, we well ask, is "new" here? Jesus elaborates that this *new* command is to love as Jesus himself loves: "Just as I have loved you, you also should love one another" (v. 34b). So disciples are to love as Jesus loved. And if that is not challenging enough,

Jesus amplifies that his way of loving is also God's way of loving: "As the Father has loved me, so I have loved you; abide in my love" (15:9). So Jesus loves as God loves and disciples are to love likewise. As if for emphasis, Jesus repeats, "This is my commandment, that you love one another as I have loved you" (15:12)—which is as God loves. Of course we can never do so perfectly, and yet this is the amazing holiness/authenticity to which God in Jesus challenges and graces disciples.

Indeed, the great "holiness code" that God revealed to Moses proposes the same ideal. It begins with, "You shall be holy, for I the LORD your God am holy" (Lev 19:2). Jesus echoed this sentiment when he encouraged disciples to "be perfect...as your heavenly Father is perfect" (Matt 5:48). So trying to love like our God is the heart of the holy authenticity to which we are called; we need a consistently practiced spirituality that nurtures us toward this grand ideal.

Amazing as it seems, we can aspire to at least approximate—if only gradually—such holiness in daily life because, as Paul explained, "God's love has been poured into our hearts through the Holy Spirit that has been given to us" (Rom 5:5). Thus, by the grace of the Holy Spirit at work in our lives, we can attempt to live into the wholesome holiness and authenticity that Jesus proposed, satisfying a deep hunger of our hearts.

In light of our calling to be holy like our one and triune God, we can further elaborate the integrity and mutuality that such authenticity invites. First, to have integrity that reflects the oneness of God "[who] is love" (1 John 4:8) encourages us to aspire to generous love—*agape*—toward oneself. We can readily forget this third leg of the greatest commandment. Yet God made it a law in that original holiness code (Lev 19:18)—where Jesus first learned it—that we are to love *ourselves*, letting this be the measure of love for neighbor. True self-love is the foundation of our own integrity; the more we love ourselves truly, the more we experience the love of God.

Such integrity is anything but a selfie solipsism. It requires taking care of one's own health and well-being, insisting on one's personal dignity and rights, guarding one's body as a "temple of the Holy Spirit" (1 Cor 6:19), getting the rest and recreation we need, being good stewards of our food and drink, developing the talents and gifts that God gave us, and ever attempting to flourish as a human being. Integral self-love prompts us to see all acts of genuine self-care as spiritual practices when done out of faith conviction.

Following on, personal integrity that leads into mutuality demands honesty in all our human exchanges: being truthful and trustworthy; fulfilling our commitments; developing and sharing our gifts; informing, forming, and following our conscience; being a person of hope, especially in the midst of adversity; finding joy and meaning in the everyday of life; and the list goes on.

Likewise, there are very practical dimensions to the *mutuality* of Christian holiness. Most obviously, mutuality demands that we love God and neighbor with our whole mind, heart, and strength—with all our soul. Then, mutuality demands living the social values demanded by Christian faith and as modeled by Jesus. So Christian holiness demands compassion toward all in need, with special favor for the poor and those whom Jesus favored most—the least, the lost, and the last.

Reaching beyond love and compassion, the mutuality of Christian authenticity requires working for justice, opposing all social arrangements and cultural practices that deny people their human rights and dignity. As noted earlier, the biblical understanding of both *justice* and *holiness* is right and loving relationship with God, self, others, and creation; they are two sides of the same coin. It is impossible to practice a *Christian* spirituality of mutuality and grow into authenticity after *the way* of Jesus without embracing the social responsibilities of Christian faith, living with and working for justice. And Christian holiness demands mutuality with God's creation, which means to be responsible toward the environment and to respect all living creatures.

Christian spirituality that nurtures holiness toward authenticity as personal integrity and communal mutuality surely sounds overwhelming, especially if heard (and often echoed in *new age* spirituality) as a call to "pull yourself up by your own bootstraps." Gratefully, it is by the grace of the Holy Spirit, inflowing and outflowing, working from within and without, that sustains our own best efforts to grow toward such authentic holiness.

All of our prior reflections on God's free and freeing grace echo resoundingly here. Christian spirituality is ever a covenant partnership of God's Spirit working through our own spirits and then through a faith community and our life in the world. And even for the most authentic of Christian persons, the journey into holiness as integrity and mutuality remains *lifelong* and *gradual*, ever in need of God's grace and mercy along the way.

To cite Paul again, it is through the Holy Spirit that God's "abundant grace in Jesus Christ" can make effective our own spiritual practices. As the love "between" the Father and Son, the Spirit functions for us as God's effective love—grace—at work in our lives and world, continuing God's liberating salvation in Jesus Christ. To embrace such a spirituality, however, most of us Christians are sorely in need of expanding our imaging of the Holy Spirit.

OUR HOLY SPIRIT IS TOO SMALL

We mentioned earlier that a challenge to our reaching for wholesome holiness of life and authenticity as persons is that our sense of the Spirit is also too small; this needs elaboration.

Orthodox and Eastern Catholics, and Pentecostal Christians too, have a well-founded criticism of mainline Christians that we, in fact, pay scant attention to the Holy Spirit. We need "remedial work" in this regard. Now, while not intending to defend our inattention, let me note that the traditional terms of *Father* and *Son* lend concrete images, familiar from daily life, whereas *Spirit*—well, it is hard to imagine. Indeed, since the first King James Bible translation (1611) up until the Second Vatican Council, the favored name for the Third Person of the Blessed Trinity in English was "Holy *Ghost*"—more spooky than friendly.

Likewise, Christian art typically depicts the Spirit as a small dove. This reflects the account that John the Baptist saw "the Spirit descending from heaven like a dove" upon Jesus (John 1:32). But to settle for a small bird image falls infinitely short of reflecting the dynamic Spirit that is the source of all creation. The same might be said of the first Pentecost symbol when small "tongues, as of fire" (Acts 2:3), appeared over each person present.

But pause and think about it for a moment: *the Spirit of God is the energy of the whole universe—past, present, and future.* Genesis 1:3

155

reflects that God's *ruah* (spirit) is the causal force of creation. Einstein established that all that exists is caused and held in existence by *energy*. Thus, God's Spirit sources *the Energy of the universe*, stretching back across billions of years and empowering its emergence and evolution since the beginning in time out of time, and reaching on into eternity. As the new cosmologists contend, the universe emerged with a "big bang" some 13.8 billion years ago, triggered by a subatomic particle (the Higgs boson) that gives everything else its energy and mass. The natural sciences have long referred to this as "the God particle." How right they are!

From a faith perspective then, and resonating with the sciences, God's Spirit sources the energy that sustains the whole universe with all of its adaptation and selection. And this cosmic evolution continues now by the energy of God's Spirit throughout billions of galaxies, each with billions of planets and stars, ever contracting and expanding with limitless energy. God's Spirit has been at work from the beginning of the universe, the reason why there is anything rather than nothing.

In the Nicene Creed, Christians profess faith in the Holy Spirit as "the giver of life." The Book of Wisdom claims that "the spirit of the Lord has filled the world" (1:7) and now we can add, "the universe." Of course the pinnacle product of God's creative energy—again reflected in both Genesis Creation accounts—is the human person. Scientists estimate that life began to emerge on planet earth from microorganisms and bacteria some 3.8 billion years ago. Then, comparatively recently, *homo sapiens* emerged some 150,000 years ago (the present estimate). Even as human life came forth from God as the pinnacle expression of God's creative Spirit, we realize that all plant and animal life is also an expression of the divine energy—that we recognize now as God's *agapaic* love.

That we can have heightened access now to the empowering energy of this Spirit of God through Jesus Christ is a central conviction of Christian faith. Surely the Spirit who brought forth the whole universe can help to satisfy the hunger of our own spirits to become holy and authentic, gracing us to follow *the way* of Jesus in daily life. The Spirit that makes and sustains galaxies can surely empower people's integrity and mutuality toward holy authenticity on this wee planet earth.

PAUSE FOR REFLECTION

- Reflect on your own imaging of the Holy Spirit. How might you expand it?

- Why would becoming authentic call to personal integrity and mutuality with others?

- The Holy Spirit as sourcing the energy of the universe; how might this enrich your sense of the Spirit at work in your own life?

THE SPIRIT IN THE HEBREW SCRIPTURES

Scientific cosmology suggests to Christians that God's Spirit has been at work as the dynamic source and creative energy of the universe since its beginning—perhaps with a "big bang." This echoes the faith conviction reflected in the Hebrew Scriptures, though they portray six hardworking days and a seventh day of divine rest. Whichever one prefers and as revealed to the Israelite people of old, God originates and sustains the universe, not as an impersonal energy but as a personal God of loving-kindness.

God's spirit is not portrayed as a distinct divine person in the Hebrew Scriptures (thus I do not capitalize in this section); this will come later with the Christian revelation of the Blessed Trinity. Yet the Hebrew Scriptures clearly and repeatedly attest to the work of a spirit of divine origin throughout creation. And this witness begins on the very first page of the Bible, with its second verse, Genesis 1:2. Here, for the first of some four hundred times, we encounter the Hebrew word *ruah*, in Greek *pneuma*.

Ruah is variously translated as "wind," "breath," or "spirit." The modern Bible editions render *ruah* in Genesis 1:2 as "wind"—so "a wind from God swept over the face of the waters." Older translations, however, have "the *spirit* of God," and this echoes the sentiment of later books of the Bible. For example, the Psalmist praises God's spirit as creator of all living creatures: "When you send forth your spirit, they are created; and you renew the face of the ground" (Ps 104:30). Then, as a feminine word, *ruah* is used as referring to God some one hundred times. Overall, we find a portrayal of the works of God's spirit very similar to what the New Testament later attributes to the Holy Spirit. To begin with, God's spirit in the Hebrew Scriptures reflects divine presence and assistance.

There is no more moving statement of the divine spirit's presence and care for people than Psalm 139:7–10. The Psalmist begins with a rhetorical question: "Where can I go from your spirit? Or where can I flee from your presence?…If I take the wings of the morning and settle at the farthest limits of the sea, even there your hand shall lead me, and your right hand hold me fast." A few verses later, the Psalmist adds, "For it was you who formed my inward parts; you knit me together in my mother's womb. I praise you, for I am fearfully and wonderfully made" (vv. 13–14). Clearly, the spirit is omnipresent to us, beginning with our conception.

It is also clear throughout the Hebrew Scriptures that God's spirit calls the Israelite people to personal integrity and communal mutuality, with both demanded by their covenant with God. For while each member was called to holiness and held accountable, yet it was as a community that God engaged the ancient Israelites to be "a people holy to the Lord your God" (Deut 14:2). Their covenant demanded that they live as persons-in-community and as a community-of-persons.

No place is the personal and communal nature of biblical spirituality better summarized than in "the holiness code" of Leviticus 19—already referrenced. Addressed to the whole people of Israel through Moses, it epitomizes a holiness that demands both integrity and mutuality. As seen already, it begins with, "You shall be holy, for I the Lord your God am holy" (19:2). As we read on, being holy demands caring for "the poor and the alien" (v. 10), being honest and truthful in all dealings, being kind to all in need, respecting people's good name, and living "with justice" (v. 15). In its great both/and verse we read,

"You shall love your neighbor as yourself" (v. 18). And it clarifies further, "You shall love the alien as yourself" (v. 34), mandating love for all—not just fellow Israelites.

We also see the integrity/mutuality dynamic of holiness reflected in the Hebrew Bible's sense of God's spirit as source of personal wisdom for life *and* demanding justice for all. The biblical understanding of *wisdom* evolved in the Hebrew Scriptures and is eventually represented as a person-like collaborator with God in the work of Creation (see Prov 8:30). Overall, however, divine wisdom encourages living as wise people by keeping the divine/human covenant.

Biblically, a person becomes wise by living wisely, in other words, by integrating what one professes with how one lives. People are recognized as wise by their integrity of life. Similarly, living wisely is done in solidarity with the whole community. So, the wise woman or man lives a life of holiness by keeping the covenant, which demands integrity to their wisdom and solidarity with their people.

Then, a constant theme throughout the Hebrew Bible, and in its prophetic books especially, is that God's spirit requires people to live justly. The prophet Micah can say, "I am filled…with the spirit of the LORD" and thus "with justice and might" (3:8). Through Isaiah, God makes clear that the true fasting and worship as demanded by the covenant is "to loose the bonds of injustice, to undo the thongs of the yoke, to let the oppressed go free, and to break every yoke…to share your bread with the hungry, and bring the homeless poor into your house; when you see the naked, to cover them, and not to hide yourself from your own kin" (Isa 58:6–7).

A little later, Isaiah anticipates that "the spirit of the Lord GOD" will "anoint" the Messiah "to bring good news to the oppressed, to bind up the brokenhearted, to proclaim liberty to the captives, and release to the prisoners; to proclaim the year of the LORD's favor" (61:1–2). No wonder Christians later would confess in their Nicene Creed that "the Holy Spirit…has spoken through the prophets."

So, God's spirit in the Hebrew Scriptures has multifaceted functions in creation and among God's people. By way of encouraging them to live toward holiness of life, God's spirit works both within people's hearts and through the covenant community, demanding personal integrity and communal mutuality, with their covenant inviting them to become holy as their God is holy—authentic and true like their God.

HOLY SPIRIT IN THE GOSPELS

The Gospels present the life of Jesus as empowered by the Holy Spirit and as the catalyst for God's outpouring of the same Spirit upon disciples. Needing to be selective again, we highlight how the Spirit calls to a spirituality that nurtures the personal integrity of Jesus's disciples and likewise their outreach with compassion and justice to others and especially the poor. To live into the holiness of Jesus by the power of the Spirit is to contribute to God's reign both within and without, having it rule in one's heart (Luke 17:21) *and* working for its realization "on earth as it is in heaven" (Matt 6:10).

Spirit in the Life of Jesus's Mother Mary: The story of the Holy Spirit in the Gospels begins with Mary's conception of Jesus—as reflected in the faith of the first Christian communities. We are so familiar with Luke's "Christmastime" account of Mary's conceiving Jesus that the miracle reflected here can pass us by and likewise the crucial role that Mary played by the power of the Holy Spirit in God's work of liberating salvation. Pause here and read again—even if in July—Luke 1:26–38.

First, note that the angel Gabriel appears to Mary who has "found favor with God." Gabriel announces, "You will conceive in your womb and bear a son, and you will name him Jesus," and he "will be called the son of the Most High"—God.

Mary reasonably asks, "How can this be, since I am a virgin?" and receives the amazing response, "The Holy Spirit will come upon you, and the power of the Most High will overshadow you; therefore the child to be born will be holy; he will be called Son of God." As later Christians would name her, and by the power of the Holy Spirit, Mary was truly the "mother of God." And her response was one of amazing faith: "Let it be with me according to your word," accepting her august role in God's plan of liberating salvation.

Then the Spirit that conceived within Mary turned her outward with love and compassion. The angel messenger alerted Mary that her cousin Elizabeth, though "in her old age," had conceived as a gift from God and was now six months pregnant (Luke 1:36). Instead of dwelling on her own amazing experience, Mary "set out and went with haste to a Judean town in the hill country" (1:39) to support her old cousin. Accepting Luke's account as embedded in the faith-memory of the first community of disciples, from Nazareth to "the hill country" of Judea would have been at least a week's journey over difficult terrain. But the Spirit within always prompts outward with love and compassion toward those in need.

When they meet, the baby in Elizabeth's womb "leaped" for joy. Then, "Elizabeth (also) was filled with the Holy Spirit and exclaimed... 'Blessed are you among women, and blessed is the fruit of your womb'" (Luke 1:41–42). Note that by Luke's account, the first two recipients of the Holy Spirit in the new covenant that God was forging with humankind through Jesus were both women.

Mary's personal integrity and loving mutuality with Elizabeth continues to be reflected in how she spoke of God's care for all humankind. In her Magnificat prayer immediately following (Luke 1:46–55), Mary portrays God as her holy "Savior" who has boundless mercy for every person, and yet favors "the lowly," and fills "the hungry with good things." Mary's spirituality reflected her resources within and her turn outward toward those in need.

Jesus Empowered by the Spirit: We previously noted that at the beginning of Jesus's public ministry an extraordinary theophany took place during his baptism by John the Baptist at the Jordan River. There, the Spirit "descending like a dove" on Jesus, and "a voice came from heaven" saying, "You are my Son, the Beloved" (Mark 1:9–11). For the new covenant in Christian faith, this is the first time that all three Persons of the Blessed Trinity are revealed simultaneously. Thereafter, Jesus was "full of the Holy Spirit' (Luke 4:1) throughout his public ministry of incarnating *the way* and working miracles to advance God's reign.

We reviewed in chapter 4 how on a Sabbath morning in his home synagogue at Nazareth, Jesus claimed to fulfill the greatest messianic prophecy of all—Isaiah 61:1–2 (cited earlier and see Luke 4:16–21). A few verses before this launch of his public ministry, "Jesus, filled with the power of the Spirit....began to teach...and was praised by everyone"

(Luke 4:14–15). Later, Jesus would claim that he cast out demons "by the Spirit of God" and explicitly pointed to such overcoming of evil as a sign that "the kingdom of God has come" (Matt 12:28).

Jesus himself "rejoiced in the Holy Spirit" (Luke 10:21). He assured disciples that when put on trial for their faith, "the Holy Spirit will teach you at that very hour what you ought to say" (12:12). Indeed, Jesus promised that God will "give the Holy Spirit to those who ask" (11:13); the Spirit is available to all people.

The most developed New Testament sense of the role of the Holy Spirit is found in John's Gospel, running throughout and then climaxed by Jesus's discourse at the Last Supper. To begin with, while John has a different version of Jesus's baptism than the three Synoptics, he has the Baptist testify, "I saw the Spirit descending from heaven like a dove, and it remained on him" (Jesus) (John 1:32). Likewise, John atests that Jesus "baptizes with the Holy Spirit" (v. 33). In his discourse with Nicodemus (John 3), Jesus said that no one can "enter the kingdom of God without being born of water and Spirit" (3:5; note Jesus's feminine imagining of the Spirit—only a woman can give birth). And Jesus promised often that all "believers in him" would receive the Spirit (see John 7:39).

Then, in his final discourse on the night before he died, Jesus assured the disciples, "I will ask the Father, and he will give you another Advocate, to be with you forever" (John 14:16). The Greek term *parakletos* is variously translated as Advocate (as in a court of law) and Comforter; so the Spirit both champions our well-being and consoles our hearts as needed. Jesus also assures disciples that this is "the Spirit of truth" who "abides with you, and will be in you" (John 14:17).

Immediately following in John, we hear Jesus say that this same "Advocate, the Holy Spirit, whom the Father will send in my name, will teach you everything, and remind you of all that I have said to you" (14:26). This makes clear that the Holy Spirit will continue Jesus's work of teaching, so suffused with the call to integrity and mutuality, helping disciples to remember his gospel that they are to live and bring to the world. Indeed, "when the Advocate comes…the Spirit of truth… will testify on my behalf" and likewise will help disciples "to testify" on behalf of Jesus (15:26–27).

Further, Jesus's gift of the Spirit will lend his community the power to forgive people's sins in God's name, knowing well that we would often need mercy for our lack of integrity and mutuality (John 20:21–23). Clearly, the Spirit whom God sends to disciples will nurture their holiness, both within their own hearts and for their outreach to the world.

The Spirit Comes at Pentecost and Remains: At the beginning of Acts, we read of Jesus, now the risen Christ and about to ascend into heaven, saying to disciples, "You will be baptized with the Holy Spirit not many days from now" (1:5). He assured them that "you will receive power when the Holy Spirit has come upon you; and you will be my witnesses…to the ends of the earth" (1:8). After this, Jesus "was lifted up" into heaven (1:9). Then, the disciples, along with Mary the mother of Jesus and other women disciples, about 120 persons in all (1:14–15), began their wait for the coming of the Spirit. This momentous event unfolded on Pentecost Sunday, some fifty days after Jesus's resurrection. Acts 2 tells the dramatic story:

> When the day of Pentecost had come, they were all together in one place. And suddenly from heaven there came a sound like the rush of a violent wind, and it filled the entire house where they were sitting. Divided tongues, as of fire, appeared among them, and a tongue rested on each of them. All of them were filled with the Holy Spirit and began to speak in other languages, as the Spirit gave them ability. (2:1–4)

Note well that "all of them were filled with the Holy Spirit"—men and women, apostles and disciples, all 120 there present. Then, having received the Spirit, the first miracle was to enable disciples to preach "in other languages" as they moved outward to evangelize the world with the gospel of Jesus Christ.

The Book of Acts follows with a mighty sermon delivered by Peter. He insists that Jesus had fulfilled the messianic prophecy found in the biblical Book of Joel 2:28–32, that "in the last days it will be, God declares, that I will pour out my Spirit upon all flesh" (Acts 2:17). Peter explained how Jesus was crucified, and yet "God raised him up" (2:24). Then he cites more prophecies attributed to King David—ancestor to

Jesus—all pointing to Jesus as the promised Messiah. Peter concludes by saying that now being exalted "at the right hand of God," Jesus has "poured out" the Holy Spirit (2:33).

Many listeners were moved to faith in Jesus and asked Peter what they should do. His response: "Repent, and be baptized every one of you in the name of Jesus Christ so that your sins may be forgiven; and you will receive the gift of the Holy Spirit" (2:38). Thereafter, those first disciples began to call people into the community of Jesus's disciples, baptizing them, as the risen Christ had instructed, "in the name of the Father and of the Son and of the Holy Spirit" (Matt 28:19)—to share in the triune life of God.

And this outpouring of the Holy Spirit is constantly recounted throughout the remainder of Acts. Since then and forever, the Holy Spirit continues to empower Christians to live for God's reign by *the way* of Jesus with personal integrity and communal mutuality; this is our path to holiness of life and authenticity as persons in the world.

PAUSE FOR REFLECTION

- How might this review of the Holy Spirit portrayed in the life of Mary and Jesus deepen your sense of the Spirit at work in your life?

- Reflect on the Holy Spirit as Advocate of truth. What truth might the Spirit be encouraging you to recognize and live at this time?

- Consider the Holy Spirit as Comforter. What comfort do you need to ask of the Holy Spirit? How might the Spirit empower you to comfort other people?

LIFE IN THE SPIRIT

The rest of the New Testament, and especially the writings of St. Paul, re-present Christian discipleship as "life in the Spirit" (perhaps read

Paul's summary review in Rom 8:1–17). So the time after Jesus—this time now—is the period of the Spirit. It is by the Holy Spirit that God continues within human history the work of liberating salvation in Jesus. The grace of the Spirit moves people from within and without, for integrity and mutuality, through our own spirits, through faith community, and through the sacramentality of life in the world—the arena of God's grace.

Let us reflect briefly on what it means to "live life in the Spirit" today. We will highlight: (1) how the Holy Spirit acts in and through the whole Church, and (2) in and through the life of each Christian, with the communal and personal in symbiosis.

The Holy Spirit in the Life of the Church: Remember John's account of Jesus's Last Supper and his emphasis on the Spirit as the source and guide to *truth*. Well, the most riveting example of how the Holy Spirit began to guide the new Christian community toward truth was at a very early gathering of leaders in Jerusalem, often referred to as the first of many Church councils. We find the story of the Council of Jerusalem in Acts 15.

The first Christian disciples were devout Jews. They tended to presume that the requirements of Mosaic Law still applied in full, and that living as Jewish was a prerequisite for being Christian. As Gentiles began to embrace Christian faith, however, the issue arose, did they really have to obey all of Mosaic Law? The most pressing issue was around male circumcision, and then the dietary laws. And Jesus had left no specific teaching on the question. On the one hand, he had said that he had come not to abolish the Law but to fulfill it (Matt 5:17). Yet he could also say, "You have heard that it was said…but I say…" (5:38–48) as if reinterpreting some sacrosanct precepts of the law.

The issue first arose as a disputed question in Antioch regarding Gentiles converted by the preaching of Paul and Barnabas (see Acts 14:26). The church at Antioch appointed "Paul and Barnabas and some of the others" (15:2) to take the controversy to "the church" in Jerusalem and to "the apostles and the elders" there (v. 4). "Much debate" (v. 7) ensued in the assembly of the Jerusalem church. Peter argued that "God…testified to them [the Gentiles] by giving them the Holy Spirit, just as he did to us" (v. 8) and "has made no distinction between them and us" (v. 9). But others argued for retaining the full force of the law. The upshot was a negotiated compromise, whereby the council reiterated some dietary aspects of Mosaic Law but dispensed Gentile men from circumcision—a momentous decision.

Worth noting, however, was how the leaders in Jerusalem prefaced their decision to the church in Antioch and consequently to all the churches: "It has seemed good to the Holy Spirit and to us" (15:28). In other words, those first Christian leaders saw the teaching ministry of the Church as functioning through good human discourse and by the guidance of the Holy Spirit, or better still, with the Holy Spirit working through the discernment of the faith community. With this the Council of Jerusalem had put in place the teaching mode of the Church that prevails down to the present day. As the Second Vatican Council echoed almost two thousand years later, this has enabled "this tradition which comes from the Apostles [*to*] *develop* in the Church with the help of the Holy Spirit" (*Dei Verbum* 8).

There are many other examples throughout the Book of Acts of the Holy Spirit working in and through the Church for God's reign in the world. All who believe and are baptized receive the Holy Spirit (19:5–6), sometimes even before baptism (10:44–48). Likewise, the Holy Spirit designates new people for ministerial functions in the Church who are then commissioned by those who are already leaders who "laid their hands" on the Spirit-selected candidates (13:1–4).

The work of the Holy Spirit is not limited to the Christian community; God can pour out the Holy Spirit on all people of good will (Acts 10:45). For sure, the Spirit continues God's work of liberating salvation in Jesus, effective in a paradigmatic way through the Church. Yet, as Jesus explained to Nicodemus (John 3), just as "the wind blows where it chooses" (3:8), so does the Holy Spirit.

God's Spirit at Work for Integrity and Mutuality in People's Lives: While the Holy Spirit is guiding the whole Christian community, Paul makes clear that the Spirit gives distinctive gifts to particular members who then contribute these to the life of the Church. There are many texts where Paul emphasizes that each Christian has gifts to contribute to the mission of the community, but none more forcefully than 1 Corinthians 12.

First, Paul makes clear that "no one can say 'Jesus is Lord' except by the Holy Spirit" (1 Cor 12:3); faith in Jesus is always a Spirit-gift. Then, Paul makes a sweeping summary statement regarding the gifts that the Holy Spirit grants to particular members of the faith community. "Now there are varieties of gifts, but the same Spirit" (v. 4) and "to each is given the manifestation of the Spirit for the common good" (v. 7). In other words, while every disciple has gifts, they are not to benefit the person alone but the whole faith community.

Paul lists some enhancing gifts that the Spirit can give to people, such as the following: wisdom, knowledge, faith, healing, miracle-working, prophecy, discernment, languages, and interpretation (12:8–10). He concludes his listing by saying, "All these are activated by one and the same Spirit, who allots to each one individually just as the Spirit chooses" (v. 11). Lest any Christian think that their particular gifts are for their benefit alone, Paul makes explicit (and repeats elsewhere, e.g., Eph 4:11–12; Rom 6:6–8) that just as in the human body, all parts are needed and have a unique function, then "so it is with Christ" (12:12). As always for Christian holiness, the personal and communal work hand in hand.

Still in 1 Corinthians 12, Paul emphasizes again that the Christian community is to function together as closely as the parts of the human body. As in our own bodies, every member is important, cherished, and vital to the well-being of the whole, so with Christ's Body—the Church—in which Christians are bonded by the Holy Spirit through their shared baptism. "For just as the body is one and has many members, and all the members of the body, though many, are one body, so it is with Christ. For in the one Spirit we were all baptized into one body—Jews or Greeks, slaves or free—we were all made to drink of one Spirit" (12:12–13; note: in Gal 3:28, Paul adds the couplet "male and female"). So the whole Christian community is to engage and empower the Spirit-granted gifts of each member.

Paul's punch line runs, "Now you are the body of Christ and individually members of it" (12:27). He notes again the diversity of gifts in the community, this time naming specific functions of ministry: "apostles...prophets...teachers...deeds of power...gifts of healing...of assistance...leadership, various kinds of tongues" (v. 28). He reiterates that not all have the same gifts and yet all are to contribute and work together for the mission of the whole community.

In another cherished text, Paul proposes a listing of the "fruits" or blessings that the Holy Spirit lends to people's lives. Paul writes, "The fruit of the Spirit is *love, joy, peace, patience, kindness, generosity, faithfulness, gentleness,* and *self-control*" (Gal 5:22–23, emphasis added). Note that all these gifts are to be lived, realized as a *living* faith. Note, too, though they are personal blessings, yet each one—beginning with love—promotes both integrity and mutuality, personal and communal holiness of life.

Elsewhere, Paul adds other blessings and fruits of the Spirit. So the Spirit brings freedom, "where the Spirit of the Lord is, there is freedom" (2 Cor 3:17). His reflections in 1 Corinthians 12 flow on into chapter 13; ultimately the gifts of the Spirit are "faith, hope, and love…, these three; and the greatest of these is love" (1 Cor 13:13). Paul knew well the ultimate rule and measure of Christian spirituality for holiness/authenticity of life—love for God and neighbor as oneself.

HOPE FOR OUR HEARTS

All the desires of our hearts are, in their own way, *spiritual* because they arise from and can help to satisfy some facet of our diamond-like human soul. For this reason, all the hungers are permeated by what we propose in this chapter as our distinctly spiritual desire for holiness of life. This might be well understood by postmodern ears as satisfying the hunger for authenticity as persons, which for Christians means to grow in integrity and mutuality after *the way* of Jesus.

There are myriad genres and types of spiritual practices, and as noted before, many readily accessible on today's "market." Indeed, all the great world religions, each in its own way, amount to traditions of spiritual wisdom for life and propose a distinctive path to holiness and authenticity. Christianity does this "in spades." However, in order to draw wisely upon the resources of other traditions, it is important to know their defining perspectives, the kind of holiness they propose, and how it might be or might not be compatible with Christian spirituality.

Whatever we borrow should reflect the personal and communal emphases of Christian faith, promoting both our integrity and mutuality.

Otherwise we can get a bit lost, not knowing our Christian spiritual home nor how to find our way there. While Jesus said, "In my
Father's house there are many dwelling places"—so lots of homes
within God's family—he also made clear that he himself was preparing
a special "place" for disciples (John 14:2). We all need a spiritual home
within God's family, and there is certainly none better than the one prepared by Jesus. When confident in our own home, we might well sally
forth and be enriched by spiritual gifts from other "dwelling places."

Toward such good grounding, this chapter summarizes a Christian spirituality that nurtures holiness/authenticity, focusing on the
Holy Spirit as our Sanctifier. Colloquially we can say that within the
Blessed Trinity, encouraging sanctity of life is the Spirit's assignment.
Meanwhile, our understanding of God and of Jesus Christ from the previous chapters are most relevant to our practice of Christian spirituality
as well. Likewise, all the chapters in part 2 of this work will highlight
particular aspects of "Catholic" faith that can enrich the spiritual journey of any person.

Truth is that God's Spirit, the source of all creation, is ever at work
in the lives of Christians, calling to integrity and mutuality as holiness
and authenticity after *the way* of Jesus. This defining core of a Christian
spirituality requires our allowing the Spirit to work from within our
own hearts and personal practices and from without—through participation in a Christian faith community and from our experiences of life
in the world. Such a spirituality responds to the hunger of our hearts for
a wholesome holiness toward the authentic people we can become—
fully alive to the glory of God.

As human beings, we cannot suppress our spiritual potential and
the hunger it prompts in our hearts for holiness/authenticity. Yet we can
neglect or misdirect it. Simply recognizing ourselves as spiritual beings
does not inevitably make us holy and authentic—for sure. We need to
intentionally nurture our spirituality; though the Holy Spirit is ever at
work in people's lives, we must honor our side of the covenant.

I proposed already that a practiced Christian spirituality entails all
the stories and symbols, prayers and practices, patterns and perspectives that,

graced by the Holy Spirit, nurture people's efforts to live with integrity and mutuality as disciples of Jesus into holiness of life and authenticity as human beings. In other words, to have "gas in the tank" for living Christian faith, each of us needs to engage spiritual sources that can nurture our growth, by the grace of the Spirit, into holy authenticity. Let us review briefly each of the potential sources—stories, symbols, prayers, practices, patterns, and perspectives—of a functioning Christian spirituality.

The whole *Story* of Christian faith is a prime resource to our spirituality. Yet each of us needs to find our "anchor texts" within the great Christian Story, the substories that engage our own heart and personally inspire. For myself, one core text is the Gospel story of Luke 4:16–21—Jesus launching his public ministry and claiming to fulfill the messianic promise of Isaiah 60:1–2. Then, for a *personal* anchor story, I constantly remember how my grandmother, though blind and paralyzed from the waist down during her last twenty years of life, never missed Sunday Mass. She had to be carried into and out of the church, with great discomfort to her. Every time I'm tempted to miss Sabbath worship, I remember the story of Granny—and off I go!

Likewise, we all need sacred *symbols* that can call and nurture us to holiness. Again, for Catholic Christians, the primary and most effective symbols are the sacraments, with Eucharist having pride of place as "the sacrament of sacraments" (Aquinas). Regular reception of Eucharist, "the bread of life" (John 6:35), is a powerful nurture to a wholesome holiness. From God's side of the covenant, no other sacred symbols are more assured as means of grace for our lives than the seven we celebrate as a community. Again, of course, all the sacraments require us to respond as covenant partners with God. Then, a more personal symbol that helps sustain my spirituality, and especially toward hope, is the painting of the Last Supper by the Polish artist Bodhan Piasecki with the women and children included at the table.

Our spirituality also needs the nurture of both personal and communal *prayer*. Personal prayer can be traditional or innovative as long as it helps to nurture our response to the Spirit's call into holiness/authenticity. Communal prayer also can take many forms but is most effectively encountered in the worship of faith communities. Simply put, it is not possible to grow in Christian discipleship without practices of personal and communal prayer.

Then, we need some particular *practices* in our working spirituality. Catholic tradition offers myriad options. The most imperative practice is to actively belong to and contribute our gifts to the mission and ministries of a faith community. Another rich practice is spiritual reading or listening (podcasts). Studying and praying with the Bible, alone or with others, is an enriching spiritual practice, and likewise reflection and faith sharing in small faith communities. Add, too, practices like doing works of compassion and justice, of making pilgrimage, of taking retreat time, of availing of spiritual mentoring, and the list goes on.

Then we need *patterns* of lifestyle, spiritual habits we can follow without much deliberation. These emerge as our practices become routine, like when keeping Sabbath is one's pattern of life, not needing decision from one week to the next. Here, too, we can include lifestyle patterns that reflect spiritual poverty toward money, possessions, pleasure, and ambition. And we can all develop a pattern of bringing gospel values to the public realm of our lives, allowing Christian faith to shape our politics as well as our prayers (our theme in chapter 10).

And there are foundational *perspectives* that can help to keep us keeping on into authenticity/holiness. In many ways, foundational perspectives are the overall spiritual resource offered by this book. So, our imaging and understanding of God, of Jesus the Christ, and here of the Holy Spirit, are grounding perspectives to shape our practice of spirituality. Who and how we believe God Is for us, the reign of God commitment of the historical Jesus, God's liberating salvation through the risen Christ, and the sanctification that is empowered by the Holy Spirit are perspectives that can well sustain and shape our operative spirituality.

The chapters that follow will pick up other perspectives that distinguish Catholic Christian faith and how they can enrich any person's practice of spirituality. This includes its communality, sacramentality, and commitment to a *living* faith that lends hope and encourages the works of social justice. The fundamental perspectives we choose are key to growing in holiness as disciples of Jesus and toward authenticity as human beings.

PAUSE FOR REFLECTION

- Imagine what it might mean for you at this time to embrace "life in the Spirit."

- What gifts of the Spirit does your Christian community need now? What particular gifts do *you* have? How might you put your gifts to work for the whole community?

SPIRITUAL PRACTICE: DISCERNMENT OF SPIRITS

The confidence of Christian faith is that the Holy Spirit constantly prompts our own spirits to live as disciples of Jesus. However, the scriptures and traditions also make clear that the "spirits" that move within our own hearts are not always from the heart of God. We can be prompted by evil spirits as well, or, if you prefer, by our own hardness of heart and proclivity for sin. So the sentiments that arise in our hearts need to be "tested" for their origins. As the author of 1 John writes, "Beloved, do not believe every spirit, but test the spirits to see whether they are from God" (4:1). How might we "test the spirits" that may be moving in our lives and discern the best ones to follow?

Again, St. Ignatius of Loyola lends another good practice. He personally recognized that there were good and bad spirits working in his life and devised a helpful way of discerning between them. He proposed that good spirits lead us to consolation, whereas bad spirits bring desolation. For Ignatius, consolation is not just a happy feeling but rather what disposes us to live and love as disciples of Jesus and thus to be at peace. Desolation, by contrast, leads us away from God's desire for us and into darkness and turmoil. So, we must discern where any movement of spirit might be coming from and what it is leading us to do.

The key question for discernment of spirits, then, is to ask what are the likely fruits—or weeds—from a particular movement of our spirit. Of course, we have the teachings of Jesus and the Church to help us discern aright, yet we must also ask the Holy Spirit to guide us personally in concrete circumstances. If we discern an outcome as encouraging discipleship to Jesus, we can trust that the Holy Spirit is prompting, and follow accordingly. If some movement leads away from *the way* of Jesus, we must resist it.

FOR FURTHER READING

Groome, Thomas, and Colleen Griffith, eds. *Catholic Spiritual Practices: Treasures Old and New*. Orleans, MA: Paraclete Press, 2014. A reclaiming of many Catholic spiritual practices as proposed by some leading scholars and spiritual writers.

Lennan, Richard, and Nancy Pineda-Madrid, eds. *The Holy Spirit: Setting the World on Fire*. Mahwah, NJ: Paulist Press, 2017. A collection of essays on the Holy Spirit by some Boston College theologians.

Locklin, Reid B. *Spiritual but Not Religious: An Oar Stroke Closer to the Farther Shore*. Collegeville, MN: Liturgical Press, 2005. Makes a convincing argument that spirituality needs the raft of religion and communal commitment to get to the "farther shore."

Interlude

So Where Are We Now?

TAKE A BREAK

During my summer vacations from high school and college, I worked on a farm. That it was owned by my grandfather made the work no less backbreaking (nor better paid), from 8:00 a.m. to 6:00 p.m., six days a week. What made it bearable was an old farmhand named Joe Kane, who had labored there all his life. I loved to pair off with Joe as work companions. He had rich and hard-won wisdom from life and told the best of stories, always as if true—though they seldom were. Our chat got both of us through the day.

Every afternoon around three o'clock, Joe would pause whatever we were doing, sit down, and ask, "So where are we now?" Then he'd review what we had accomplished so far (how many drills of potatoes, or cocks of hay, or stacks of corn), and he'd imagine what more we might get done before day's end. This step back from the work face lent a welcome respite, celebrated our progress, and was an opportunity for Joe to enjoy his pipe. All day I'd look forward to Joe's "so where are we now" interlude. I take one here!

CATHOLIC PERSPECTIVES FOR THE IMAGINATION OF THE HEART

Thus far we have reflected on some of the human heart's deepest longings: for fullness, for love, for happiness—and a reliable way to achieve it—for freedom, and for a wholesome holiness of life toward authenticity as human beings. We proposed foundational Christian convictions concerning who and how God Is for us, about the historical Jesus as the Christ of faith, and of the sanctifying role of the Holy Spirit.

With the "assurance of faith" (Heb 10:22), the convictions proposed can lend great spiritual wisdom for responding to the hungers of our hearts. They can guide our desires toward the most fulfillment possible on this side of eternity, and not only for ourselves but through us for the common good of all people and creation. The loving relationality of our one and triune God makes self-fulfillment of any hunger—as if only for the self—an idolatrous and destructive quest. Christian spirituality and its quest for authentic holiness requires "all for one and one for all."

Now, in part 2 we turn to some distinguishing "Catholic" perspectives on Christian faith and how they might lend spiritual wisdom to help satisfy other pressing hungers of heart. While the previous chapters have drawn upon some distinctly Catholic sources (like Vatican II and the Catechism), their sentiments and spirituality could be readily embraced as mainstream Christian. Here we turn to perspectives that are more distinctly—though not uniquely—"Catholic." I continue to hope, however, that with the ecumenical progress of our age, the spirituality of every Christian will find them fitting, even if not like an old shoe.

In this part 2, then, we review four of Catholicism's most constitutive aspects, namely its communality of personhood (chapter 7), its sacramentality of life (chapter 8), its accent on living faith for hope (chapter 9), and its emphasis on a faith that does justice (chapter 10). While their combined collage helps to distinguish Catholicism, they can be encountered and lived out in any community of Christian faith.

We search out the spiritual wisdom of these deep structures of Catholicism because wisdom is precisely what the heart needs to guide the right fulfillment of its desires. As noted in the prologue, the heart can lead us aright or lead us astray; the key is the wisdom we bring to guide it. With the Psalmist, we must strive to "gain a wise heart" (Ps 90:12) because the foolish heart does evil (Ps 14:1). In Christian faith, of course, the path to spiritual wisdom is *the way* taught by Jesus of Nazareth—none wiser. Rightly do the Gospels portray him as wiser than Solomon (Luke 11:31), the paradigm of biblical wisdom, and Paul calls Jesus "the power...and the wisdom of God" (1 Cor 1:24).

There is a strong biblical sentiment that whether our hearts lead us to wisdom or foolishness depends on "the imagination of the heart," in how we imagine fulfilling its hungers. With a moment of reflection, we recognize this as patently true. As human agents, we continually make choices. To fulfill the longings of our hearts, we must first imagine how best to do so; what we image as their fulfillment surely shapes the choices we make. So the "imaginings of our heart" greatly influence the lives we choose to live and especially how to fulfill our desires.

Surely this is why the first commandment urges us to put God at the center of our lives; a *pesel*—"graven image"—there will lead us astray (see Exod 20:4). As human beings, God entrusts us with a fundamental choice *and* the freedom to choose. Nowhere is this reflected more vividly than in Deuteronomy 30:19. There, God speaks through Moses to the Israelite people: "I have set before you life and death, blessings and curses. Choose life so that you and your descendants may live." So we have momentous life choices to make. When the imaginings of our hearts are guided by a rich spiritual resource like "Catholic" faith, we are more likely to choose wisely for life and blessings rather than foolishly for death and curses.

The perspectives we raise up in this part 2 from the spiritual treasury of Catholic faith have particular appeal to the imagination. This is likely because Catholicism's deepest layers of faith are experientially encountered through symbols and realia that invite us to imagine (bread, wine, water, oil, washing feet, etc.). Its instances of institutional shortcomings notwithstanding—and now all too patently on display—at the core of Catholic faith we find a rich tradition of spiritual wisdom that can guide the imagination of any heart toward fulfilling its deepest desires and living into holiness and authenticity of life.

If left to our own imaginations, so influenced by what Charles Taylor calls the "social imaginary" of our secular cultural context, we can readily go astray and even presume that we are going aright. Meanwhile, the communality, sacramentality, living faith for hope, and social justice commitments of Catholicism can appeal to the imaginations of every heart and lend spiritual wisdom to help satisfy their hungers.

PART II

CHAPTER 7

A "Catholic" Sense of Ourselves

Our Hunger to Be Good and to Belong

"It Takes a Village"

I experienced the wisdom of this old African proverb firsthand, growing up in a rural community in Ireland. To begin with, my core family was nigh a village unto itself; I was the youngest of nine children and we had copious aunts, uncles, cousins, and two maternal grandparents nearby. Then add in the neighbors, a motley crew that reflected the whole medley of humanity—with all of its sins and graces. If the poet Frost be right, that "home is the place where, when you go there, they have to take you in," then I surely had a home in that village.

My mother's best friend was Molly Gorman. Her son Kevin was one of my best buddies too, and Molly was like a second mother to me. One day, I got into some trouble that I imagined would bring down my mother's wrath. Rather than facing the music, I decided to hightail it over to Molly. I confessed to her; I've forgotten what my crime was, but after hearing my story, I've never forgotten her response. She said, "Well don't worry about it Tom; your mother knows that you're a very good boy. Go on home now and she'll be *happy to see you." So assured, I ventured home, and behold, Molly was right. My Mom was even worried about me.*

I believed Molly that day, and the conviction of my innate goodness as a person, even in spite of my sins along the way, has remained with me ever since. Likewise, that village lent me a sense of belonging and the conviction that I'm better off in relationships and community instead of trying to go it alone. My family and village gave me a fundamental perspective that we become our best selves as persons-in-community and within a community-of-persons.

OUR HUNGERS TO BE GOOD AND TO BELONG

Regarding the first of this symbiotic duo, the reader may well be surprised that I name as a deep hunger of the human heart a longing to *be good*. One could well rejoin (and quote copiously from the morning paper or selectively from the Bible) that the more foundational human drive is toward sin and evil than toward doing and being good. A little against the grain then, I invite the reader to consider that a pressing hunger of our hearts is to be a good person and to be recognized as such.

Second, I propose that as human beings we long to be included and in communities that encourage our innate goodness, recognize us as being "as good as" anyone else therein, and welcome our contribution to the common good of all. So, to *belong* means to be accepted, to be respected, to be included in—as fully as others. More than a passive presence, *belonging* also means to actively participate in, contribute to, and be held accountable by our communities. Let us unpack each of these reciprocal claims—our need to *be good* and to *belong*—a little further.

To begin with, no person wants to see themselves as innately evil. Even psychopaths try to convince that their evil deeds are done for some good. Hitler likely convinced himself that his horrendous destruction of Jews, gypsies, and homosexuals served some noble cause. It is as if the human heart cannot choose barefaced evil; when we do it, we need to justify it somehow—in order to look ourselves in the mirror. I propose that our fundamental human disposition, and thus a desire of the heart, is to be and do good, and to be thought of likewise.

Patently, we are eminently capable of doing terrible evil. And somewhat ironically, we can so choose by our God-given freedom. Yet when we do bad things, we know that we are falling short of who we really are, diminishing our authenticity as human beings. When we justify acts of evil to ourselves or others, we recognize, at some deeper level, that we are in bad faith—as Hitler must have! Rather than persisting in bad faith, however, to honestly recognize our failings can prompt us to ask God's mercy and aspire again to being the good person that is our heart's desire.

Then, for us to become the good people we long to be, we need others to recognize and encourage us as such; we need to belong! This is because we are inherently communal beings. I say "inherently" because it is not as if we are persons first who then choose to engage in relationships and community. Instead, our social environment shapes who we are to begin with; in a sense, our sociality is prior to our individuality. So we need relationships and the context of community to become authentically human; we cannot become *persons* by ourselves. A standard conviction within the social sciences is that we are "looking glass" selves. In other words, we *tend to become* what our sociocultural environment reflects as who we are to be.

I highlight "tend to become" because I do not believe that we are determined by our relationships and sociocultural context—as if we are no more than the sum of our circumstances. While some social scientists claim as much, from a Christian perspective, God's grace can always empower our own agency and enable us to resist negative influences, though often requiring a mighty struggle. Yet this being said, our relationships and communities have enormous influence on our identity as persons. We are most likely, then, to grow into our own goodness by being included in communities that image us as good, empower us to be good, and welcome our contribution to the common good of all. For this reason, belonging to affirming communities is another deep hunger of the human heart.

Our hungers to be good and to belong, like all of our desires, arise from our souls. Again, they eminently reflect our spiritual nature as made in the image of our one and triune God—a community of infinite Goodness. For this reason, we need a spirituality that nurtures our goodness and fosters our belonging. While this is a deeply human calling, our growth in goodness is more likely within the context of a faith community that encourages as much. And we need a faith community that has good-encouraging traditions, stories, and symbols, that proposes perspectives, practices, patterns, and prayer ways that nurture the potential goodness and communality of its members. Christian communities have a unique potential—and responsibility—to so provide.

Anticipating what we develop below, a Christian faith community can be measured by how effectively it provides what we need to grow spiritually and thus in our potential for personal goodness as communal beings. And given its copious spiritual charisms and traditions, a Catholic community has some inestimable assets in this regard. Then, the empowerment to be good by belonging to a Christian base community should permeate how we belong to and participate in all the other communities of our lives, reaching from our immediate relationships into the public realm.

We all belong to many communities of family, friends, neighborhood, work, leisure, politics, etcetera, and then to our society at large. If our varied communities are to nurture our potential goodness and foster our sense of belonging, we need them to recognize that we are "as good as" other members and welcome our contribution to the common good of all. If any communal context diminishes us as somehow "less than" others, it inhibits our potential goodness and reduces our contribution to the whole. Every person longs for their dignity to be respected, their human rights to be honored, their gifts to be engaged, and their equality recognized—to truly belong. All those longings require that our communities recognize us for being as good as anyone else and welcome us to contribute the good we are and do for the common good of all.

Patently, all forms of social and cultural discrimination (sexism, racism, homophobia, ageism, etc.) are based on the false premise that some people are not "as good as" other humans. There is no pain greater to our hearts than to be disrespected, excluded, or made to feel that we don't belong—at least not fully—because we are not as good as some other members. A Christian faith community and its spirituality should empower people to disbelieve and resist all such forms of discrimination and social injustice. Following on, it should offer the spiritual resources that prompt people to imagine their potential goodness and lend a sense of belonging within God's family where all are recognized as equally made in the divine image and likeness.

Clearly then, to become good persons as communal beings for the common good of all, we need a spirituality that encourages us to imagine ourselves as such, and then spiritual resources that nurture us to so live. My proposal is that a "Catholic" Christian community has unique potential to lend such spiritual resources and support. More than most other faith traditions, it affirms our innate *goodness* as persons and the *communality* of both our human estate and of Christian faith. These are inspiring imaginings to shape a life-giving spirituality and the practices to sustain it.

At its best—and even, as often, when falling far short—a Catholic Christian community can be a powerful sacrament of God's grace to people's lives, encouraging their innate goodness to flourish, lending a deep sense of belonging, and encouraging their contribution to the common good of society. So the invitation is to craft a spirituality that reflects Catholicism's good and communal imagining of ourselves and to participate in forging a faith community that reflects and empowers as much. Such a spirituality can enable us to imagine how to live Christian faith in the midst of the world as disciples of Jesus, fulfilling our hungers to be good and to belong.

PAUSE FOR REFLECTION

- When you look into your own heart, do you recognize a deep hunger to be ever growing as a good person? Name some "next steps" that such progress might include.

- What do *you* think? Do you need a faith community to nurture your own spiritual goodness and sense of belonging? Why or why not?

GOOD PEOPLE TOGETHER: A THEOLOGY OF OURSELVES

By way of crafting a Christian spirituality that nurtures a *living* faith, there is nothing more foundational than how we image ourselves as human beings. Who we imagine us to be, personally and communally, has a pervasive influence on who we become and how we live our lives together. And while our personal dispositions and our socio-cultural environment are powerful forces on our identity, there is, I propose, a God-given core to all human beings that shapes who we can become—by God's grace.

To ground a Christian spirituality, then, we must imagine who we can become from the perspective of our faith in God and as revealed in Jesus Christ. This amounts to asking, "Who does our Creator create us to be?" and then, how might this God view encourage us to imagine ourselves and all people.

Given our both/and nature, personal and communal, we can first imagine, and only for the sake of analysis, a theological *anthropology* of ourselves—as *persons*-in-community. Then, because God made us inherently relational, we need a theological *sociology* as well, imagining who we are as a *community*-of-persons. Though these two aspects—the personal and communal—are symbiotic, for clarity sake we will reflect on them in turn. I reiterate, however, that we must not imagine them as being separate or sequential—as first one and then the other. Existentially and for a "Catholic" imagination, we are always to be *persons*-in-community and a *community*-of-persons.

Good Persons at Heart: Many times already we have referred to the two great mythical accounts of Creation that we find in Genesis 1 and 2. And just as their teaching is echoed throughout the Bible, we return to them again here because they constitute the first foundation of a Catholic anthropology and suggest (below) a sociology as well. In sum, they claim that God made humankind in God's own image and likeness—whom Christians believe to be both personal and communal, one and triune—and that we are alive by the life-breath of God.

The first mythical account has the "spirit of God" working across six days to forge first the cosmos, then plants and all living creatures, and finally, as the pinnacle of Creation, humankind. Note its rich conviction that all of life comes forth from God. At the end of the sixth day, the account represents God as saying, "Let us make humankind in our image, according to our likeness" (Gen 1:26). Then, as if after consulting within the Godhead, "God created humankind in his image, in the image of God he created them; male and female he created them" (1:27). As God looked upon the creation of the sixth day—which included "living creatures of every kind" (1:24) as well as people—God saw it as "*very* good" (1:31, emphasis added), the only time the superlative is used.

The whole human rights tradition, at least of the Western world, has been based on the profound truth taught by this biblical myth, namely that all people—regardless of gender, race, ethnicity, orientation, physical or mental abilities, etcetera—are created equal (e.g., the American Declaration of Independence). We might say that we have dignity, equality, and respect as persons "by copyright" to our God. The clear teaching is that every person is equal to and as good as any other.

The second account portrays God making *ha adam*—a gender-inclusive term meaning *humankind*—"from the dust of the ground," and then God "breathed into [*adam*]...the breath of life; and [*adam*] became a living being" (Gen 2:7). So all people are alive by the very life-breath of God. While this account applies no superlative to humankind, we can well surmise that whatever breathes from the life-breath of God is good; how could it be otherwise? Indeed, thereafter God commissions humankind to be good stewards of God's creation (see Gen 2:15), intimating both our ability and responsibility to be partners with God and each other. So far, so *good*!

Then, in Genesis 3, we read the other familiar myth of what Christians have long named as "the fall." Though most theologians no longer take it as causative of our human condition, this mythical story reflects our own proclivity for sin and our need for God's help. More recently, it has been interpreted to have both negative ("original sin") and positive consequences (desiring a conscience for "knowing good and evil" [3:5]). For sure it reflects an honest appraisal of our human situation—that we can choose to do bad things. The key question, however, is what is our dominant disposition, for good or evil? Theologically we might ask, was God's original grace in creation negated by some original sin of humankind, and did this corrupt to evil all of us who came thereafter?

This symbolic question became a divisive one at the time of the Reformation. The Reformers (Luther and more so Calvin) interpreted Genesis 3 as reflecting a complete fall from grace by humankind into a totally sinful condition. In Calvin's phrase, Adam and Eve's disobedience reduced us to a *massa peccati*, a mass of sin and inherently corrupt. The Reformers were rightly emphasizing the need for God's saving grace over against a Catholic freneticism about performing good works as if we must earn salvation by our own efforts.

The classic Catholic posture, however, was to acknowledge our "proclivity for sin" (term used by the Council of Trent) and yet to insist that humankind always remains in the divine image and likeness, and thus are inherently good. Original grace, as it were, outweighs original sin. This has remained the standard Catholic position ever since. In our time, the *Catechism* reiterates, while "human nature bears the wound of original sin," we more so "desire the good" and ever "remain an image of our Creator" (*CCC* 1707 and 2566).

Perhaps the most compelling rationale for this classically "Catholic" position is not so much the story of Adam and Eve as of incarnation. Simply stated, God could not have taken on our human estate in Jesus, God's own Son, if being human is inherently evil. While we share in God's life, in Jesus we believe that God shared in ours, so it must be good. As theologian Karl Rahner has well argued, Jesus is the fullest expression of our humanity, not only revealing God to us but us to ourselves. In Jesus we recognize the potential goodness that is ours, the more fully human we become persons as he was.

Further, as reviewed in chapters 4 and 5, Jesus not only models for us how to live for God's reign, but in his paschal mystery released an abundance of God's grace that empowers us to so live. We are always capable of choosing and doing the good because "God who is at work" in us empowers us "both to will and to work" for our "salvation" (Phil 2:13).

By way of the relationship between our own agency and God's grace, the Catholic position, classically expressed by St. Thomas Aquinas, is that grace works through and enhances our nature, as in a partnership. In other words, God's grace—the Holy Spirit now at work—both prompts and empowers our best efforts to be and do good. And while God's grace is always *gratia*, yet, and as stated throughout, every grace comes to us as a responsibility—to play our part.

The great Catholic theologian Bernard Lonergan well described our partnership with God as encouraging a "realistic optimism" about ourselves and who we can become. *Optimism* is the defining noun, but we must be realistic about our capacity for evil as well. Meanwhile, sin is always against our better nature. Molly Gorman was right; we are, at heart, good people.

That we are graced to do the good does not mean that we always so choose, as we well know from personal experience and the morning paper. The reality of every human person is that we sin, and as St. Augustine noted, we often "sin boldly." Even the greatest of saints were forever lamenting their sinfulness and how far short they fell in living their goodness as disciples of Jesus for God's reign in the world.

For this reason, Catholic faith wisely recognizes a gradualism in living into our potential goodness; as Pope Francis suggests, "Ordinarily, [grace] takes hold of us and transforms us *progressively*" (*Gaudete et Exsultate* 50). To echo chapter 6, growing into holiness and authenticity is a lifelong journey that is never completed until we finally rest in God. The crucial Catholic conviction about ourselves, however, is that in spite of our sins and "proclivity" to sin, we remain essentially good and ever more disposed toward good than evil. Indeed, to believe that we are inherently sinful encourages a self-fulfilling prophecy, as well as a denial of the power of God's grace through Jesus Christ.

To concretize a positive anthropology, imagine an example from parenting. A child tells a lie or steals something. What to do? Instead of saying, "You're a liar," or "You're a thief," better by far to say, "You're *not* a liar; so why are you lying?" or "You're *not* a thief, so why are you stealing?" By way of their self-understanding—how they imagine themselves—it is far wiser to encourage the positive, even while confronting them with their wrongdoing.

Made for Each Other: Social scientists can diverge in their portrayal of the human person with some emphasizing our individuality and others our communality. Likewise, traditional cultures tend to prioritize the community, whereas postmodern ones emphasize the individual.

Christian faith, however, and Catholicism in particular, emphasizes both—the dignity and rights of the person *and* our communal nature that makes us responsible for and to our neighbor and for the common good of all.

This both/and posture of Catholicism begins with that same biblical text of Genesis 1:26–27—that God made humankind in God's own image and likeness. That it affirms our dignity, rights, and potential goodness as persons, we have already well noted. Now, the God subsequently revealed in Jesus as triune lends Christians the warrant for claiming that God made people as communal beings.

That our God is a Trinity of Divine Persons points to our own communality; otherwise we would not image our God. Further, to reflect God as right and loving communion means that people become most authentically human by living in right and loving relationships. So no wonder that Jesus posed the greatest commandment as to love God, neighbor, and ourselves with our whole being. Given our God-given nature, we simply must relate with others, and our highest human potential is to relate with love within community.

This being said, the Christian conviction about our communal nature has deep roots in Hebrew faith as well. Long before Jesus's revelation of God as one and triune, the Hebrew Scriptures reflect over and over that God entered into a covenant not with individuals per se but with the Israelites as a community: "I will walk among you, and will be your God, and you shall be my people" (Lev 26:12).

Not only did their covenant make them personally and communally responsible to God, the Israelites realized that they were likewise responsible to and for each other. All the biblical covenants with God are also a covenant among the people themselves, binding them together to care for each other; only thus can they live their vocation as a *people* of God. Indeed, we can say that throughout the whole Bible, to live humanly is to live in partnership with God among a people of God who are responsible to and for each other.

Note, too, that Israel's biblical mandate to so live reached beyond their own community and was to include all humankind. As God revealed in the covenant with Abraham, the Israelites' partnership with

God as a people was to be a means of blessing for "all the families of the earth" (Gen 12:3).

Repeatedly the Hebrew Scriptures remind the Israelites that their covenant with God requires them to treat not only each other but also "the alien" (persons of other races) with dignity and respect. "You shall not wrong or oppress a resident alien" (Exod 22:21); rather, "you shall love the alien as yourself" (Lev 19:34). So to be in covenant with God bonds with the whole human family, making all humanity brothers and sisters. We are responsible to and for all people because they are all God's own.

It was to be expected, then, that Jesus, steeped in his Jewish faith, would reflect a communal understanding of the person and preach a gospel that forged a community of faith. From the beginning of his public ministry, Jesus went out into the highways and byways and invited all into a *community* of disciples. And not only were they to "follow" him, but also they were to be participants together in his mission of God's reign, which required community building. In the first account of his recruiting disciples, Jesus called Simon (Peter) and Andrew to follow him so that they might all "fish for people" together (Mark 1:17).

And as elaborated in chapter 4, Jesus's outreach and call into community was radically inclusive. He called and included women and children, poor and rich, farmers and fishermen, tax collectors and prostitutes, the whole host of humanity. Scripture scholars agree that the most radical symbol of the inclusivity of Jesus's community was his table fellowship; he welcomed all to the table, in the world of his time so symbolically laden.

Then, as noted many times, Jesus taught that our ultimate human capacity and the greatest communal good we can do in life is to love. This is why he wove together his greatest commandment (uniting Deut 6:5 and Lev 19:18) as a symbiosis of loving God, ourselves, and others—even enemies—with all of one's mind, heart, strength, and soul. And this summarizes "all the law and the prophets" (Matt 22:40).

No wonder then how Jesus described God's final judgment of our lives (Matt 25:31–46). It eminently reflects that we are responsible to and for each other, and especially for those most in need. But Jesus did not propose such a spirituality as simply a test to decide reward or punishment later. To honor our communal nature is its own reward now and this is realized by living as good people who are made for each other. To live in right and loving relationships reaps "a hundredfold" *now*, as well as "eternal life" hereafter (Mark 10.30).

That Jesus's disciples recognized that he intended them to bond as a faith community is evident from the very beginning of the Church. Here we need only echo again Paul's rich image of the Christian community as so bonded by baptism as to constitute the very body of Christ in the world. Paul writes, "Now you are the body of Christ and individually members of it" (1 Cor 12:27). Note Paul's both/and emphasis, on the community and the person. And all are to work together at the service of the whole (12:28–31), and "for building up the body of Christ" in the world (Eph 4:12).

PAUSE FOR REFLECTION

- Do you agree—or disagree—with Catholicism's emphasis on our dual nature as personal and communal? Explain your rationale!

- Why might living in right and loving relationships be its own reward—now?

- What does your good and communal nature mean for your own sense of yourself?

NEEDED: A TRULY CHRISTIAN FAITH COMMUNITY

A faith community is where we most likely can satisfy our spiritual hungers to be good and to belong. Rather than trying to "go it alone," a community of faith can lend the resources we need and opportunities to contribute our own gifts and goodness. While this is true of all people, regardless of religious tradition, it seems eminently true for people who aspire to a Christian spirituality, given the personal/communal nature of its grounding faith and imagining of who we are. A "private Christian" is a contradiction in terms. We are most likely to grow in *living* faith as disciples of Jesus by being persons in *Christian* community and within a *Christian* community of persons. Let us reflect a little on the kind of Christian community we need and that we must try to build up by contributing our own gifts and goodness.

Here we could digress into a vast topic that theologians refer to as *ecclesiology*—the study of the Church. Instead, and from a "Catholic" imagining of ourselves and of our hungers to be good and to belong, we limit here to five brief reflections: (1) why belong to a Christian faith community; (2) the kind of community Christians are called to become; (3) who is to belong; (4) how we are to belong; and (5) a recognition of how far short of its own faith that our institutional Church can fall, and yet how to keep hope alive, in these particularly more challenging times.

1. *Why Belong to the Church?* Given the personal/communal nature of ourselves and likewise of Christian faith, we are most likely to satisfy our spiritual needs to be good and to belong as disciples of Jesus through membership in a Christian faith community. Simply stated, *living* Christian faith—ever the intent of its spirituality—requires the resources and opportunities to be found in the Church. Indeed, by baptism all Christians have the *right* to a base faith community that nurtures our goodness and fully includes us as members. Of course, this *right* also brings its *responsibilities*.

Revisiting a text we encountered before, John's Gospel has Jesus recognize that there are many homes within God's universal family. He explains, "In my Father's house (*oikia* also meant *family*) there are many dwelling places" (14:2). This text puts us in mind of the great world religions, and the rich and distinctive spiritual homes they offer within God's human family. It would seem that Jesus favored everyone to find a particular "dwelling place"—be it his or some other home.

Then immediately following, and directly addressing the disciples, Jesus adds "I go to prepare a place *for you*....I will come again and will take you to myself, so that *where I am*, there you may be also" (John 14:2–3, emphasis added). So Jesus clearly intends his own disciples to have a distinctive Christian home within God's universal family; we must need as much! Indeed, bonded with the risen Christ through baptism, Jesus now takes us *to himself* and coabides with us in our shared "dwelling place." This fulfills his promise that "where two or three are gathered in my name, I am there among them" (Matt 18:20). We can find such a Christ-encountering faith home through actively participating in the life of the Church.

Belonging to a "Catholic" faith home should encourage the positive and communal imagining of ourselves previously described, and then give access to its stories and symbols, practices and patterns, perspectives and prayer ways that enable us to live into authentic holiness of life. Its spiritual assets can encourage both our growth in goodness and our active belonging. In a Christian community, too, we can find people of like faith to pray and worship with, to do the works of compassion and justice with, to repent and find forgiveness with, and to journey in faith with, helping to support each other along the way.

2. *What Kind of Christian Community?* For imagining a baptism-bonded community of Christians, there is no more vivid image than Paul's posing of the Church as the "body of Christ" in the world. As such, and by the power of the Holy Spirit, this *Body* has the mission to continue God's work of liberating salvation in Jesus. As a community, then, we must try to embody all the values reflected in the life of the historical Jesus, empowered now by God's abundant grace through the risen Christ.

In another rich communal image, Paul said that Christians are "members of the household of God, built upon the foundation of the apostles and prophets, with Christ Jesus himself as the cornerstone" (Eph 2:19–20). Everything about us then should reflect our firm foundation and location in *the way* of Jesus. And when we fall short, we must help each other to recognize as much, repent, and ever renew our efforts to live faithfully as a community of Jesus's disciples.

So the Church universal and every local Christian community is to reflect all the compassion and care, peace and justice, mercy and forgiveness, inclusion, outreach, and hospitality that we see reflected in the praxis and preaching of Jesus. Above all, we must imagine ourselves as a community of radical love that reaches within and without—even to enemies. And worth repeating, we are to show particular favor for those who need some favor most, the poor of whatever kind.

We have referred a number of times to the inclusivity of Jesus's original community. Reflecting Jesus's values, Paul insisted likewise that this Body of Christ should be marked by its egalitarian spirit and inclusivity. Paul portrayed all members as on equal footing because "in the one Spirit we were all baptized into one body" and "we were all made to drink of one Spirit" (1 Cor 12:13). No Christian is any more baptized than any other. Then, for those "baptized into Christ....There is no longer Jew or Greek, there is no longer slave or free, there is no longer male and female; for all of you are one in Christ Jesus" (Gal 3:27–28). A defining commitment of every Christian community must be to give all members a sense of unqualified belonging and with equal rights and dignity.

Only in such an inclusive and egalitarian community can we begin to satisfy our hunger to be good and to belong, with everyone considered just as good as everyone else. Sustained and empowered by such a Christian *body*, we are more likely to function in all our communities— family, workplace, neighborhood, and society at large—as agents of inclusion and for the common good of all. The graces that the Holy Spirit mediates to Christians through the Church, continuing God's liberating salvation in Jesus, are always meant "for the life of the world" (John 6:51).

We noted earlier that at least 35 million people in the United States alone identify themselves now as "former Catholics"; they appear to be *dones* more than *nones*. The great majority, however, eventually find and join another faith community, so typically their leaving is not from loss of faith. Statistically, one half of all U.S. Catholics leave the Church at some time in their lives; about 10 percent return, leaving some 90 percent who do not. And many who stay away express bitterness toward the Church (we return to more depressing statistics below).

One has to wonder, then, what are we Catholics doing that is so effective in driving people away, even making many embittered? Though this pressing question cannot be easily answered, it must be faced, and I suggest some of the alienating factors and how to address them below. For now, let us be clear that instead of *driving people away* the Church must make every effort to *bring people along*. We must give every would-be member a deep sense of belonging and without fear of being judged, regardless of the circumstances of their faith journey or their disagreements with Church teachings and disciplines that are not central to the faith itself. And think about it: no Christian lives perfectly the radical gospel of Jesus—loving enemies, doing good to those who hate us, turning the other cheek, going the extra mile. So *who* is entitled to send anyone else away?

3. *Who to Belong: Saints* and *Sinners!* From great image makers like Jesus and Paul, it is abundantly clear that all the baptized must be welcomed and equally included in the Church, local and universal. Having already highlighted this general inclusivity, let us emphasize here that the Church must ever welcome both saints and sinners, or better, people who are becoming *saints* as repentant *sinners*. We focus first on our vocation to become saints.

In chapter 6, we proposed that all Christians are called to a wholesome holiness of life and that our sanctification is particularly the work of the Holy Spirit. For disciples of Jesus, to become holy/authentic means to continue growing in *living* faith for the reign of God as he incarnated and taught, and that the Spirit's grace now empowers our own good efforts to so live.

St. Paul echoes often this call to sanctity; some seventy-five times he addresses or refers to Christians as "saints." So he writes "to the saints and faithful brothers and sisters in Christ in Colossae" (Col 1:2). Likewise, he addresses "all God's beloved in Rome, who are called to be saints" (Rom 1:7). The Second Vatican Council retrieved this sense of sanctity as a universal calling for all Christians. The title of chapter 5 of Vatican II's Constitution on the Church (*Lumen Gentium*) summarized it well: "The Call of the Whole Church to Holiness," and went on to explain that this includes every baptized person. All Christians are to imagine themselves as becoming saints. Then, what of us sinners?

In the early centuries of Church history, a heretical movement emerged called *Donatism*. The Donatists claimed that only "saints" could belong to the Church and that sinners were excluded. St. Augustine (345–430), who for long had lived a sinful life himself, made and won the argument that the Church must welcome sinners as well. And he based his argument on the claim that the Church is to be *katholos*—"catholic." So the Church's claim to catholicity demands that we welcome saint and sinner alike. Thank God!

Far from excluding us sinners, an integral aspect of the Church's mission from Jesus is to be a community that mediates and assures all of God's mercy while ever encouraging our better selves. Jesus said of himself that he came "to call not the righteous but sinners to repentance" (Luke 5:32). He repeated the teaching of the prophet Hosea, imagining God to say, "I desire mercy, not sacrifice" (Matt 9:13). As Pope Francis frequently and rightly insists, "God's name is mercy," and "mercy is the heart-beat of the Gospel" (*Gaudete et Exsultate* 97). A Christian community is constituted of sinners becoming saints and of saints who are forgiven sinners, and all are most welcome.

4. *How to Belong?* There is an old attitude among Catholics, going back at least to the Council of Trent (1545–63) and still lingering, that does not encourage us to be agents of our faith but dependents instead. The hierarchical ordering of the Church can be stereotyped as doers and done for, providers and provided for, teachers and taught, clergy and laity, with a qualitative line of demarcation between them. It reflects a pedestalizing of Church leaders made up of an ordained elite on which all *merely* baptized members depend for access to God's grace and the gospel.

This posture was epitomized in the oft-quoted statement of Pope Pius X (1835–1913): "The Church is essentially an *unequal* society, that is, a society comprising two categories of her sons, the Pastors and the flock, those who occupy a rank in the different degrees of the hierarchy and the multitude of the faithful....The one duty of the multitude is to allow themselves to be led, and, like a docile flock, to follow the Pastors" (*Vehementer Nos* 8 [1906]). Though written over one hundred years ago, this papal encyclical reflected the typical attitude of the Catholic Church down to Vatican II (1962–65), and its traces continue to this day.

By welcome contrast in our time, Pope Francis has repeatedly insisted that such clericalism is the antithesis of the egalitarian and participative community that Jesus envisioned and Paul championed. On at least six different occasions, in one way or another, Jesus warned the leaders of his community not to "lord it over" others. He went so far as to encourage that "whoever wishes to become great among you must be your servant," and precisely because he himself "came not to be served but to serve" (Mark 10:42–45). Jesus is ever the model of servant leadership to which *every* Christian is called by their baptism into Christ's Body.

Repeating a little, Paul made very clear that within this Body of Christ "there are varieties of gifts, but the same Spirit" and adds "to each is given the manifestation of the Spirit for the common good" (1 Cor 12:4, 7). So every member is to contribute their gifts for the good of the faith community and for the life of the world. All are to put our gifts to work "for building up the body of Christ" (Eph 4:12) and actively participating in its mission.

As generally agreed among scholars, one of the great achievements of the Second Vatican Council was its returning Catholic consciousness to the conviction that all the baptized constitute "the common priest-hood of the faithful," and share with the ordained "in the one priest-hood of Christ" (*Lumen Gentium* 10). We might say that by baptism all Christians are "ordained" as in commissioned to participate in the mission and ministries of the Church in the world.

The Council insisted that this "priesthood of the faithful" calls every baptized person to be a fully-fledged participant in the life of the Church. For by baptism, all Christians "share a common dignity from rebirth in Christ"; there is to be "no inequality" among us on any basis (*Lumen Gentium* 32). Indeed, all the baptized are "made sharers in the *priestly*, *prophetic*, and *kingly* [governance] functions of Christ" (no. 31, emphasis added).

The Council went on repeatedly to unpack this traditional triad of Christ's functions and ours. So baptism calls every Christian: to "full, conscious, and active participation" in worship (*Sacrosanctum Concilium* 14)—our *priestly* function; to side with those "who are poor or in any way afflicted" (*Gaudium et spes* 1)—our *prophetic* function; and "to express opinion on things which concern the good of the Church" (no. 37)—to have voice in Church *governance*. By baptism, then, every Christian person and local community is invited—nay mandated—to actively participate in the Church's mission to continue God's saving work in Jesus.

Catholics are slowly making progress, if only inch by inch, on becoming active agents rather than passive recipients of the Church's mission to the world. Nothing less will be true belonging and the full realization of our baptismal rights and responsibilities.

5. *Falling Far Short, yet Keeping Hope Alive.* We already noted the welcome presence of sinners in the Church, and thank God—or I could not belong myself. Yet we must recognize that while the effectiveness of the Church as a sacrament of God's grace is always assured from God's side of the covenant, from our side we often fall too far short. Indeed, there is ample evidence to challenge the idyllic portrayal of the Church offered above as if only a pipe dream. Some egregious failures, local and universal, encourage a healthy skepticism as well as renewed resolve.

All the empirical studies of religion in America indicate a falling off not so much in belief as in *belonging* to a faith community—our interest here; this is particularly true of mainline Christian churches. For example, in 1980, only 4 percent of Americans listed themselves as "none" regarding religion; now (2017) more than 25 percent so identify and the number keeps growing. When asked why they chose "none," some 65 percent say that all religions do more harm than good. Likewise, a significant percentage see religious faith as contrary to science, seeing them as competing rather than complementary ways of knowing.

That some 75 percent of Americans still claim religious belief is significantly higher than in other Western countries, yet a growing number are what the sociologist of religion Grace Davie designates as "believers without belonging." This seems to be particularly true of millennials (those born between 1980 and 2000, approx.) For example, some 90 percent of Catholic millennials say that they believe in God somehow (certain or fairly certain), 85 percent claim that their faith is very or somewhat important to them, and 75 percent pray regularly. This most likely means that they also put good Christian values to work in their daily lives and that their faith shapes their identity. Yet about 75 percent do not actively belong to a Christian community. Why not? There are a great variety of reasons, all of which need to be and can be readily addressed.

Often cited are hardened official positions on what would appear to be debatable topics (e.g., women's ordination, artificial means of birth control), or stringency about rules that are literally "man-made" (e.g., priestly celibacy). Another significant reason is the Church's rejection of the medical science that gay and lesbian orientations are biological and psychological dispositions; in other words, created by God in the womb. Meanwhile, the Church insists that same-sex attraction is deliberately chosen and "intrinsically disordered" (*CCC* 2357). And while the percentage of people with same-sex orientation may be relatively small in the overall population, they have parents and families who resent their loved ones being treated as not fully belonging—unless they remain celibate.

And there are many other alienating postures that drive Catholics from their faith home. Even a short list would include the following: male dominance in Church leadership and governance; lack of accountability on the part of Church leaders; lack of opportunity for laity to lead and to share their gifts; sexist language and imagery; a judgmental attitude, especially around matters of sexuality; priests who are unduly focused on their *presiding* (at liturgy) role to the neglect of *preaching* and *pastoring*; a grossly inflated imaging of the ordained to the diminishment of the baptized—what Pope Francis well names the "curse" of clericalism—and the list goes on.

While Francis has brought a new openness and an emphasis on reaching out to the margins with mercy and welcome for all, he follows after some thirty-five years of more rigid pontificates that alienated many Catholics, at least in Western cultures. And though our postmodern era may be more open to the spiritual, it is less disposed toward organized religion.

These negative factors that make belonging to the Church more difficult and impossible for many must be challenged and changed; all can be rectified and the core convictions of our faith demand as much. Nothing compares, however, to the desolation of spirit and the challenges to people's faith posed by the clergy sex-abuse scandal. It is now evident across all cultures (and so throughout the Church); though some contexts may not have exposed it yet for varied reasons (e.g., church cover-up or lack of a free press). This represents an immense tragedy, first and foremost for the victims/survivors and their families, and then it has inflicted a deep wound on the whole Catholic community. The breadth and frequency of such reports belie the claim that the statistics are no worse among Catholic clergy than other professions (as if this would be any consolation).

To resolve and then move beyond the present crisis caused by clergy sex abuse, the Catholic Church needs to practice what is referred to now as "transitional" justice. This is the kind needed to move successfully from a situation of institutional injustice to a time of reparation and then to structural changes that guarantee that the injustice does not continue. Applying transitional justice to the sex abuse of children and minors by clergy (includes priests and vowed religious men and women), the first step would be to address the root causes of the abuse and its crimes; to ask, "Why did it happen?" and then to make needed changes to eradicate the sources.

Here again Pope Francis specifically names clericalism and the whole pedestalized culture that has surrounded Catholic clergy as a prime cause (see "Letter to the People of God," Aug. 20, 2018). This is echoed by social scientists who claim that their exalted and exaggerated status can encourage Catholic clergy in a sense of entitlement, as if "above the law." This is augmented by the Church's insistence that *all* priests be celibate (not optional), making them *exceptional* in such a vital aspect of human identity as sexuality. Celibacy has never been viewed as theologically essential to priesthood; witness the traditions of married priests in the Eastern Catholic and Orthodox churches. And its "sign" or witness value has surely been diminished, at least in public perception, by recent scandals. Clearly the Catholic Church needs to craft a contemporary theology (in the spirit of Vatican II) regarding the nature, purpose, and requirements for ordained ministry, and increased stewardship of who is admitted to seminaries and novitiates.

Second, transitional justice would hold all clerical perpetrators publicly accountable with total truth telling about their crimes. Because their actions were criminal (not just sinful), this would include reporting to the police and civil authorities, with all credible accusations made public and, insofar as possible, prosecuted in courts of law.

Third, there must be reparation made to all survivor victims. This includes financial compensation, assistance with needed therapy, and public apologies from the pope, local bishop, and church leaders. Further, the crimes should be somehow memorialized as a deterrent to them happening again.

Last, the Church must put in place policies and structures that ensure that this dreadful abuse never happens again. The U.S. Bishops made a step in the right direction with their "Charter for the Protection of Children and Young People" (2002). However, that charter stopped short of holding negligent bishops accountable for the cover-up of such crimes. The next and needed step is to put in place tribunals (perhaps one in every diocese) made up primarily of laypeople, which hold bishops accountable for the protection of children from sex abuse by clergy. Beyond this, every local parish and faith community must implement policies and procedures (e.g., careful background checks, special training of all pastoral ministers) to ensure that Catholics can confidently say "never again" of this terrible scandal.

This crisis prompts larger questions about the general governance of the Church and highlights that the present structures allow for very little participation by laypeople. We might say that the Catholic Church is the last absolute monarchy, at least in the Western world; this is not likely to be effective going forward. Though the *Code of Canon Law* of 1983 encouraged pastoral and financial parish councils and the possibility of diocesan synods, these canons—the official law of the Church—have been sparsely implemented. Perhaps one way that God may draw good out of the evil of clergy sex abuse is a major reordering of the structures of governance in the Catholic Church, and, in particular, with far greater and substantive participation by lay leaders.

Meanwhile, and on a hopeful note, a central achievement of Vatican II was to remind all Catholics that "we" are the Church. All the baptized must take responsibility to enable the Church, local and universal, to be the kind of community that Jesus intends us to be. We must keep alive the vision that in spite of our often glaring failures, personally and as a community, the Church can, with the help of the Holy Spirit, encourage and mentor people in *living* faith as disciples of Jesus. Not by its own deserts but by the gratuitousness of God's grace, every Christian community can be a sacrament of God's liberating salvation, high-pointed in its celebration of the liturgical sacraments (a theme in chapter 8).

Rather than simply lamenting our shortcomings as a community, baptism gives every Christian the responsibility to continue the struggle to make the Church all that the Holy Spirit enables it to be—through our cooperation. With the help of the Spirit, we *can* become a holy and wholesome community of Christian faith that encourages people's goodness and lends all a heartfelt sense of unconditional belonging. Even when we experience the Church being egregiously less than what it should be, we must cling to and work for the vision of a faith community where all are included, are safe and respected, their potential goodness nurtured, and their gifts engaged for the common good of all. This is the Christian faith to which we belong and that belongs to us, even when our church as human institution falls far short.

Though "we hold this treasure in earthen vessels" (2 Cor 4:7, NAB), our faith is a treasure nonetheless. Growing a Christian faith community that reflects and lives the values of Jesus is an ideal worthy of our best efforts and struggle. By the grace of the Holy Spirit, we can keep hope alive and work together toward the dream that Jesus had for his community of disciples.

HOPE FOR OUR HEARTS

On a purely human level, it surely lifts our hearts to imagine ourselves as good people who are fully entitled to belong—in Church and society. Such life-giving convictions are deepened all the more when we imagine that this is who and how we are by divine design. God made the whole human family to be good persons-in-community and a good community-of-persons.

Christians can top this off with the conviction that such an understanding of ourselves and of our faith community was championed by Jesus and empowered by God's work of liberating salvation through him. As a result, we are assured that the Holy Spirit continues God's work in Jesus, lending us the grace to grow in goodness and to deepen our belonging to our faith community. As full participating members, we can enhance our own and our Christian community's goodness and outreach into society for the common good of all. For our spiritualty as Christians, we always have the grace needed to be good and to belong. What hope for our hearts!

Such a hopeful image of ourselves, our communities of faith, and the potential of us together is foundational to a "Catholic" spirituality. It can help to satisfy our hungers to be good and to belong, beginning with belonging to God's universal family, and then finding our own spiritual home and having access to God's grace at work within the Christian family of Jesus. This positive and collaborative perspective lends a far more empowering spirituality than the self-sufficiency that many postmodern people presume and the hybrid sources they draw upon to nurture their holiness of life. As proposed in chapter 6, we can be most enriched by other homes within God's family when we feel at home in our own "dwelling place"—as prepared for us by Jesus (John 14:2).

It can be a huge challenge to believe in our own goodness in the face of some powerful counterforces that beset us in life, personally and socially. Most of us experience, at some time or other, people or systems that want to project negative self-images on us; they can be very hard to withstand. Our resistance is strengthened, however, when we deeply imagine that our own goodness and worth are from God; what more compelling rationale could we have!

Likewise, we can readily fall into self-destructive patterns of behavior that are largely self-chosen and yet become addictive, robbing us of our freedom. If we begin to think that we are no more than our addictions or circumstances, then we lose our agency and descend deeper into the abyss. A powerful counterforce to self-destruction is to cling to the spiritual conviction that we are essentially good people—no matter what we have done. Further, we *can* ever reclaim that goodness and our own agency, precisely because this is how God made us to be; and we always have the help of the Holy Spirit—"Higher Power"—to live into our potential.

Similarly, and by way of our belonging, most of us encounter social and cultural contexts where we are excluded for one reason or another. Sadly, we can begin to believe that this is what we deserve; we tend to interiorize our oppressions. Again, it can be a powerful spiritual antidote to know that we *are* "as good as" everyone else. We are entitled to fully belong to this human family precisely because it is God's family; membership is our birthright from God.

Sadly, our faith community, local and universal, can fail miserably at times to grant every member a sense of full inclusion and to welcome their gifts and goodness into the life of the community. Existentially, the Church can make some people feel as if they are somehow "less than" some others in the eyes of God. While Catholicism proclaims that all are made in the divine image and likeness (it must, if not to be heretical to its own core faith), it can treat some people—women, gays, the poor, minorities—as if they are less than fully included.

Here again the spiritual perspective that God and Jesus intend all members of the Christian community to be treated as equals, as fully belonging and contributing members, can help to sustain one's sense of unconditional inclusion. This requires recognizing that the Church is wrong when it excludes or diminishes anyone for any reason. Likewise, it requires our committing to work for the Church to become the inclusive and egalitarian community that Jesus intends. Here again, God's grace can empower our spiritual commitment; indeed without it we surely lose heart.

We recognize, of course, that people have lived into great goodness and deep belonging through the spiritual wisdom and practices found in the faith communities of all Christian churches and likewise in the great world religions. Meanwhile, the Catholic Church has a rich treasury of spiritual wisdom about ourselves and our communality that can encourage any person's spiritual growth and mediate the grace needed for holiness and authenticity of life. Belonging to such a base faith community will enrich how we belong to other communities, for our own good and the common good of all.

In sum, then, Catholic faith and the spiritual community that carries it offer rich spiritual resources for how to respond to our hungers to be good and to belong. Its imagining of who we are and then the *stories* and *symbols*, the *practices* and *patterns*, the *perspectives* and *prayer ways* it accesses can provide a spiritual treasury for us to become good and to have a deep sense of belonging, beginning with a faith community and flowing out from there. To embrace the imaginings of "Catholic" faith about our good selves and full inclusion will encourage a spiritualty that brings its own reward. It will help to satisfy two deep hungers of the human heart—to be good and to belong.

PAUSE FOR REFLECTION

- What might be your next steps for growing into your own potential goodness?

- Imagine what gifts you can bring to your faith community. How might you put them to work there?

Spiritual Practices: Putting the Bond of Baptism to Work

Having engaged here with the symbiosis of ourselves as *personal* and *communal* beings, let me suggest a spiritual practice for each reciprocal facet of our humanity and spirituality. The first is about praying with the saints and for the souls; the second about integrating oneself into a Christian faith community. Both encourage us to put the bond of baptism to work.

Praying with the Saints and for the Souls: There is a long Christian tradition going back to the very early Church of praying *with the saints* and *for the souls*. Both reflect the conviction that the bond of baptism is never broken, not even by death. Instead, our belonging to Christian community continues on into eternity, uniting us with the great communion of saints and sinners who have gone before us. The former can pray with us and for us, and the latter can benefit from ours. I offer a word about each practice; first, praying with the saints!

Just as we can ask people to pray for us and with us while living, we can do likewise with the saints gone ahead into eternity. Having lived this earthly life, they surely know "from the inside" and with sympathy our challenges and needs. And being in God's eternal presence, we can well assume that their praying for us and with us is all the more effective.

This ancient practice is sometimes misunderstood as if Catholics are asking the saints to personally answer our prayers; this would make them tantamount to God—idolatry. Only God can answer our prayers. Instead and just like the living, those already among the communion of saints can pray with us and for us, continuing to honor our shared baptism. And let us not limit our partnership to officially canonized saints. We can surely be confident that those departed who loved us in life—parents, grandparents, old friends—are all the more likely to pray for and with us now. Indeed, being in God's eternal presence, they are still present to us, albeit in a whole new way.

Amidst the great Communion of Saints, of course Mary the mother of Jesus holds pride of place. She was the first to experience the Holy Spirit in the new Christian covenant (Luke 1:35). Mary's acceptance of her august role in God's work of salvation through her son Jesus—to bear him in her womb—is the model of a trusting faith for all of her son's disciples. Then, as a fully human person, Jesus had to be taught, and Mary with Joseph surely taught him well; look at his values.

Mary was with Jesus from the beginning, throughout his life, and John's Gospel has her at the foot of the cross, among other women disciples (see 19:25). Her prayers can surely still support our own. Recall that Jesus, with some apparent reluctance, was prompted to work his first miracle at Mary's behest at the wedding feast of Cana (John 2:1–12). Might we still be confident that Jesus is all the more likely to hear his mother's prayers on our behalf now? Of course the time-honored personal prayer to her is the "Hail Mary," asking her to pray for us as the "Mother of God." What an august title—and rightly!

Then, by *praying for the souls* we continue the ancient Catholic practice of interceding through prayer and good works for those who have died but may not have been immediately ready for the eternal presence of God. Instead, they needed to pass through a process of "purgation"—traditionally referred to as *purgatory*—to ready them for the divine presence. This Catholic practice has certainly been abused and is easily misunderstood; indeed, the selling of "indulgences"—

measured credits for the souls in purgatory—was one of the abuses that triggered the Protestant Reformation.

Yet, and speaking personally, I still find consolation in the notion of purgatory. It means that even if I have not reformed my life entirely and transcended all my sins by the time of death, God will still cut me a bit of slack, allowing me a chance to put things right, even when beyond the grave. And it is consoling to imagine that my purgation will be hastened by the prayers and good works on my behalf by those who love me and live on. While their love prompts them to intercede for me, our bond of baptism makes their intercession all the more effective.

Seek out and be an active member of a Christian faith community. If not already so, search out and join a life-giving parish community or congregation. Then, become an active member, contributing your threefold resources of *time*, *talent*, and *treasure* to make your Christian faith community an effective sacrament of God's reign in its local context.

By tradition, Catholics are somewhat hardwired into belonging to their *local* parish—within their geographic area. However, the varied quality of parishes now advises one to seek out a "good" parish. Simply stated, this is a Catholic community that will nourish our faith, foster our goodness, engage our gifts, and welcome us as fully included. This is not invariably one's nearest parish; one may need to shop around and travel a bit to find a truly *catholic*—all are welcome—faith community.

Having joined a parish community, remember how we defined *belonging*. It demands participating in, contributing to, being held accountable by, and giving our gifts to whatever community we commit. At a minimum, such belonging begins with regular participation in Sabbath liturgy (Saturday evening or on Sunday). Then look at the various activities, services, committees, and projects of the parish that are in need of participants, and look at your own gifts and availability. Balancing both, choose a match that will welcome your particular contribution. Your investment will be well rewarded by the nurture of your own faith and your deepened sense of spiritual belonging. Remember, all of us need a particular home within God's family.

FOR FURTHER READING

Martin, James. *Building a Bridge: How the Catholic Church and the LGBT Community Can Enter into a Relationship of Respect, Compassion, and Sensitivity*. New York: Harper Collins, 2017. A courageous and much needed book; the title says it all.

Rolheiser, Ronald. *The Holy Longing: The Search for a Christian Spirituality*. New York: Image, 2014. A moving spiritual response to the longings of the heart.

Saraceno, Michelle. *Christian Anthropology: An Introduction to the Human Person*. Mahwah, NJ: Paulist Press, 2015. A readable theological reflection on what it means to be human—the key to a "Catholic" spirituality.

CHAPTER 8

A "Catholic" Sacramentality

Our Hunger for Meaning and Purpose

Sacramental Moments

    A central conviction of Catholic faith and its spirituality is that daily life offers the constant possibility of experiencing "sacramental" moments. I referred to them earlier as "mystical" in that they can mediate divine presence and grace. Beyond and beneath the seven great liturgical sacraments, sacramentals are things, events, places, or people that remind us of our faith and encourage our imaginations, as Ignatius of Loyola proposed, "to see God in all things." Such sacramental or mystical moments "happen" in the ordinary and everyday of life; we do need to be alert for them. The key to a "Catholic" spirituality, then, is to develop a sacramental consciousness toward everyday experiences.

    For myself, a daily possibility of sacramental moments is mediated by our little dog, Riley (all nine pounds of him). Few aspects of my life in the world assure of God's unconditional love more than Riley. When I look into those big eyes, I imagine them to say, "I love you and God loves you too." I can be gone for an hour, a day, or a week, but no matter; when I come home, Riley smothers me with an over-the-top welcome. He likes nothing better than to climb on my lap and lick my hands, as if smothering me in kisses. Now maybe he just likes the salty taste of my skin sweat. But if you knew Riley, you too would be tempted to imagine that Divine love is ever present to your life—no matter how long you might be away!

THE HUNGER FOR MEANING AND PURPOSE

To find meaning in life is as intense a hunger as any of the heart, though at first blush it may seem more like a concern for our reason. As we make our way through life as reflective persons, we inevitably try to make sense of it all, to figure out the purpose of our being in the world. So at first blush, desire might not be as prompting in this quest as, for example, our hunger for love. Yet that we find life meaningful and worthwhile is an intense longing of the heart, as deep as any other.

We have an emotional need to find rhyme and reason in our daily lives. Indeed nothing is more painful than feeling that our lives in the world have little value and less purpose. And as with all the facets of our diamond-shaped heart, this *reasonable desire* permeates all of our longings. Our hungers for love, happiness, freedom, authenticity, and so on will starve unless we can imagine our lives to have meaning and purpose.

This chapter describes how a sacramental consciousness encourages us to imagine that life is profoundly meaningful and worthwhile. Its defining conviction is that we come forth from God to journey home to God and eternal happiness. Then our lives in the world and everything along the way can have meaning because God is ever present to us, aiding and abetting our journey home. Rather than having to *make meaning* out of life by and for ourselves—as the "buffered self" of postmodernity—our lives are worthwhile as a *given*, as gift from God. Because "in [God] we live and move and have our being" (Acts 17:28), our meaning is grounded in an Ultimate Horizon, our God of unconditional love. Indeed, we give glory to God just by being alive in the Divine image and likeness, with life's final purpose—home to God—all the more assured as we live by *the way* of Jesus.

In the previous chapter, we reflected on Catholicism's essentially positive anthropology/sociology and our understanding of ourselves and our communal nature. Here, we find the same positive sentiments echoed in the *cosmology* that Catholic faith encourages—one's outlook on life in the world. For ancient Greek philosophers, *cosmos* referred to a world that is meaningful and patterned, rejecting its opposite, *chaos*. Echoing this fundamental stance, and without denying the reality of evil, suffering, and the absurd, a "Catholic" imagination encourages the outlook that the world that God creates and likewise all that humans create as culture and society are essentially good and can be put to meaningful purpose.

Of course, we can choose to live otherwise, rejecting the good potential of life in the world, putting creation and what we create within it to evil purpose. Yet, of itself and like ourselves, nothing of creation—God's or our own—is inherently evil or absurd. Life in the world has meaning, purpose, and goodness because it is grounded in Divine meaning, purpose, and goodness, and God's grace enables us to so live. This classic Catholic perspective on life in the world encourages and is encouraged by a sacramental imagination.

When Catholic Christians hear the word *sacramental*, most tend to think of the seven great sacraments that they celebrate in church. But as we will see presently, the "principle of sacramentality" reflects and yet is far broader than the sacred seven. It encourages an outlook on all of life as suffused with God's effective love and presence—grace— inviting us to recognize and respond to the *more* amid the *ordinary*, the *mystical* in the *everyday*.

This aspect of Catholic spirituality encourages us to live with a sacramental consciousness; in effect, to bring a faith perspective to everything of life. Such an imagination encourages us to glimpse the Eternal in the temporal, the Transcendent in the immanent, the Creator in the created order, the Ultimate in the immediate. This is not to be blind to the reality of evil, suffering, and the absurd in life. In fact, a sacramental consciousness should make us all the more alert to what is contrary to God's will for us and the world. And because our God is of unconditional love and infinite goodness, what is contrary to the nature of God cannot finally triumph.

Because their work so engages the imagination, poets (and the poet within each of us) know best this principle of sacramentality. Let me offer a few of my favorite instances.

Many poems by the Irish poet Paddy Kavanagh are suffused with the convictions that "God is in the bits and pieces of Everyday" (from *The Great Hunger*). For example, the first verse of his poem 'The Long Garden" reads,

> It was the garden of the golden apples,
> A long garden between a railway and a road,
> In the sow's rooting where the hen scratches
> We dipped our fingers in the pockets of God.

Likewise, the poetry of the English Jesuit Gerard Manley Hopkins constantly reflects,

> The world is charged with the grandeur of God.
> It will flame out, like shining from shook foil…
> —"God's Grandeur"

And in her epic poem "Aurora Leigh," Elizabeth Barrett Browning, echoing Moses's experience before the burning bush (Exod 1:1–15), wrote,

> …Earth's crammed with heaven,
> And every common bush afire with God;
> But only he who sees takes off his shoes,
> The rest sit round it and pluck blackberries

So we can simply "sit round and pluck blackberries," or we can open our imaginations to "see God in all things." Such a spiritual imagining makes our lives appear eminently meaningful and worthwhile, with all of life in the world being the theatre of God's grace, where God's unconditional love is ever at work on our behalf. In sum, a sacramental outlook can help to satisfy our deep hunger of the heart for a sense of meaning and purpose to our lives.

PAUSE FOR REFLECTION

- Recall a significant sacramental experience—a God moment—in your own life. Dwell again in the memory of this mystical encounter. What does it help you to imagine about your life in the world?

- What do you think it takes to regularly imagine God's presence and grace in the ordinary and everyday? How might you nurture such a sacramental imagination?

THE WORLD AS THEATRE OF GOD'S GRACE

Our English word *sacrament* comes from the Latin *sacramentum*, which refers to something made sacred (*sacrare*) or holy. However, in translating the New Testament from its original Greek to Latin, *sacramentum* was used for the Greek *musterion*. This roots our English word *mystery*, and its etymology suggests something mystical, requiring an alertness in order to be recognized. So the word *sacrament* conveys the sacred and holy, while its Greek equivalent, *mystery*, hints at something concealed that needs to be revealed and acknowledged.

It is important to note that a sacrament and the sacramentality of life is not magic, as if working automatically without our engagement. As the word implies, sacrament reflects that something sacred is given as gift, and yet as mystery it requires the recognition and response of participants. A sacramental *outlook* is on the *lookout* to *see* the more—the presence of God—and to respond. Otherwise, in the imagery of Barrett Browning, we miss "the bush afire with God" and just pick its berries.

St. Paul often used the term *musterion* to refer to the whole mystery of God's work of liberating salvation in Jesus Christ. He described this as "the mystery that has been hidden throughout the ages and generations but has now been revealed" (Col 1:26). The ultimate mystery/sacrament of Christian faith, then, is the liberating salvation that God has effected in Jesus Christ and continues now by the Holy Spirit. Mark's Gospel echoes

214

this sentiment when he refers to "the secret of the kingdom of God" and notes that some "may indeed look, but not perceive, and may indeed listen, but not understand" (4:11–12). It takes the eyes of faith working through imagination to *see* what can be seen and to *hear* what can be heard of God's mystical presence and its inbreaking in our daily lives.

So, antecedent to celebrating sacraments in our churches—and to heighten their effect—Christians need a sacramental consciousness by which we imagine that the whole world and our life within it is the theater of God's grace. This is *now the time and place* where God is present, outpouring the "abundant grace" of which Paul wrote so often, all made possible by Jesus's life, death, and resurrection, and effected now by the Holy Spirit at work in the world. The ordinary and everyday of our lives is where and how God comes looking for us with effective love that encourages us to respond. It is first and foremost in the daily of life—not in our churches—that we encounter God and live out our covenant as disciples of Jesus toward God's reign.

So the ultimate mystery—*the* sacrament—revealed in Jesus is that the backdrop of all creation and the unfolding of history is God's reign being brought about by God's grace and engaging people of faith to live as covenant partners in its realization. All that comes our way and everything we do well with our lives in the world—even the most menial of tasks or functions—can contribute to realizing God's reign "on earth as in heaven." What greater meaning and purpose could our lives have than to so live. And such *living* faith now leads on into the "kingdom that will have no end" (Nicene Creed).

A defining potential of "Catholic" spirituality, then, is to encourage people in a sacramental outlook on life. This is a spiritual tipping point because our basic worldview shapes our whole way of *being* as both noun and verb—*who* we are and *how* we live. We all have a tint to our lenses that colors how we see and engage in the world. Whether we view the glass as half full or half empty makes a huge difference to how we live our lives. With its positive cosmology, and the conviction that God's grace is ever at work in the theatre of the world, "Catholic" spirituality encourages us to imagine that our glass of life is always more than half full; indeed, as the psalmist portrayed, our "cup" often "overflows" (Ps 23:5).

CHOICES AND CHALLENGES OF A SACRAMENTAL OUTLOOK

There is nothing automatic about developing a sacramental *consciousness*; as the latter term implies, it requires intentional alertness on our part. To begin with, it invites us to view everything from the stance of faith in God and to imagine God's presence and grace at work "in all things." This calls for a faith perspective toward who we are, what we do, and the history unfolding around us. It encourages us to see everything within the backdrop of God's reign that is being realized by God's grace, working through all of humanity and throughout history.

Then, a sacramental consciousness prompts us to imagine how best to put our faith to work in every circumstance and situation. Toward what we initiate and what simply comes our way in life, it encourages us to wonder what God might be up to, to imagine how God's Spirit is moving and how best to respond. A sacramental consciousness reflects a confidence grounded in faith, and especially in times of adversity, that, in the immortal words of Julian of Norwich, "in the end, all will be well." Even in the face of suffering or evil, this sacramental outlook imagines that God can draw some good out of them. Of course, this is never to bless suffering or justify evil but to be confident that God is always "greater."

A sacramental imagination, then, encourages a very positive though realistic posture toward life in the world. While some people seem to have this as their natural disposition, all of us, at varying times, need to choose it deliberately as an act of faith and to have spiritual practices that help to sustain it. Such practices require us to use our imaginations to anticipate the mystery of life unfolding and are aided by recalling previous experiences of God's grace at work. When we look back over our lives, we can often recognize what we did not "see" at the time. Such memories can fuel our imaginations going forward.

A particular challenge for a sacramental consciousness is to be alert for the subtle hints of God's love at work in the very ordinary and everyday—the humdrum Mondays of our lives. Rarely does God beat us over the head with God's presence; it is always *musterion*— mystery—requiring our recognition. On the other hand, there can be moments when God's presence is palpable; we should relish such mystical experiences to sustain us at times when we feel God's absence (more below). In a metaphor from Celtic spirituality, there are some special times and places, encounters and events that become "thin moments," as if the veil between the Creator and life in the world becomes threadbare, enabling us to see through more clearly. Such *thin* moments can help sustain us in the *thick* ones!

To recognize even a spark of God's presence can light up a whole situation. And Jesus encouraged us not to place such light "under the bushel basket" but to let it "shine before others" (Matt 5:15–16). As always with our covenant, the grace of sacramental moments brings responsibility to share the light.

All this being said, a sacramental outlook is anything but naive; in fact, it requires *critical social* consciousness. (We elaborate this at length in chapter 10 on social justice.) Briefly here, recall that our perspective on life is greatly shaped by our sociocultural context. Rather than helping us to "see God in all things," our historical circumstances can blind us to God's presence and discourage us from responding. Likewise, it can lull us into accepting what is clearly *not* of God's reign as if it is. This seems all the more likely in our *secular age* that bans religious symbols and discourse from the public square. Indeed, our context can make what is eminently *not* of God's reign seem like *normal* or to be accepted as "just the way things are." Here one can think of racism, chauvinism, homophobia, and discrimination of every kind, people dying of hunger, destruction of the environment, and the list goes on.

Because it is of God, a sacramental consciousness should make us keenly aware of our own sins *and* help us to recognize sinful social arrangements and cultural mores. It should sharpen awareness of our own failures to live as disciples of Jesus and heighten our perception of and resistance to all political structures and cultural ideologies that cause injustice and oppression; otherwise, our *outlook* is not of God. Clearly, then, a sacramental consciousness requires a critical and discerning perspective on every aspect of our lives in the world.

Note again that in Jesus's description of our final judgment (Matt 25:31–46), both the sheep and the goats admit that they did not "see" God. The only difference between them is that the sheep *did* see the poor and needy and responded to them, whereas the goats failed to see them and thus *did not* respond. In other words, by way of *seeing* what we ought to see, God desires a sacramental outlook that first recognizes and responds to those in need of any kind. Rather than seeing God first and then the needy, God prefers the reverse sequence in case we might not get to what we should do. Through recognizing and responding to those whom God favors most—the poor of every kind—we are more likely to imagine God's presence as well.

Even more than in Jesus's time, our cultural prejudices and social structures can blind us to injustice and hide the poor and needy, allowing us to presume that some government agency is taking care of "them," sometimes even that they deserve their lot. A sacramental imagination should help us to "see through" to the suffering of others and encourage us to resist every injustice, exclusion, and oppression.

This being said, a sacramental outlook on life is well challenged by the reality of human suffering, whether caused by the freedom of nature or of persons. How can one "see" God's presence, for example, in the midst of a great natural tragedy or a humanly made one? In chapter 2, we attempted to address the mystery of a provident God of unconditional love and the reality of suffering and evil. It will rise again in chapter 9 around the issue of hope, but let us reflect on it briefly here from the perspective of sacramentality.

First, note the paradox that oftentimes amid suffering and misfortune, people experience the presence of God more intensely, not as causing their misery but as being in solidarity with them. For Christians, of course, this divine solidarity in suffering is intensely symbolized in the crucified Jesus. The poor, oppressed, and marginalized often seem to have a keener sense of God's presence and of Jesus's solidarity with them than those of us doing quite well. This being said, the question of suffering and evil again verifies that a sacramental consciousness is anything but naive.

It may be helpful here to recall an old distinction in Christian spirituality between a *kataphatic* and an *apophatic* perspective. *Kataphatic*—literally "with images"—is a spirituality that readily sees signs of God's presence in creation and the everyday, in the midst of ordinary human experiences. It reflects a high sacramental consciousness, readily recognizing God's immanence and nearness. By contrast, *apophatic*, literally "without images" and sometimes called "the negative way" (*via negativa*), more keenly experiences the absence of God. Its defining experience is of God's total transcendence and otherness, of God's absence more than presence.

Though different emphases, the kataphatic and apophatic traditions are two sides of the same coin of Christian spiritualty. Both are grounded in the deep faith that God *is* ever present with God's empowering grace, even when we do not experience as much. Simply put, both kataphatic and apophatic perspectives recognize that there is no time or place where God is not *our* God. And as Christians, we remember that Jesus crucified was raised up by God; the risen Christ remains forever the sign and source of victory over all suffering and evil. Meanwhile, it is very understandable to experience a kind of divine absence amid suffering. Yet *our* felt sense is not what determines whether God is present or not.

The truth is that we are always enveloped in God's unconditional love. Yet we are entitled to lament when we do not experience as much, but instead God's absence. Of the 150 psalms in the Bible, over a third are of lament, more than any other type. And echoing one of those Psalms (22:1), even Jesus cried out in protest from his cross, "My God, my God, why have you forsaken me?" (Mark 15:34). Surely so can we!

The greatest of saints have complained about their experience of what the spiritual writers call "a dark night of the soul." The dark times, however, can remind us of how limited we are in our understanding of God and yet draw us all the more deeply into believing and responding to God's love in the midst of suffering.

Mother Teresa of Calcutta told of having a profound personal encounter with Jesus, even as if the risen Christ was fully present to her. She could name the place and date—on a train to Calcutta on September 10, 1946. From this vivid personal encounter with Jesus, she drew the inspiration for her great lifework among the poorest of the poor, and to found the Missionaries of Charity. For the remainder of her life, however, she spoke and wrote often of living in spiritual darkness. Yet Mother Teresa's "dark night" inspired her all the more to *see* and serve Jesus in the sick and poor of Calcutta and throughout the world.

In the words of Erasmus cited previously, "Bidden or unbidden; God is present."

PAUSE FOR REFLECTION

- Where or when do you most often experience your life in the world as "the theatre of God's grace"?

- How can you deepen your own sacramental imagination?

- What can help you to recognize the paradox of God's love and presence in the face of human suffering?

CHURCH: LIKE A SACRAMENT WITH SEVEN SACRAMENTS

So, Catholic spirituality invites to a sacramental outlook on life, to imagine God's presence and grace at work in the everyday and how best to respond. It can help people to see their life in the world as the arena of God's grace, to find great meaning and purpose as they put their faith to work in the daily.

Then, in "Catholic" traditions especially, the sacramentality of life in the world gathers into particular climatic symbols of powerful effect—the seven sacraments. They are like seven great tips of the iceberg that reflect the sacramentality of life and of all creation. Traditional Catholic theology (echoing Thomas Aquinas) understands a sacrament as *a sacred symbol that causes the grace it symbolizes*. In other words, a sacrament's effectiveness, at least from God's side of the covenant, is guaranteed by the power of the Holy Spirit.

Note again that this guarantee of grace is only from God's side; to reiterate, sacraments are always acts of faith rather than magic. As such, they require the recipient's response to the general and particular graces mediated through each sacrament. And yet, they gather the sacramentality of life into climatic symbols that have a heightened power to mediate God's grace. For example, while a meal with friends can be a sacramental moment, the celebration of Eucharist by a faith community has heightened effectiveness in mediating God's grace.

To appreciate the seven sacraments, however, we need to start—as always for Christian faith—with Jesus. In a real sense, we can look on Jesus as God's most effective sacrament to the world. He was God come among us as a person, who by his life, death, and resurrection catalyzed God's abundant grace into human history. Think about it: God could not have been any more effectively present to us than in the historical Jesus; in him the Divine "Word became flesh and lived among us"—fully embracing our human estate (John 1:14).

God's work of liberating salvation in Jesus and the powerhouse of grace that his paschal mystery released into human history continues now by the Holy Spirit. So we can think of Jesus as the supreme Sacrament of God's grace and presence. Indeed, each of the seven is a kind of personal encounter with the risen Christ Jesus.

Following on from Jesus as God's supreme Sacrament, we can recognize the Church, too, as a kind of sacrament. While the Holy Spirit continues God's liberating salvation in Jesus throughout all of creation and human history, the Spirit does so in a particularly effective way through the Christian faith community. As noted earlier, the Gospels make very clear that Jesus gathered a community of faith around him to participate in his mission and ministry to the world. Jesus promised and God sent the Holy Spirit to empower this faith community to continue God's work of liberating salvation.

Now, the Holy Spirit works particularly through the Church to carry forth Jesus's mission, making it an effective symbol and source of God's saving grace. As the Second Vatican Council taught, in an "analogous" way we can say that the Church—the whole Christian faith community of the baptized—"is a kind of sacrament of intimate union with God" (Lumen Gentium 1). It is within and through this community of faith that Christians can celebrate and receive the graces of the seven sacraments for their lives in the world.

To think of the Church as the special sacrament of God's grace heightens again the need for us to be an effective and credible symbol, causing what we symbolize as a community. In other words, the sacramental nature of the Church challenges Christians to "practice what we preach," to help cause what we symbolize—the inbreaking of God's reign. Likewise, to be a sacrament of our triune God demands that the Church reflect the unconditional love within Godself and toward all humankind. Recognizing the trinitarian ground of the Church's life and sacramentality demands that it be a community of boundless mercy and compassion, and of inclusion and hospitality toward all who wish to belong.

Made up of saints and sinners like ourselves, the Church, as well reviewed in chapter 7, often falls far short of its sacramental function. Rather than making us sanguine, however, our vocation to be an effective symbol of God's grace to the world demands that we ever renew our efforts to reform the Church. This being said, its effectiveness as a sacrament does not depend—thank God—on the adequacy of its structures or the holiness of its members. The Church as all the baptized united into the Body of Christ is an effective symbol of God's grace, like a sacrament, because the Holy Spirit works through it to continue God's work of liberating salvation.

Seven Great Sacraments: Each of the seven is a unique and effective way of encountering the risen Christ, and is so by the power of God's Spirit acting through the ministry of the Church. All mediate God's sanctifying grace—to make us holy—and then a particular grace that each sacrament symbolizes. We might name their particular graces as *bonding* (baptism), *empowering* (confirmation), *sustaining* (Eucharist), *forgiving* (reconciliation), *healing* (anointing of sick), *serving* (holy orders), and *uniting* in love (matrimony).

Note, too, that the core symbols of all seven sacraments are something from the "ordinary" of life, like community, bread, wine, water, oil, touch, words, gestures, and lovemaking in marriage. This reflects the continuity between the sacramentality of life in the world and what we high-point in celebrating the seven.

Baptism symbolizes all human experiences of bonding and belonging to community and the responsibilities that come with them. Its sacramental grace is to initiate people into the bond of the Body of Christ, the Church, empowering them to live as disciples of Jesus within a community of disciples toward the reign of God. St. Paul also tells the baptized that "you...have clothed yourselves with Christ" and that they "belong to Christ" now; this is why the bond of baptism transcends all divisions, making all as "one in Christ Jesus" (Gal 3:27–29).

All the baptized are called and graced to participate in the Church's carrying forth of Jesus's mission to the world. Every member has "gifts" to be used "for building up the body of Christ" (Eph 4:11–12). As we reviewed in chapter 7, Vatican II reclaimed this radical theology of baptism—that "we" are the Church, with all to function together as a "priesthood of the faithful." For example, "The baptized, by regeneration and anointing of the Holy Spirit, are consecrated into a spiritual house and a holy priesthood" (*Lumen Gentium* 10).

Confirmation symbolizes all the hopes and dreams, the courage and resilience, the efforts and agency of the human spirit. Then, through this sacrament the Holy Spirit empowers Christians with the particular grace needed to mature as witnesses of *living* faith, and to play their part as fully-fledged members of the Body of Christ. Confirmation is the sacrament of "growing up" in God's grace, deepening our initiation.

By confirmation the Holy Spirit enables the baptized to live all the more faithfully as disciples of Jesus in the midst of the world. It *confirms* Christians in their baptismal faith, with the Spirit offering them adult-like gifts such as wisdom and prudence, fortitude and temperance, and the strength they need to bear witness as disciples of Jesus. Likewise, it deepens—beyond baptism—the fruits of the Spirit in people's lives. As noted previously, St. Paul lists such fruits as "love, joy, peace, patience, kindness, generosity, faithfulness, gentleness, and self-control (Gal 5:22–23).

Eucharist symbolizes all in life that sustains and nourishes, that lends vitality and responsibility, promotes peace and justice, encourages care and compassion, and more. Thomas Aquinas well named Eucharist as the *sacramentum sacramentorum*—the sacrament of sacraments (and thus why Christians capitalize). And the Second Vatican Council described it as "the fount and apex of the whole Christian life" (*Lumen Gentium* 11).

In celebrating Eucharist and by the power of the Holy Spirit, the faith community can encounter the risen Christ present in its assembly, in the Scriptures proclaimed, and climatically in the consecrated bread and wine as Jesus's own "body and blood" presence. By offering such "a sacrifice of praise" (Heb 13:15) to God, participants receive Jesus as their sustaining "bread of life" (John 6:35). Eucharist brings the promise "to live forever" and the responsibility to go forth (*missa*—mass) to "announce the Gospel of the Lord" (a final dismissal in Roman Rite).

Reconciliation symbolizes and reflects all human efforts of repentance and forgiveness, of mercy and clemency, of peacemaking and restitution. For Christians, the sacrament requires people to recognize, admit, repent of, and confess their sins. Its particular grace is a personal encounter with God's never-ending mercy that assures repentant sinners of forgiveness. Here, by the Holy Spirit working through a priest representative of the Christian community, we are assured of God's mercy, no matter the sin, and are counseled and graced to amend our lives to live more faithfully as disciples of Jesus.

Such living faith demands that we ourselves become agents of God's reconciliation and peacemaking in the world. As St. Paul writes, "In Christ God was reconciling the world to himself...entrusting the message of reconciliation to us" (2 Cor 5:19). And, as if to drive home the point, Paul adds, "We are ambassadors for Christ, since God is making his appeal through us" (v. 20)—on behalf of God's mercy, reconciliation, and peace.

Anointing of the Sick symbolizes all human efforts at healing the ill, caring for the elderly, and consoling the dying. The sacrament's particular grace is to mediate God's healing power to restore people to health— spiritual, physical, or psychological—if it be God's will. If a person's life is ending, this sacrament of the sick forgives their sins and lends them hope for eternal life with God.

Holy Orders symbolizes all vocations of loving service, all work done with integrity toward God's reign. Its sacramental grace is to designate and ordain people to function as leaders in the Christian community's ministries of *preaching* God's word, *presiding* at the celebration of the sacraments, and *pastoring with* the faith community. Their pastoring function in particular is to empower the "priesthood of the faithful," engaging the gifts of all members and enabling them to work well together, with "holy order."

Matrimony symbolizes all human acts of friendship and support, of love and commitment, of ethical human intimacy and integrated sexuality. Its particular grace is to unite a married couple in a permanent and exclusive covenant of life and love, and to lend them the graces they need to live their vocation in faithful partnership. After baptism, marriage is a couple's shared calling to holiness—together.

It is significant, too, that in Catholic tradition, the marrying couple—not the presiding priest or deacon—are the celebrants of the sacrament. And further, their sacramental union is enacted in their first act of lovemaking—after the wedding ceremony. So their sacrament is realized not at the altar but in their marriage bed. What a beautiful affirmation of the sacramentality of human lovemaking, which continues throughout a couple's marriage.

As stated already and worth repeating, the effectiveness of a sacrament depends both on the action of the Spirit and on the response of the person and community celebrating it—as always, a covenant. True, sacraments mediate God's love at work, but they also bring the *response-ability* to live the particular graces that each sacrament effects. So Eucharist enables people to encounter the real presence of the risen Christ *and* it sends us to "announce the Gospel of the Lord" by the lives we live. And this is likewise for living the particular grace of all seven sacraments.

HOPE FOR OUR HEARTS

As meaning makers by Divine design, we have a deep hunger of the heart to find life purposeful and worthwhile. There is no worse feeling than that all may be pointless and absurd. And whether we find life meaningful or not depends in large part on the perspective we bring to it, on *how* we imagine things. That tint to our lenses can make the glass seem half full or half empty; so much depends on our perspective. So, we hunger for a cosmology—an outlook on life in the world—that helps us imagine *cosmos* rather than *chaos*, meaning rather than absurdity, a firm foundation rather than the abyss. For such a positive imagining there is none more effective than a "Catholic" spirituality that lends a sacramental outlook on life.

It surely helps to satisfy our hunger for meaning and purpose if we have an enduring sense of God's presence to us—exactly what a sacramental consciousness fosters. It helps us to imagine God being present in life's ordinary and everyday as well as in high-point events and moments. When we can "see God in all things"—and even when we cannot but have faith that God is with us, nonetheless—such a spirituality can make all seem purposeful and worthwhile.

There is no feature more identifying of "Catholic" spirituality than its principle of sacramentality, climaxed in the celebration of seven great sacraments. A sacramental imagination encourages us to see God's grace-full presence at work in the world and in our own lives. With unconditional love, God has the best of intentions for us all and intends to draw us home to Godself for eternity. Along the way, we can see everything in life as situated within the ambit of God's presence and effective love and imagine the eternal horizon into which God ever invites us. What a gift to our hearts!

"Catholic" spirituality nurtures such a sacramental imagination and encourages us to make it our own. Add to this, then, the gift and effectiveness of the seven sacraments. In the previous chapter, we recognized our need to belong to a Christian faith community that can sustain our spiritualty toward *living* faith. Within a Catholic community, participants can call upon the particular grace of each of the *permanent* sacraments we might receive—baptism, confirmation, and holy orders—or upon the grace of the *repeatable* ones of Eucharist, reconciliation, anointing of the sick, and marriage (latter can repeat sometimes).

The sacraments that we celebrate through the Church further assure us that we can always access the graces we need, empowering our own good efforts to live life well and to the fullest. They assure that God's grace is always at "high tide" toward us. No matter the circumstances, the grace of the sacraments can sustain us in living as disciples of Jesus. Our lives can have no more satisfying meaning and purpose than to so live.

I said at the beginning of this chapter that the poets most readily reflect a sacramental consciousness, and this because imagination is their tool of trade. I close by sharing another poem that deeply nurtured my own sacramental imagination when I first learned it *by heart* in high school. The author, Joseph Mary Plunkett, was an Irish poet and mystic as well as a revolutionary. He was executed (at age twenty-nine) for his leadership role in the Irish Rising that began on Easter Monday, 1916 (recall Yeats's "terrible beauty"). Reflecting the Cosmic Christ, Plunkett's poem writes large the sacramental imagination. Read it slowly and let it touch your own heart as it did mine—over fifty years ago.

> I see his blood upon the rose
> And in the stars the glory of his eyes,
> His body gleams amid eternal snows,
> His tears fall from the skies.
>
> I see his face in every flower;
> The thunder and the singing of the birds
> Are but his voice—and carven by his power
> Rocks are his written words.
>
> All pathways by his feet are worn,
> His strong heart stirs the ever-beating sea,
> His crown of thorns is twined with every thorn,
> His cross is every tree.
>
> ("I See His Blood upon the Rose")

PAUSE FOR REFLECTION

- What might help you to be alert for the signs of God's presence and grace at work in your daily life?

- How might Sabbath celebration and reception of Eucharist help to sustain your sacramental outlook throughout the week?

SPIRITUAL PRACTICES: NURTURING A SACRAMENTAL IMAGINATION

Here I suggest some spiritual practices that can sustain and deepen one's sacramental consciousness.

Be Alert in the Daily for Sacramental Moments: In chapter 1 we encouraged the practice of an *Examen of Consciousness* at day's end, looking back over it for the God-moments and how well we responded. However, we can also develop an alertness for sacramental moments as the day unfolds.

We can sharpen our sacramental imaginations by pausing at the beginning of each day with the old practice of a "morning offering" of our lives to God. Though there are lots of traditional ones, I suggest that you craft your own. You can fashion it any way you like, as long as it renews your sense of God's presence, to look with faith to the day ahead, to renew your commitment to live as a disciple of Jesus, and to ask God for the graces you need.

For what it's worth, I made up one with my son when he was in preschool; we still say it together (though I don't know how much longer). "Thank you, Loving God, for a good night's sleep and a brand-new day. We place ourselves in your hands this day. Our Brother Jesus, help us to live it well. God's Holy Spirit, guide, direct, and protect us, Amen." We follow with an Our Father and Hail Mary, usually praying for some particular intention, like an upcoming test or a friend in need.

Stop to Smell the Roses: In Christian spirituality and as noted earlier, meditation is identified as *talking* to God, whereas contemplation is more like *listening* to God, allowing God to take the initiative and speak—so to speak—to our hearts. Bringing a contemplative attitude to daily life can help to recognize how God's presence and grace are reaching out to us. Most often such contemplation amounts to noticing the gifts that may be staring us in the face, if we would but "stop to smell the roses." Indeed, we can find a likely source of such mystical moments within nature, as the Psalms often attest. For example, "All the trees of the forest sing for joy before the LORD" (Ps 96:12–13).

On that note, I must confess that for reasons I do not understand, I can experience the majesty of the great trees outside my office window as sacramentals. They prompt me to look up and out and to imagine God's presence—and even more so if there are birds singing from their branches. To cite another poet, Joyce Kilmer well wrote, "Poems are made by fools like me, but only God can make a tree."

Celebrate Eucharist with Your Faith Community: The Second Vatican

Council insisted that all Christians are called "to fully conscious, and active participation…[as] demanded by the very nature of the liturgy" of Eucharist. It added that "such participation by the Christian people…is their right and duty by reason of their baptism" (*Sacrosanctum Concilium* 14). So while Eucharist is our "right," it is also our "duty." How could it be otherwise for us, called to be a sacramental people as we are? What a gift this "bread of life" (John 6:35) can be for all the hungers of our hearts. And to access God's grace to our lives, there is no more effective source than to join with a Christian faith community for the Sabbath celebration of Eucharist.

FOR FURTHER READING

Cooke, Bernard. *Sacraments and Sacramentality*. Rev. ed. Mystic, CT: Twenty-Third Publications, 1994. A classic written by a renowned Catholic theologian.

Day, Dorothy. *The Long Loneliness*. New York: Harper & Row, 1952. The spiritual autobiography of one of the greatest saints of American Catholicism, marked by a deep sense of life's sacramentality—found especially among the poor and those most in need.

Ross, Susan A. *Extravagant Affections: A Feminist Sacramental Theology*. New York: Continuum, 2001. Adds a necessary perspective to our sacramental imagination as a source of the equality and justice that God intends for all.

CHAPTER 9

A "Catholic" Faith

Our Hunger for Hope

Hope against Hope

On my grandparent's farm, Friday afternoon was the butter-making time. Granny would sit on a high stool in the subterranean dairy (long before refrigeration in rural Ireland) to supervise this sacrosanct weekly event, while my mother rhythmically rolled the churn. It could take up to an hour before there was any sign of butter. Granny used the wait time to tell stories and offer her commentary on all the momentous happenings in our village, holding forth from two vantage points—her high stool and hard-won wisdom from a good long life.

As a little kid, I loved to be there for the butter making. There was something magical about seeing the white milk go in, the golden butter come out, and to hear granny's stories while we waited. On one such Friday (I was about seven at the time) when I wondered aloud if the butter would ever appear, she told a churning story that has shaped my life. It is also the best explanation I know of St. Paul's paradoxical phrase of "hoping against hope" (Rom 4:18).

As Granny told it, one day two little frogs made their way into the farmer's dairy and were playing around on a shelf above the milk urns. They fell off and into a big half-full urn beneath them. They swam to the side but of course there was no way out. They tried jumping but the urn was too high, and its conical neck made it all the more difficult to leap out of there. One little frog soon concluded—and reasonably—that their situation was hopeless, gave up, and sank to the bottom. The second one decided to keep on splashing around in the milk, though all seemed hopeless, and did so until it passed out from exhaustion. When this little frog woke up, it was sitting on a pile of butter.

That granny story has encouraged me to hope always and to work for my hopes, even when the odds are stacked high otherwise.

OUR HUNGER FOR HOPE

The whole symphony of heartfelt hungers that marks our human condition is permeated with a hunger for *hope*. Our longings for fullness and freedom, for love and happiness, for holiness and authenticity, for purpose and meaning, and so on, all need hope to sustain them. Only with hope can we keep on swimming like that second little frog; without it, we give up and likely sink to the bottom.

This chapter proposes that a Christian spirituality that imagines and nurtures a *living* faith can be a powerful resource to sustain our hope. The great theologian, Thomas Aquinas, was convinced that faith is the necessary ground of hope. So even as the focused hunger here is for hope, we elaborate further the *living* faith needed to sustain us as hopers. In particular, we focus on the human capacities that need to be engaged and shaped by Christian faith if it is to suffuse our lives and ground good hope. Such faith engages, metaphorically, our *heads*, our *hearts*, and our *hands*—the whole *being* of people. And the more all our capacities are put to work in *living* Christian faith, the more assuredly it grounds our hope.

Christian faith that grounds hope must reach beyond the general understanding of "faith." Typically, it is heard as synonymous with *belief*—as in assenting to proposed truth claims. As we will see, it has a believing dimension, but Christian faith is to define who we are and shape how we live. However, even our language patterns resist this sense of *living* faith as proposed throughout this book. We speak of faith only as a noun, never as a verb or adverb, as if it is something static, something we *have*—or don't have. So we speak of hope and hoping, love and loving, but "faithing" just set off my spellcheck. In fact, Christian faith is to be realized as both noun and verb, shaping *who* we are and *how* we live.

In one of his parables, Jesus compared two kinds of faith—one built on rock and one built on sand (Matt 7:24–29). When the "storm" came, the one on rock "did not fall," whereas for the one on sand "great was its fall." The difference between them was that one "heard" and "acted" on their faith, while the other simply heard. A *living* faith that permeates our identity and lifestyle is like a rock of hope that can sustain us in any storm.

There is a kind of positive thinking involved in Christian hope, yet it is more than optimism. The latter can be naive at times, and true hope is eminently realistic. Real and reliable hope faces into life, experiencing its challenges and tragedies, joys and sorrows, and yet remains hopeful that somehow, even when we don't know how, things will "turn out" and all can be well.

Hope is marked by the determination to see the light, if only a flicker, rather than to curse the darkness. Whether facing the everyday burdens that come our way, or some great cross like serious illness, or the calamities, sufferings, and injustices that beset the world at large—and our Church—hope can sustain us to keep on swimming.

Conversely, despair is to give up hope (*de-sperare* literally means "without hope"), and surely there is no greater pain to the human heart. When we despair, the burdens can become unbearable, with the dreadful potential to bring us to some form of destruction. Despair is directly contrary to the will to life; it can cause us to give up as hopeless on any and all the hungers of the heart.

From a Christian perspective, the ultimate source of hope is the dying and rising of Jesus and its promise of eternal life for all. We return to this "final" hope at chapter's end but note it here for its symbiosis with faith. Powered by faith in the paschal mystery of Jesus Christ, Christians can always hope against hope that our life journey, no matter its trials and tribulations, will lead us home to God. In the promise of eternal life, we can imagine realizing the fullness of our hope. St. Paul explained that "through Jesus Christ our Savior" we can "become heirs according to the hope of eternal life" (Titus 3:6–7). So the ultimate hope of Christians is the promise, grounded in faith, of eternal life with God. Meanwhile, how do we manage to keep on swimming toward partial fulfillment of our hopes—for now?

As Paul also attests, hope is primarily a gift of God's grace. This then begs the question, what about our side of the covenant? I propose that sustaining hope rests upon *living* faith precisely because it requires our own agency—as well as God's grace. Without our good efforts to realize it, no matter how feeble, hope is only fantasy or wishful thinking. By growing in *living* faith, we sustain our hopes as well. However, to presume that all will be well without our good efforts (all by God's grace) is what Christian tradition describes as the sin of presumption (see *CCC* 2092).

Thomas Aquinas well described *faith*, *hope*, and *love* together as the three *theological* virtues. He called them "theological" precisely because all three are gifts from God—by grace. Though gifts, the same Aquinas constantly insisted that "grace works through nature." In other words, the graces of faith, hope, and love divinely empower *and* likewise require our own agency. As people in recovery through AA will attest, their hope depends on the help of a Higher Power and yet demands their own mighty efforts—attending meetings, avoiding temptation, supporting each other, and so on.

Aquinas further posed these three theological virtues as both cumulative and circular, with faith grounding hope that is to lead on into love, which in turn leads back into and renews our faith. Ironically, the Christian emphasis on faith and love tended to downplay the imperative role of their connector—hope. Here we give *hope* its moment in the sun. Without hope, both faith and love collapse, whereas sustaining hope depends upon a *living* faith that is realized most eminently in love.

In effect, faith and hope combine as our basic life stance. The Letter to the Hebrews unites them thus: "Faith is the assurance of things hoped for, the conviction of things not seen" (11:1). St. Paul also explains that "in hope we were saved" and then clarifies, "Now hope that is seen is not hope. For who hopes for what is seen? But if we hope for what we do not see, we wait for it with patience" (Rom 8:24–25). As Paul implies, hope is always a stretch—for something not yet "seen"—and we reach by *living* faith. The more we grow into such faith—engaging head, heart, and hands—the more we can keep on in hope and never despair.

We already described *living* faith in chapter 3 as being *alive, lived, and life-giving for ourselves and others.* And as elaborated in chapter 7, Christian faith is lived in and through a Christian community toward God's reign. Indeed, given that Christian spirituality is to encourage us in *living* faith, hope has been a constant theme throughout this book, with a designated section in every chapter—*Hope for Our Hearts.* So far, however, our description has focused more on the products of *living* faith when realized in people's lives, the fruits that it bears—when alive, lived, and life-giving.

Here we try to reach further back to the source of such fruits—to describe the tree needed to produce them. Of course, the two aspects function as cause and effect; a tree is an apple tree only because it bears apples. Yet, for analysis sake, we can distinguish the human capacities to be engaged toward *living* faith from the fruits that it bears in our lives, to be *alive, lived,* and *life-giving.*

So I propose that from within our personhood, we have three constitutive human capacities for *living* faith, all to be actively engaged. I summarize them as our abilities for *believing, trusting,* and *behaving,* and as engaging our *heads,* our *hearts,* and our *hands.* Such faith is needed to sustain our hope as well.

PAUSE FOR REFLECTION

- Think about the challenges to your hope at this time. What helps you to keep on in the face of them?

- Imagine how *living* Christian faith can be a source of hope, no matter one's burdens and challenges.

- What might hope ask of us in the face of Church failures, like clergy sex abuse?

OUR WAYS FOR LIVING FAITH

The Balancing Act of Faith: A little historical background may help to highlight the vital role of all three human capacities—believing, trusting, behaving—in forging the kind of *living* faith that lends hope. With only a little hyperbole, we might say that Christians have fought wars over the question, "What do we mean by faith?"; think of the "Thirty Years War" (1618–48; aftermath of the Reformation), and the traces of the conflict that linger to this day (e.g., Northern Ireland).

As echoed in chapter 5 regarding the relationship of nature and grace, here we dip again into the core controversies at the time of the Reformation (usually dated from 1517 and Luther's famous Ninety-five Theses). The Reformers made *sola fide* a battle cry, claiming that we are saved by "faith alone" and understood faith as "a bold trust in God's grace" by which we are "justified" (Luther). So their emphasis was on faith as *trust* in God, and this realized *sola gratia*—solely by God's grace.

As previously noted, the Reformers rightly wished to emphasize the gratuitousness of God's grace as the effective source of our liberating salvation, or what they preferred to call our *justification*. However, can Christian faith be reduced to a blind *trust* and this by grace alone; does grace not always come, as said so often throughout, as a responsibility that requires our own capacities and good efforts in response?

The Reformers could selectively cite St. Paul as their authority that faith as *trust* in God is what saves and this by *grace alone*. So, "by grace you have been saved through faith, and this is not your own doing; it is the gift of God—not the result of works, so that no one may boast" (Eph 2:8–9). Another text, much favored by Luther, was Paul's classic statement found in Romans 5:1–5. There Paul asserts boldly that "we are justified by faith" and "have peace with God through our Lord Jesus Christ." Paul rightly goes on to explain that such faith "produces hope, and hope does not disappoint us, because God's love has been poured into our hearts through the Holy Spirit."

Conversely, many times Paul also described *living* faith as demanding our own good works, especially that of love. For example, "The only thing that counts is faith working through love" (Gal 5:6). Indeed, in that same Letter to the Romans, Paul wrote repeatedly of "the obedience of faith" (e.g., 1:5; 16:26, etc.), making clear that *living* faith reaches beyond trust in God and must "get done"—the covenant again.

When the Catholic Church regrouped and began its own reform with the Council of Trent (1545–63), it could agree that we are saved by faith but insisted that *living* faith must be realized in *good works*. The Catholic-favored scripture text to buttress its position was the Letter of James 2:14–26. James argues repeatedly that *living* faith (the kind that you could "show me," v. 18) demands our good works—or it is not *living* faith. He concludes with the resounding summary that "just as the body without the spirit is dead, so faith without works is also dead" (v. 26).

So, good works are integral to *living* Christian faith. And it is not as if we have faith first that then prompts good works; rather, the good works are constitutive of the faith, and vice versa, neither being realized without the other. Indeed, faith that is not lived is sin rather than faith. James had it right: faith is literally *dead* without good works!

In as much as Reformation polemics led Protestants to overemphasize faith as trust and solely by grace, and Catholics to overemphasize good works and as if by our own efforts, both sides at the time got it wrong. Happily, Catholics and Lutherans finally reached agreement on this controversy with their *Joint Declaration on the Doctrine of Justification* of 1999 (yes, it took almost five hundred years), and since then signed by many mainline Christian denominations. The key passage reads, "By grace alone, in faith in Christ's saving work and not because of any merit on our part, we are accepted by God and receive the Holy Spirit, who renews our hearts while equipping us and calling us to good works" (note the careful wording, honoring both sides). So much for Christian faith as *trusting* and *behaving*; then what of *believing*?

In the aftermath of Trent, and when directly addressing the faith life of ordinary people (rather than theological debates with the Reformers), the Catholic Church began to put huge emphasis on *belief* as if synonymous with faith—rather than one constitutive aspect. Perhaps this was understandable, given that many of its core beliefs had been challenged by the Reformers.

The *Catechism of Trent* (first published 1566, also known as *The Roman Catechism*) was by far the most influential text in disseminating the Council's reforms. It defined faith as "that by which we yield our *unhesitating assent to* whatever *the authority of our Holy Mother the Church* teaches us to have been revealed by God" (emphasis added). The text goes on to explain that any kind of questioning or doubt about Church teachings reflects a lack of faith—even a sin against it. This is as if *belief* is the sum total of Christian faith and to be embraced out of obedience to the teaching authority of the Church rather than by personal conviction. Indeed, Trent's insistence on faith as unquestioning belief in Church teaching remained in place up until the Second Vatican Council and is still in vogue among more traditionalist Catholics.

The challenge is to fully include and with equal emphasis all three constitutive activities of *living* faith—*believing, trusting, behaving*—and these by God's grace that engages the agency of our *heads, hearts,* and *hands.* We can find the warrant for such a holistic understanding of faith in what is to be the cumulative outcome of faith and hope, namely love, and this suggested by how Jesus preached his greatest commandment—the ultimate mode of *living* faith.

The Greatest Commandment as Clue to Living Faith: Aquinas's portrayal of the three great virtues as cumulative and circular suggests the kind of faith needed to originate the sequence toward hope and lead on into love. Working backward from faith's outcome of love, recall that the greatest commandment as Jesus taught it requires love of God and neighbor as ourselves and with *our whole being.* The listing in Deuteronomy 6:5 that Jesus cited (and coupled with Leviticus 19:18—"love your neighbor as yourself") reads "with all your *heart,* and with all your *soul,* and with all your *might*" (emphasis added).

None of the three Synoptics has the terms precisely as this original, yet all name such loving in a holistic way. So, Mark puts on the lips of Jesus: "With all your *heart,* and with all your *soul,* and with all your *mind,* and with all your *strength*" (12:30, emphasis added). Then the Pharisee who repeats the greatest commandment back to Jesus lists "with all the *heart,* and with all the *understanding,* and with all the *strength*" (v. 33, emphasis added). Luke has a lawyer quote the greatest commandment to Jesus as "with all your *heart,* and with all your *soul,* and with all your *strength,* and with all your *mind*" (10:27, emphasis added). And Matthew has "with all your *heart,* and with all your *soul,* and with all your *mind*" (22:37, emphasis added).

Whatever combination of terms we list, the point surely is that we are to love with our *whole being*, rhymed above as with all our *head, heart,* and *hands,* and thus to engage our *intellect, emotion,* and *will.* The faith that grounds such love must also be a holistic affair, engaging our whole being. Any lesser faith could not be the origin of hope, nor receive back the nurture of a love that demands all of our mind, heart, and strength—our very soul.

Taking our cue from what is required to fulfill Jesus's greatest commandment, let us imagine the *living* faith that grows from such loving as also engaging our minds, our hearts, and our wills, all the basic capacities of the human person. *Living* Christian faith, then, engages our *heads* in *belief as personal conviction,* our *hearts* in *trusting and bonding relations,* and our *wills* ("hands)" in *the praxis of discipleship to Jesus.* Though we can separate them out for analysis, the three constantly interweave as the tripod source of *living* Christian faith, which is the rock that sustains our hope.

Faith as Belief by Personal Conviction: As noted previously, the most common association with faith is *belief,* understood as an assent of the mind to truth claims. While there is a deep *believing* aspect to Christian faith that thoroughly engages our minds, we need to qualify in two key ways. First, Christian *belief* that can partner with *trust* and good *works* to ground a hopeful faith is best reached by personal conviction and not simply by submission to teaching authority. This seems all the more imperative for postmodern people (chapter 1), so insistent on personal agency. Second, the belief involved in Christian faith refuses modernity's claim that our mind is most reliable when it excludes emotion, favoring dispassionate thinking. Instead, the conviction that undergirds Christian faith must be both *mindful* and *heartfelt.*

First, let us note that *conviction* in Christian faith is not a purely personal matter. Every Christian is to be informed and guided by the teaching authority of their Church as it articulates the shared beliefs that constitute their common faith. Guided by the Holy Spirit, "the Spirit of truth" as Jesus promised (John 16:13), an old Catholic tradition is that the whole Church is to participate in discerning its shared faith. To this end it has a threefold coalition of collaborating sources: the *common faith* of the baptized; the *scholarship* of its scholars in Bible and theology; and then the *magisterial* function of the Church's episcopal/papal leaders that articulates the consensus of the whole faith community. All three partners—people, scholars, and bishops/pope—are vital to preserving and developing the truth of the faith handed down, and to the effective functioning of the Church as teacher (*magister*).

However, and contrary to the *Catechism of Trent* (as cited above), embracing the Church's shared faith need not be by blind submission. Catholic Christians should never be expected to believe something as true just because their Church says so; it is true for better reasons—which is why the Church says so! Particularly in our time, the Church cannot legislate the truth; it must persuade to it. So all Christians are entitled, indeed well advised, to bring their own critical reasoning to their faith beliefs, to become critical believers. Christian belief is more likely to ground *living* faith for hope when embraced out of personal conviction, and this by sound reasoning.

Here note the long-standing Catholic tradition that faith and reason are essential partners. Summarizing, the First Vatican Council (1869–70) declared that "faith and reason are mutually advantageous. Right reason demonstrates the foundations of faith and faith sets reason free." Indeed, religious faith without the monitor of critical reason can become dangerous, leading to fanaticism or fundamentalism; whereas reason without the resource of faith can lead to total relativism or enslaving ideologies. Of course, reason alone cannot bring us to Christian faith; as Paul well said, faith is always "the gift of God" (Eph 2:8). Yet we are entitled to bring all the powers of our mind—reason, memory, and imagination—to examine, understand, judge, and embrace the teachings of Christian faith with personal conviction, making our *living* it all the more likely.

For coming to personal persuasion about Christian beliefs, the work of the great Catholic scholar Bernard Lonergan on the dynamics of authentic cognition can be helpful. Lonergan says that to truly know something as our own, there are four mental functions that we need to perform and do so intentionally. Indeed, we can readily recognize these dynamics in our own consciousness—we enact them a thousand times a day.

In brief, we must begin by paying *attention* to the data of what is to be known; in this case the teachings of Christian faith. Then we must strive to understand the data—to make sense out of them; it is imperative that we *understand* the teachings of Christian faith if we are to personally believe. In explaining the parable of the sower, Jesus emphasized that *understanding* the seed of God's word is needed in order to bear the fruit of discipleship (see Matt 13:18–23).

Following on, we must make our own *judgments* about what we understand, whether it be true or false, right or wrong, and come to see for ourselves if it makes good sense. Finally, we must reach our own *decisions* about it and whether to embrace the particular teaching into our own faith framework. It would seem that all four of these dynamics— attending, understanding, judging, and deciding—are essential for people to come to personal conviction of the beliefs of Christian faith.

Our second point to highlight is that the kind of belief required of Christians must reach beyond what we typically mean by intellectual assent—as if purely cognitive—vital as this may be for *living* faith. The New Testament Greek term *pisteuo*, usually translated as "to believe," has a far deeper meaning than assent of the rational mind. It is better described as a deep-down conviction, a rock-solid confidence, an unshakable affirmation that is mindful and yet heartfelt as well. Such an epistemology is echoed now in postmodernity's emphasis on the emotive and experiential alongside of critical reason, with all essential for life-giving knowledge.

While the Synoptics use *pisteuo* often, the word is writ large in John's Gospel, occurring some one hundred times. Two of John's classic texts give a *feeling* for how deeply he understood "belief" and particularly belief in Jesus. In John 3:16, we read that God sent God's own Son Jesus into the world "so that everyone who *believes* in him may not perish but may have eternal life" (emphasis added). A little later, John has Jesus repeat, "All who *see* the Son and *believe* in him may have eternal life" (6:40, emphasis added). Such believing includes and reaches far beyond the mind; it is to be embraced in the very depths of one's being, in what the poet Yeats called "the marrow bone."

With personal and critical conviction, then, there are specific truths, values, and wisdoms for Christians to embrace as the belief aspect of their *living* faith. Our most esteemed symbol of beliefs, of course, is a creed that we recite at Sabbath worship. There Christians stand together—

highlighting our shared conviction—to confess heartfelt belief in God as triune and what this means for our lives. The etymology of creed is *credo* and has roots in *cor dare*, literally "to give the heart." So our Creed is no dispassionate declaration of the mind alone but confesses a heartfelt conviction and commitment. Then, add all the dogmas and doctrines, values and virtues, symbols and wisdoms, and all the common teachings that constitute the corpus of Christian faith.

Of the teachings of Christian faith, we also do well to remember, as the *Catechism* points out, that they reflect a "hierarchy of truths" (*CCC* 90, quoting Vatican II). In other words, some teachings are more central "to the foundation of Christian faith" (ibid.) than others, and those that are further from the center (or lower down on the hierarchy) are less requiring of our belief. This is important to recall regarding matters of Catholic teaching that remain debated amidst the *sense of the faithful*, the *research of the scholars*, and the Church's official *magisterium*—the threefold sources of Church teaching referred above.

Faith as Trusting and Bonding Relations: In so many ways, faith is an affair of the heart. To cite the greatest commandment again, its Deuteronomy text and all versions in the Synoptic Gospels have "with all your heart" in its demands. Christian love and thus Christian *living* requires our whole heart, the best of our emotions. More than its partners of *mind* and *strength*, the *heartfelt* faith that gives hope and grounds love calls us into right and loving relationships all across the board.

As Jesus commented of the Pharisees and scribes, quoting the Prophet Isaiah (29:13) regarding true worship of God, "This people honors me with their lips, but their hearts are far from me" (Matt 15:8). *Living* faith—the measure of true worship of God—always demands our hearts.

As previously noted, biblically the *heart* stands for the whole person. Yet taking our usual meaning of *heart* as referring to human affectivity and emotion, the heart's contribution to a *living* faith can be summarized as *trust*. Indeed the Latin *fidere*, the root of "faith," means precisely *to trust*. And here we can well appreciate the emphasis of the Protestant Reformers.

The *trust* of Christian faith calls us first and foremost to give over our hearts entirely to God, with unbounded confidence in God's unconditional love and grace at work in our lives. And it is by God's love at work—grace—that we can be confident of our liberating salvation, or what Luther preferred to call our "justification." With this term, Luther intended the legal echo, claiming that Jesus erased the debt owed to God for our sins, making us righteous—just—before God. As he liked to quote, we "are now justified by [God's] grace as a gift, through the redemption that is in Christ Jesus" (Rom 3:24).

Whatever metaphor we favor, *living* faith calls us to embrace Luther's unbounded trust that the paschal mystery of Jesus's dying and rising has affected our liberation from the power of sin and from all that might hold us bound. We can trust entirely in God's saving will for us all, beginning here and completed in eternity. Spiritually speaking, to sustain us in such trusting faith we need to nurture our relationship with God by worship, prayer, and spiritual practices. The trust of *living* faith calls us, with the help of the Holy Spirit, to grow into the two-way love of God—to embrace ever more deeply God's love for us and to develop our loving relationship with God. God's outreach to us is always an invitation into divine friendship.

The trusting dimension of Christian faith also invites us into a deeply bonded friendship with Jesus Christ. In his final discourse, Jesus named the disciples as "friends" (John 15:15), and so for all Christians. Integral to *living* faith, then, is to become friends with Jesus, and to grow this friendship throughout our lives. We are to "abide" in Jesus, bonded as intimately as the vine and its branches (15:5). The *General Directory for Catechesis* summarizes that the purpose of all Christian education in faith is to "put people in communion and intimacy with Jesus Christ" (*GDC* 80, echoed in *CCC* 426). This is not, however, to be a cozy or exclusive "me and Jesus" relationship. Rather, as we elaborate below, it calls us to discipleship—which the *Directory* describes as "full and sincere adherence to Jesus's person and the decision to walk in his footsteps" (*GDC* 53). Disciples to Jesus must "walk the walk."

Baptism bonds all Christians into a personal and trusting relation-ship with Jesus. To describe as much, Paul uses a number of images. He says that Christians "belong to Christ" now (1 Cor 3:23), are to "put on the Lord Jesus Christ" (Rom 13:14), and again, we are to "have the mind of Christ" (1 Cor 2:16), all bespeaking a deep bond of unity with him. Indeed, we are to be "ambassadors for Christ" (2 Cor 5:20), so close that we can officially represent him as an ambassador might their country.

This bonding and belonging with Jesus, of course, must lead on into our *belonging* to his community of disciples, the Church. We have cited many times Paul's imagery of the Church as the Body of Christ in the world. The trusting or emotive aspect of *living* faith is to bond us into right and loving relationship with a Christian community, all uniting like the parts of a body and lending us a sense of belonging that we experience firsthand.

In chapter 7, we described such *belonging* as to be accepted, to be respected, to be counted in as a full member, to be as good as any other. Then, far more than a passive membership, *belonging* means actively participating in, contributing to, and being held accountable by our Christian communities—local and universal. So while the affective aspect of Christian faith is to bond us in love with God and with Jesus, it is also to bond us with sister and brother Christians into a community where all are welcome and every member is fully included.

Continuing on and reaching beyond our bond of belonging to a Christian community, the affective aspect of *living* Christian faith calls us to right and loving relations with all of God's people. It calls us to treat all people as our sisters and brothers, convinced that everyone belongs to the one family of God. Indeed, the trust of *living* faith also calls us into right and responsible relationship with creation, as Pope Francis has stated so compellingly (see his *Laudato Si'*). Christian faith demands that we protect our environment from destruction and prevent the waste of its natural resources.

In sum, the trust needed to ground *living* Christian faith for hope demands "all our heart."

Faith as Praxis of Discipleship to Jesus: Throughout this book, we have emphasized that *living* faith—as the term clearly implies—must be *lived* by Christians, realized in their daily *behavior*. Here we echo the Catholic emphasis on faith as "good works." As the third aspect in our tripod of *living* faith, it calls us beyond *believing* and *trusting* to *behaving* as disciples of Jesus, beyond *intellect* and *affect* to *action*, beyond our *heads* and *hearts* to engage our "strength"—or metaphorically, the work of our *hands*.

As consistently lived behavior, Christian faith is to become a life-style, a habitual pattern. Rather than something that needs to be chosen from one occasion to the next, it is to become our pattern of life, after *the way* of Jesus. Of course, there are particular choices to be made (we review conscience below), yet our faith demands an overall lifestyle by which we strive to behave consistently as disciples of Jesus, letting this shape our whole way of being in the world.

When writing of faith as a pattern of Christian living, Thomas Aquinas used the term *habitus*. This is under translated by our word *habit*, which we can hear as nonreflective; we often speak of "falling into" habits as if not by choice. For Thomas, as for Aristotle from whom he borrowed the notion, a habit is a well-reasoned disposition to act in a particular way, even as acting that way deepens the habit as consistent behavior. Lived Christian faith is to become so habitual.

Here another ancient term from Aristotle can help to capture both the reflective and active aspects of lived Christian faith—the word *praxis* (also being widely retrieved). Again, praxis includes but means more than we usually mean by practice in that the latter also can be nonreflective, as in "*practicing* my golf" (badly needed, too!). For Aristotle, praxis is reflective action and action that is reflected upon in order to develop *phronesis*, by which he meant a pattern of practical wisdom. It seems like an ideal term to capture what is involved in lived Christian faith; it is the *praxis* of discipleship to Jesus that nurtures us in spiritual wisdom.

For *living* Christian faith, then, we need to develop a habitual pattern of its praxis; indeed, without this, as St. James well said, faith is "dead." We need to grow in Christian discipleship as a reflective lifestyle by which we *do* the works of faith, patterned after *the way* of Jesus. Like believing and trusting, the praxis of Christian faith is essential to sustaining our hope.

While the reflective aspect of praxis makes it more than what we might mean by *practice*, Christian faith requires as much, and especially if it is to become our consistent behavior. The practice of doing what disciples of Jesus are to do helps us "get into the habit." There is a story told of a young violinist from Ohio who had an audition at the renowned Carnegie Hall. As she exited the subway at 57th and 7th in Midtown Manhattan, she was momentarily disoriented. She knew it was around here somewhere, but which way to turn? To her relief, she saw an old man with a violin under his arm and thought that surely he would know the right direction. She approached him and asked, "Sir, can you tell me how to get to Carnegie Hall?" He paused thoughtfully and with a smile responded, "Practice, practice, practice." For developing the habit of lived Christian faith, we can say likewise; we become better at it by practice.

We proposed in the prelude that the centrality of the historical Jesus is a developing consciousness for Catholic Christians. We are still learning that discipleship to Jesus is the core of being Christian; Pope Francis is encouraging us along. Note that the Latin *discipulus* means "learner"; our vocation as Christians is to be lifelong learners from Jesus. Likewise, the Greek *mathetes*, translated as *disciple* (used some 220 times in the Gospels), in the culture of the time also meant "apprentice." Christians are called to live as perpetual apprentices to Jesus, ever learning from his example the praxis of Christian faith.

Evangelical Christians rightly focus on Jesus Christ as the core of Christian faith. However, and most often favoring the Pauline writings over the Gospels, they place little emphasis on living the social values that the Jesus of history modeled during his public ministry (there are notable exceptions, like the Sojourners Community). The typical Evangelical focus is on the Christ of faith as source of our "justification." However, the praxis of Christian discipleship requires embracing *the way* and the values of the historical Jesus, and this as a habitual lifestyle. Christians are ever called to grow as *faithful* disciples, a patterned commitment to the praxis that Jesus modeled and taught.

In chapter 4, we outlined the collage of commitments reflected in the life of the historical Jesus. Summarizing here, he calls disciples to worship and pray to the one true God as the only God of our lives. He portrays how we are to live for the realization of all the personal and social values of God's reign, doing God's will on earth, even as it is done in heaven. Apprentices to Jesus must show compassion for all in need, and imitate his favor for *the poor*, those who need the favor most.

We must imitate Jesus's witness to the dignity of all people and his radical inclusivity, welcoming all to the table. Disciples must commit to living justly ourselves and to work for justice in our church and world (our focused theme in chapter 10). Jesus summarized all in his radicalizing of the love command and in his golden rule: "Do to others as you would have them do to you" (Matt 7:12). That is the sum total of Christian praxis.

We reviewed already how *lived* faith was a central emphasis in the modeling and preaching of Jesus; we echo the same note here. We drew especially from statements of Jesus in the Synoptic Gospels that those who hear "the word" must live it (See Luke 8:1, Matt 7:21, etc.). Here, for a change, we focus briefly on how John's Gospel echoes an enriching emphasis on *doing* the truth of faith—a praxis!

John has Jesus say, "Those who *do what is true* come to the light, so that it may be clearly seen that *their deeds* have been done in God" (3:21, emphasis added). Note the imperative of *doing* the truth and that good deeds need to be *seen*, not to center on the self but on the grace of God. Recall, too, Jesus's constant conjoining of "light and life." For example, "I am the light of the world. Whoever follows me will never walk in darkness but will have the light of life" (8:12). Note again the emphasis on imitating the praxis of Jesus in order to have "the light of life." In summary, "If you continue in my word [which means to so live], you are truly my disciples; and you will know the truth, and the truth will make you free" (8:31–32). To be disciples, we must live the truth taught by Jesus; this brings us liberation—and hope.

It seems that the lawyer in Luke had precisely the right question when he asked Jesus, "What must I *do* to inherit eternal life?" (10:25, emphasis added). Jesus responded with the parable of the Good Samaritan, ending with "Go and *do* likewise" (v. 37). *Living* Christian faith requires developing the habit of doing the good works as the Samaritan did; such praxis lends us hope now and becomes our pathway into eternal life.

With this basic sense of the praxis of disciples in place, living *the way* of Jesus surely includes keeping the commandments. A rich man (described as young in Matthew) addressed Jesus and asked a similar question as the lawyer: "Good Teacher, what must I do to inherit eternal life?" Jesus's first response was to begin to list the Ten Commandments (Mark 10:17–19). Likewise, Jesus's Beatitudes in Matthew (5:1–11) are a listing of what disciples must *do*—work for mercy, peace, and justice—even at the cost of suffering. Jesus described our final judgment as whether or not we have fed the hungry, clothed the naked, sheltered the homeless, cared for the sick and imprisoned, welcomed strangers, all instances of Christian praxis (see Matt 25:31–46).

Building on the modeling and teaching of Jesus, later Christian tradition would add further guidelines for faithful discipleship with its listings of virtues that Christians are to practice. Beyond the theological ones of faith, hope, and love, disciples are called to the praxis of the *cardinal* virtues of justice, prudence, fortitude, and temperance. These are "cardinal," echoing the Latin *cardo* for "hinge," because so many other virtues turn on our living of these four.

Further, the Holy Spirit empowers us with gifts of *love*, *joy*, *peace*, *patience*, *kindness*, *generosity*, *faithfulness*, *gentleness*, and *self-control* (Gal 5:22–23); such gifts are realized only as we put them to work in our daily lives. Then Christian teaching warns us to avoid seven "deadly" sins of envy, gluttony, greed, lust, pride, sloth (as the failure *to act*), and hatred. Growing in a life of such virtue and avoiding such sins is the fidelity demanded of disciples of Jesus; such praxis is essential to our *living* Christian faith for hope.

Lastly, and echoing what we elaborated in chapter 4, disciples of Jesus must outreach with his Gospel to others; this, too, is expected of our faith praxis. Recall that the great commission by the risen Christ to the disciples on a hillside in Galilee (Matt 28:18–20) was given to all present. In other words, by baptism, Christians are called to be, in the lovely phrase of Pope Francis, "missionary disciples." Our praxis of Christian discipleship calls us to sow the seeds of faith in the lives of others (evangelization) and to help as opportune to grow those seeds as well (catechesis). In the postlude, we elaborate more fully this responsibility to share the Gospel and how we might fulfill it effectively.

In summary, all three components—*belief as personal conviction*, *trusting and bonding relations*, and *praxis of the way of Jesus*—are necessary constituents of *living* Christian faith. United as one, such *living* faith is the rock that, by God's grace, can sustain hope, especially when most needed.

PAUSE FOR REFLECTION

- In light of this holistic sense of Christian faith, how do you need to expand or reimagine your own life in faith?

- How might growing into *living* faith be a source of hope for your life? Imagine some "next steps" in your own faith-for-hope journey.

LIVING CHRISTIAN FAITH FOR HOPE

Living Christian faith can be an enduring source of hope precisely because it engages our agency, even as it assures of God's grace to mount our own good efforts to believe, trust, and live as disciples. Such holistic faith can enable us to do "as best we can" in any circumstance, and this can keep hope alive. By contrast, to cease believing the great central truths of Christian faith, to stop trusting in God's love and grace, or to "give up trying" to live as disciples of Jesus is most likely to diminish our hope as well. In the direst of circumstances, we may be reduced to no more agency than to pray our hopes, yet this may be the precise aspect of *living* faith that sustains them.

A "Catholic" spirituality emphasizes that without our own agency, faith becomes a cheap grace and our hopes no more than wishful thinking. Whereas *living* Christian faith as described here lends a solid foundation to keep hope alive. To cite a lovely phrase from the poet Seamus Heaney, *living* faith can help make "hope and history rhyme" (from *The Cure of Troy*).

It stands to reason, then, that our best source of hope is to continue to grow in *living* Christian faith. We can deepen our *personal conviction* by ongoing study and reflection, by expanding our knowledge and growing in the wisdom of Scripture and Christian tradition. Our *trusting and bonding relations* need the continued sources of worship and prayer, of belonging to a supportive Christian community, and other spiritual practices that deepen our right and loving relationships with

God, self, others, and creation. Our *praxis as disciples of Jesus* requires our ongoing embrace of the greatest commandment ("enemies" will always be a challenge) and living into all the truths, values, and virtues to be embodied by apprentices to Jesus. In other words, the efforts we make to grow in *living* faith is also the agency that sustains our hope.

The Paschal Mystery as Our Rock of Hope: Our hunger for hope requires us to return again (third time now) to its most difficult challenge—the reality of human suffering, misfortune, and sin in our lives, church, and world. While a *living* faith is our hopeful stance toward this mystery, the mystery remains. It intensifies when we find ourselves in situations for which we can imagine no good outcome, where all seems lost or over-powering, and we are challenged, to cite Paul again, "to hope against hope"—to keep on swimming (second little frog).

Christians must never propose a glib solution or minimize the suf-fering in tragic situations and injustices. Instead, we are brought to our knees by this ultimate mystery—a loving and provident God and yet the reality of human misfortune and evil. Somehow, even in the midst of what may seem like hopeless situations, Christians *can* cling to the conviction that hope endures because of the paschal mystery of Jesus's cross and resurrection.

Jesus's suffering and death on the cross is the ultimate sign of God's solidarity with us, especially in times of suffering. God was never more present to humankind than in Jesus's crucifixion. It is significant that as Jesus hung on the cross, bystanders mocked him, saying, "He saved others; he cannot save himself" (Mark 15:31). Here surely was Jesus's total solidarity with our human condition. We are never able to save ourselves by our own efforts alone; we always need help. Yet paradoxi-cally, we can help to save others.

No wonder Paul described "Christ crucified" as "a stumbling block...and foolishness" to human ken (1 Cor 1:23). Yet "God's fool-ishness is wiser than human wisdom, and God's weakness is stronger than human strength" (from 1 Cor 1:25). This is so precisely because the cross was not the end of Jesus. By God's raising him from the dead, Jesus's cross became our rock-solid source of hope—for *all* humankind and indeed for all creation. As the Second Vatican Council declared, echoing a long tradition of Catholic teaching, "For since Christ died for all people…we ought to believe that the Holy Spirit in a manner known only to God offers to every person the possibility of being associated with this paschal mystery" (*Gaudium et Spes* 22).

In chapter 5, we reviewed some consequences of God raising Jesus from the dead. In brief here, by raising up Jesus, God verified his life's work and the divine/human person that he was. God declared Jesus "to be Son of God with power…by resurrection from the dead" (Rom 1:4). Paul went on to explain that "just as Christ was raised from the dead by the glory of the Father, so we too might walk in newness of life" (6:4)—always with hope.

Because of God's raising up of Jesus and he being one of ourselves, we can rise beyond and against every cross, every suffering, every addiction, every crime, and every injustice. Precisely because God "raised us up with him" (Eph 2:6), now we always have hope. The First Letter of Peter said that Christians must be ever ready to give "an accounting for the hope that is in you" (3:15). And we can—because of our baptismal bond with Jesus in his dying and rising.

So in the most challenging of circumstances for hope, we can follow Paul's admonition and "remember Jesus Christ, raised from the dead" (2 Tim 2:8). For even "if we are faithless, he remains faithful—for he cannot deny himself" (v. 13). We might think of such dire moments of darkness as akin to experiencing the between time of Holy Saturday. Even when we cannot imagine a satisfactory outcome to suffering, tragedy, or betrayal, we are invited to wait in the interim with *living* faith that lends hope.

Here Mary Magdalene and the other women disciples who go to Jesus's tomb on Holy Saturday—not knowing yet of Easter Sunday—are our models of faith that continues to hope (Mark 16:1, etc.). Likewise, when devastated by some Good Friday in our lives, church, or world, we can go on hoping as if experiencing the between time of Holy Saturday, though we know not how, for an Easter Sunday.

Waiting in darkness, unable to imagine redress, can be unbearable and tempt us to despair. In such devastating moments, we can surely cry out with Jesus, as he cried out from his own cross, "My God, my God, why have you forsaken me?" (Matt 27:46). Yet his cry from the heart was itself a prayer, spoken out of his *living* faith. Such prayer of lament yet reflects faithfulness to our covenant with God; we still have our agency, if only to pray in protest.

Our Holy Saturday times remind us, too, that our hope in this life is ever partial. There are moments when sickness and suffering can appear to win out or oppression and injustice to prevail—at least for a time. Yet ultimately Jesus's paschal mystery always lends the hope of eternal life. In his beautiful encyclical *Spe Salvi* ("Saved in Hope"), the title echoing Paul's line "For in hope we were saved" (Rom 8:24), Pope Benedict XVI insisted that "life will not end in emptiness." Instead, God's unconditional love and gracious mercy always brings the promise of eternal life. This ever remains our final hope.

CONSCIENCE AND FAITH FOR HOPE

Living faith for hope requires us to make practical decisions in the daily of life. They can pertain to our believing or trusting, but especially to the praxis of Christian faith. Even as we grow in embracing discipleship to Jesus as a habitual pattern of behavior, there are countless particular moments in life—great and small—when the reflective aspect in the praxis of faith needs more deliberate attention. This is especially true when making ethical decisions to reflect *living* Christian faith. Here we echo chapter 1 and the fact that we must contextualize our faith, implementing it in our historical contexts, which ever requires wise discernment and decision-making.

Some moral choices are patently between good and evil, faithfulness and sin. There are situations, however, where this is not so obvious at all. Sometimes we need to choose the greater good from a number of possibilities or, indeed, at times the lesser evil. This is when we most need to draw upon a Christian conscience to guide our decision-making. Conscience is the capacity we have to look at given circumstances, weigh potential outcomes, and discern how to apply Christian principles and values to make good *moral* decisions. Clearly, conscience is vital to people's praxis as disciples of Jesus and thus to our hope.

There is a rich Catholic tradition regarding conscience that honors both our own reasoning—what Vatican II called "the voice within"—as well as the commandments and values of Christian faith, and then to discern how to integrate these two sources to reach good decisions. As the *Catechism* explains, conscience helps us "to make a right judgment in accordance with *reason* and the *divine law*" (no. 1786, emphasis added to highlight both). Let us reflect briefly on (1) right reasoning through the "voice within"; (2) on the law of God that guides conscience, especially as modeled by Jesus and taught by the Church; and (3) on discerning how to integrate these two sources—personal and communal—to make good particular decisions.

1. The Second Vatican Council summarized a long Catholic tradition as follows: "In the depths of our conscience, we detect a law which does not impose, but which holds us to obedience. Always summoning us to love good and avoid evil, the voice of conscience when necessary speaks to our heart: do this; shun that. For we have in our own heart a law written by God; to obey it is the very dignity of being human; according to it we will be judged" (*Gaudium et Spes* 16).

Note well that God's law is not something extraneous from outside of us; instead, it is written in our own hearts. This reflects the traditional Catholic position that God places a *natural law* within humankind. While we call it "natural" because integral to our humanity, it is placed in us by our Creator God. Clearly, we must listen to its promptings.

Drawing upon the natural law within engages our *reasoning* even more than our feelings. The latter regarding moral issues can be the work of our superego, making us *feel* guilty even when doing nothing wrong (I still can't have a late afternoon cookie without hearing my mom's voice, "not before dinner"). As the *Catechism* explains, conscience is "a judgment of reason" (no. 1778) that requires our own "introspection" (no. 1779), that is, discernment.

2. Then the praxis of Christian faith must also be guided by the law of God, which directs us, as Vatican II said, "to love good and avoid evil." The *Catechism* likens this second source of conscience to "the Vicar of Christ" (no. 1778) in that it represents the demands of Christian faith. So conscience must draw upon the spiritual wisdom and moral mandates that the Christian community has developed over time, beginning with the ancient people of Israel and the teachings of Jesus.

Yet the Church's moral guidelines must be appropriated and applied by people's own discernment. As Pope Francis wrote in his encyclical *Amoris Laetitia* (*AL*), the Church is "called to form consciences, not to replace them" (no. 37).

3. Listening to our own inner voice *and* to the law of God, "to reason and the divine law" (*CCC* 1786), we need to weigh both in light of each other and then come to a decision. Again to quote Pope Francis, "The faithful...are capable of carrying out their own discernment in complex situations" (*AL* 37). And having made a responsible decision, we must act upon it. For while Catholic tradition recognizes a deep freedom to such discernment and decision-making, there is an equally strong insistence that we *must* follow our conscience. Such is the sanctity of conscience; to deny either its responsibilities or its freedom would be, as the *Catechism* states, contrary to "the dignity of the human person" (no. 1780).

Practically speaking, it may be helpful to imagine four sequential "steps" in making a good decision of Christian conscience in an actual situation. Prior to any discernment, a faith-filled moral decision, especially a major one, needs to be accompanied by prayer to the Holy Spirit for guidance. Then imagine the following four steps.

First, we need to look at the circumstances of the decision to be made. As the *Catechism* advises, for good moral decision, we must first "interpret the data of experience" (no. 1788). Such discernment requires us to recognize the circumstances, the possible options, and to look to the likely consequences of any decision—for ourselves and for others.

Second, we need to discern what decision would enhance our living as disciples of Jesus for God's reign in the world. This moment should focus on what the teachings of Christian faith would command in the situation. The very word *conscience* is from the Latin *conscientia*—literally "knowing with." It reminds us to be in conversation *with* the moral teachings of the Christian community in order to make faith-filled decisions.

Third, we need to listen to the promptings of our own heart and imagine the best way to honor the will of God in these circumstances. As Vatican II stated so beautifully, "Conscience is the most secret core and sanctuary of a person. There we are alone with God, Whose voice echoes in our depths" (*Gaudium et Spes* 16).

Fourth, after looking at the data, consulting the mandates of Christian faith, and listening to our own inner voice, we must discern and decide the *living* faith way to proceed and then act upon the decision.

REMEMBER—MERCY FOREVER!

While the challenges to hope ever come our way—suffering, ill health, accidents, natural disasters, injustice, discrimination, and so on—perhaps its greatest obstacle is what we bring upon ourselves by our sins. This is because sin is the opposite to the *living* faith that brings hope. St. Paul well lamented, as a result of "sin that dwells within…the evil I do not want is what I do." And yet, when he wonders "who will rescue me" from the consequences of sin, he proclaims his faith that lends hope: "Thanks be to God through Jesus Christ our Lord" (Rom 7:17–19, 24, 25).

In Christian faith, no sin, even the worst imaginable, is unforgiveable. As Jesus assures in John's Gospel, "God did not send the Son into the world to condemn the world, but in order that the world might be saved through him" (3:17). And all three Synoptics have Jesus assure, "I have come to call not the righteous but sinners" (Mark 2:17, etc.). No matter our sin, we can always be confident in what Mary named well as God's "mercy…forever" (Luke 1:54–55). Both Jesus and Mary had learned this from their Jewish faith—that "our God…will abundantly pardon" (Isa 55:7). With such divine mercy, even our sins need not rob us of hope.

Of course, this expects us to recognize our sins, to repent of them, and to avoid committing them again. This is true of us personally and as a community of faith (*vide* the crimes of clergy sex abuse). That first step—recognizing our sins—may be the most challenging for people of this postmodern age. We can all too readily "cover up" our institutional sins, even as church. Personally, we can admit to having *issues* for counseling but not *sins* for repenting. Yet there is nothing more renewing of hope than to recognize and repent of our sins and to work for institutional reform as needed.

Recall Jesus's parable of the Pharisee and the Publican (Luke 18:9–14). The Pharisee tries to find hope by justifying himself. He prays, "God, I thank you that I am not like other people: thieves, rogues, adulterers," and goes on to list his own good works. By contrast, the Publican admits his sins and says, "God, be merciful to me, a sinner!" Jesus's punch line was that the sinful Publican "went down to his home justified rather than the other" (Luke 18:11–14).

Because repentance can be an enduring source of hope, we do well to recall here what is needed for true contrition. It has four simple but imperative steps. Speaking personally, I must (a) *admit* that I did wrong, (b) say that I am *sorry*, (c) ask *forgiveness*, and (d) *resolve* to try my best, by God's grace, not to sin again. With these four steps—as when we need to apologize to another person—we can be sure of God's mercy and receive the grace to renew our efforts of *living* faith for hope.

HOPE FOR OUR HEARTS

Every chapter of this book has a "Hope for our Hearts" section, each reviewing some particular hope suggested by the chapter topic. In a sense, then, hope is a primary theme throughout the book, reflecting that the constitutive aspects of Christian faith can nurture a spirituality that lends hope. Here our focus is precisely on the hope that is sustained by *living* Christian faith.

The hunger for hope is very deep in the human heart; indeed there is none deeper. Humanly speaking, we cannot function without hope; it is literally what gets us out of bed in the morning and keeps us going through the day. Of course, we need hope most of all in the difficult times, when the personal crosses come our way or the public affairs of the church or world at large seem all the more antithetical to the reign of God. What a gift it is to our hearts to have a Christian imagination that nurtures *living* faith for hope.

Why, even in the good times of life we need hope to enjoy them. I had an old Irish nihilist aunt who at family weddings could be heard

predicting the upcoming wakes. Perhaps she was rejoicing in our ultimate hope of eternal life, but I doubt it. For the milestones, the achievements, the blessings of life, we need hope to embrace and celebrate them.

For Christians, a personally convicted *belief* in the truths and wisdom of Christian faith can lend a well-warranted foundation to our
hope. Likewise, *trusting* in God's unconditional love and mercy is a reliable source of hope. Following on, our *trust* that in Jesus's death and
resurrection God did something extraordinary in our favor is a solid
foundation of hope. In Jesus's paschal mystery, Christians believe that
all sin and suffering—even death—have been conquered, and as said
so often here, has released an "abundance" of God's grace into human
history. Then, for Christian faith and perhaps with a particular emphasis in "Catholic" spirituality, hope arises from our *praxis* as disciples of
Jesus—from *living* faith.

Relying on God's grace, we must be agents of our hopes, participants rather than passive recipients within the divine/human covenant.
Hope is never a cheap grace. Ours is always a partnership with God,
demanding our agency to *believe*, *trust*, and *live* as disciples of Jesus for
God's reign. As we noted previously, there are Evangelical Christian
traditions that minimize the good works of faith and make as if all
depends on God's grace. But this is not the "Catholic" imagination; as
repeated umpteen times throughout, God's grace—and especially for
hope—comes to us as a response-ability.

Here I recall a youth ministry poster from many years ago that
summarized well the divine/human partnership for hope. It represented God as saying, "Without Me, you can't. Without you, I won't.
Together we can." The confidence that "with God, we can" encourages
a *living* faith that nurtures hope.

There are religions that do not encourage hope within history by
human agency, not even with divine help. For Hinduism, for example,
one may have hope for another time in the cycle of life and rebirth, but
for now, one does best to settle for the present condition. In fact, the
more people accept their lot and status, whatever it may be, the more
likely they are to be reborn with an upgrade. Again, this is not our position; on the contrary, *living* Christian faith lends hope for both here and
hereafter—and we get only one go-round at life.

In summary, and always by God's grace, the more firmly we *believe* in the central truths of Christian faith, *trust* in God's love and mercy, and *do* the good works of disciples, the more likely we are to keep hope alive. Or again, as the fruits of *living* faith, the more *alive*, *lived*, and *life-giving* our faith becomes, the more it can sustain our hope. What a gift to our hearts and world!

PAUSE FOR REFLECTION

- Choose some aspect of your life that is particularly in need of hope at this time. How might a *living* Christian faith lend you fresh hope?

- What decisions might you need to make to sustain your hope?

SPIRITUAL PRACTICE: KEEP SABBATH; LET GO AND LET GOD

A sure way for any of us to lose hope is to rely entirely on our own efforts, as if we are totally *in charge* of our lives. Even committed Christians can be tempted by this kind of selfie idolatry, especially in this postmodern age that encourages a humanism that overlooks our need for God's help. With the best of intentions, all of us can be tempted to take on too much, to presume and act as if our life outcome is entirely in our hands. A *living* faith for hope encourages us to "let go and let God" instead. While we are partners in this great divine/human covenant, God is ultimately "in charge," with even our own efforts mounted by God's grace.

Did you ever wonder why God made it *a law* that we are to rest for at least one day out of every seven? "Remember the sabbath day, and keep it holy" (Exod 20:8). God placed this Sabbath law third of the ten, after worshipping only God and honoring God's holy name, giving it high priority. To keep the Sabbath *holy* requires us to "not do any work" (Exod 20:10) and to recognize that our very selves and all we possess belong to God; whatever we think we possess is simply "on loan." The Sabbath asks us to symbolically give all back to Whom it all belongs and take a day of rest. There is no better spiritual practice than to keep Sabbath. It can nurture hope, reminding us to "let go and let God"— throughout our week as well.

This sabbath sentiment of placing everything in God's hands should be our posture every day. At the end of his *Spiritual Exercises*, St. Ignatius of Loyola crafted a beautiful prayer that powerfully expresses the sentiment of "let go and let God." It is called the *Suscipe* prayer, from its opening Latin word that means "receive." As the prayer unfolds, note that it asks God to *receive* back all that God has lent to us—because all belongs to God anyhow—granting us only God's love and grace as needed. What an ideal way to begin or end any day, and especially when our hope is under siege.

Take, Lord, and receive all my liberty,
my memory, my understanding,
and my entire will.
You have given all to me,
To you, Lord, I return it.
Everything is yours; do with it what you will.
Give me only your love and your grace,
That is enough for me.

FOR FURTHER READING

Harrington, Daniel. *What Are We Hoping For? New Testament Images.* Collegeville, MN: Order of St. Benedict, 2006. An inspiring reflection by a leading scripture scholar on the New Testament teaching on hope.

Lennan, Richard, and Nancy Pineda-Madrid, eds. *Hope: Promise, Possibility, and Fulfillment.* Mahwah, NJ: Paulist Press, 2013. An excellent collection of essays on the virtue of hope.

O'Murchu, Diarmuid. *The Meaning and Practice of Faith.* Maryknoll, NY: Orbis, 2014. Faces the challenge of embracing an adult faith for hope with a cosmic consciousness.

CHAPTER 10

A "Catholic" Politics

Our Hunger for Justice

A Great Favor and Bread on the Table
By way of the social responsibilities of Christian faith, I recognize how blest I was with the two parents I had. In particular, my mother had a deep compassion for the poor and my father was a lifelong champion of justice for all. Would that I live up to their memory!

We lived in a rural Irish community that had more than its share of poor people. Regularly, my mother would prepare more noontime dinner than our family could eat. There were always neighbors who just "happened" to be passing by at dinner time to avail. And I still remember the gracious way she had of offering food. One old friend, John, was a regular. Yet she would call out to him each time, as he pretended to walk onward, "Hello John, I cooked too much meat and potatoes again today, and I hate to see good food go to waste. You'd do me a great favor to come in and help finish it up." Of course John did my mother the favor—with his dignity intact.

While she taught me the gift of compassion, my father helped kindle a fire in the belly for justice. He was a local politician, but with a global outlook, as concerned about hunger in Africa as in the village. Though he never had an opportunity to formally study Catholic social teaching, it was the intuited platform of his politics, prompted by his faith. As I heard him say a thousand times (echoing his favorite Jesus miracle), "Christians should help put bread on the table for everyone."

HUNGER FOR JUSTICE AND A POLITICAL SPIRITUALITY

As previously compared, the hungers of the heart are like a symphony, all resonating with each other and lending their distinctive movement to the overall work. And as reiterated throughout this book, we must care for the hungers of others as well as our own, otherwise the whole symphony is thrown off-key. To care only for our own desire for love, for happiness, for meaning and purpose and so on, will land us in the idolatry of the self—with the slaveries that ensue. Humanly speaking, we are at our best and do best when we wish the best for everyone else and are diminished if we wish otherwise. So justice for *all people* is another hunger of the human heart—when true to itself.

Following on and from a Christian perspective, to be disciples of Jesus with his greatest commandment that we love God by loving neighbors as ourselves, demands that we care for the hungers of others, whatever they might be. However, this altruism gets writ large—placed front and center—when we focus on the works of compassion and justice as integral to the social responsibilities of *living* faith. Then, to keep on in our efforts to help those in need or suffering injustice requires a *political* spirituality. By this I intend a spirituality that nurtures our social consciousness and sustains our commitment to bring Christian values into the communal and public realm of our lives.

Practically speaking, works of *compassion* and of *justice* are two sides of the same coin. We have reflected often throughout on the mandate of compassion for Christians, and especially when referring to the values of the historical Jesus. As I explain below, justice reaches beyond compassion—also prompted by those values of Jesus. For example, compassion focuses more on directly feeding hungry people, whereas justice asks why they are hungry and works to change the social and economic structures that cause hunger in a society.

So while justice reaches beyond compassion—as we highlight here—we must never leave it behind. Pope Benedict wisely taught in his encyclical *Deus Caritas Est* (2005), that even if our world could fully realize justice, we would still need works of compassion toward the sufferings that inevitably come with life in the world—natural disasters, sickness, bereavement, death, and so on. Works of direct service to people in need are forever required for *living* Christian faith.

Meanwhile, our focus here is on the hunger for justice, so central to the preaching and praxis of Jesus. This was especially evident in his championing of the reign of God, a *sociopolitical* symbol and, as noted many times, the defining passion of his life. As Jesus modeled and taught, the reign of God and its justice must be placed "first" in importance by disciples (Matt 6:33). In this regard, Jesus was simply being faithful to the "radical monotheism" (H. Richard Niebuhr) of his Jewish faith; that the one true God must be the only God of people's lives, and on every level of existence, personal, communal, social, and political. There is no level or context where our God is not to be God!

So Jesus's gospel of God's reign demands that Christians put their faith to work toward the "good governance" (the Greek *politika*) of our own lives and of the public realm in which we dwell. This, in turn, needs a spirituality that can heighten, enlighten, and sustain such social commitment—a political spirimalty.

For the Bible, the spiritual quest for holiness and for justice go hand in hand. Look at the great "holiness code" that is high pointed in chapter 19 of the Book of Leviticus (the code runs from chapters 17 to 26). Its summary line begins with, "You shall be holy, for I the LORD your God am holy" (19:2). Then read on; of some fifty directives for holiness that follow, at least half pertain to works of compassion and justice. Christian holiness demands justice and requires a political spirituality to nurture it.

For many, talk of a *political spirituality* may be heard as a contradiction in terms—an oxymoron. The popular image of spirituality is of something very private and deeply personal. Indeed, a danger of claiming to be "spiritual but not religious" is of feeding into this stereotype, declining what could be the spiritual resources of a faith tradition and community, and encouraging a private spirituality of one's own making and for "the self."

This is particularly evident in new age spirituality. Google this term and what comes up will promise to help you realize your potential, improve your self-image, calm your fears, and contribute to your own good karma. While these are worthy spiritual quests, they do not directly encourage a *living* faith that helps realize the values of God's reign in the public realm.

Indeed, the history of constitutional democracy can be read to separate civic responsibilities from religious faith. When one of its great architects, Jean Jacques Rousseau (1712–78), distinguished between the *citizen* and the *individual*, he assigned the citizen to society and the individual to the Church. But this is to forget that we are one and the same person, and that Christian values are as mandatory for us in the political realm as in the personal.

That same political tradition wisely encouraged a "separation of church and state" (as in the First Amendment to the U.S. Constitution). But this good constitutional arrangement cannot allow Christians to separate their faith from how they live their lives in the communal and public spheres. Christianity, with all of its teachings on compassion and justice, is an eminently *public* faith, and requires a politically conscious spirituality to nurture its praxis.

We have a too narrow view of *politics*. Typically, people think of it only as the process of electing politicians and the work of political parties. And a term too often associated with politics is *dirty*—surely to be avoided by people questing holiness of life. Sadly, this image of *dirty* politics has become all the more warranted in our time.

But politics at its best is a noble public service (my dad was my first witness to this). And far beyond elective politics and parties, it pertains to how all of us engage in our social structures and with the cultural values (or disvalues) of our historical context. Christian faith requires of disciples a politics that puts their faith to work in the public realm and in service to the common good of all.

Having said that politics is about more than elections, yet it does pertain to the politicians we support and for whom we vote. I'm amazed by churchgoing Catholics who seem to well practice their faith in other ways but vote for politicians whose disvalues (sexism, racism, homophobia, environmental destruction, and so on) are directly contrary to Christian faith and what we describe below as Catholic social doctrine. From current voting patterns in the United States, it seems that the same can be said of many in other Christian churches.

Throughout this book, Christian spirituality is portrayed as *a people's sense of relationality with the one and triune God as the foundation of their being, and, empowered by the Holy Spirit, how they nurture this relationship to live as disciples of Jesus within a community of disciples for God's reign in the world.* Clearly, our faith in God as triune and living as disciples calls us to promote the right and loving relationships reflected in the Trinity and modeled by Jesus—across the board. We cannot do so unless our faith shapes the politics of our lives.

Then, when made operative in the life of a person or community, we described the praxis of Christian spirituality as all of *the stories and symbols, perspectives and practices, prayers and patterns that, graced by the Holy Spirit, nurture people to live as disciples of Jesus for God's reign.* Again, this calls us to deliberately draw upon all our spiritual resources in ways that enable us to bring our faith and put it to work in the public square—nurturing in us a political spirituality.

To practice a spirsualty that does not prompt the works of justice and shape our ethical engagement in society will discourage the holiness and authenticity that is the intent of Christian faith. Conversely, we are unlikely to keep on with a commitment to justice without a political spirituality to sustain us.

PAUSE FOR REFLECTION

- How do you experience the hunger for justice in your heart? How do you respond in daily life?

- Reflect on the notion of a *political* spirituality. What are your first thoughts? Recognize what is shaping your perspective.

AN OLD TRADITION EXPANDED: WHY AND WHAT JUSTICE

Beyond Compassion to Justice: We have many times noted that Jesus understood the reign of God as the central purpose of his life. His perspective was shaped by his knowledge of the Israelite prophets and how the symbol was emerging in the Jewish consciousness of his time. As such, God's reign is to reflect the *shalom* of justice, peace, and well-being that God intends for all humankind and creation. Jesus preached and lived God's reign as a *tensive* symbol, proclaiming it as both personal and social, for now and for later, as gift and responsibility, to shape people's prayers and their politics, all toward realizing the fullness of life that God wills for all "on earth as in heaven."

Add to this Jesus's praxis of compassion for the least, the lost, and the last, his working miracles to feed the hungry, cure the sick, console the bereaved, and drive out evil. Remember again the inclusivity of his community of disciples, his modeling of respect for the dignity and equality of all people, and his description of how we will be judged (Matt 25:31–46). Such social praxis was what gave Jesus's first Christians a deep commitment to works of compassion, and not only for fellow Christians but for all in need.

Over time, such social commitment was epitomized in the practices that Christians developed under the heading of *Corporal* and *Spiritual* Works of Mercy. The tradition emerged of a sevenfold listing for both forms—pertaining to the body and the spirit. Then Pope Francis recently added an eighth work to each category to include mercy *toward creation*.

The listing of the eight *Corporal* Works of Mercy now reads: *to feed the hungry, give drink to the thirsty, shelter the homeless, clothe the naked, care for the sick, visit the imprisoned, bury the dead*, and *care for creation*.

The eight *Spiritual* Works of Mercy are: *to instruct the ignorant, counsel the doubtful, admonish sinners, bear wrongs patiently, forgive offenders, comfort the afflicted, pray for the living and the dead*, and *contemplate God's creation*.

Such works of compassion will always be central to living Christian faith. Over the past 125 years, however, Christians have raised their consciousness that their faith requires them to go beyond (while still fulfilling) direct acts of compassionate service, and to live and work for justice as well. This entails addressing the political causes of human suffering and working for sociocultural change toward justice and liberation for all.

Beginning with the first great social encyclical of Pope Leo XIII (*Rerum Novarum*, 1891), Christians' sense of sociopolitical responsibility has expanded and deepened. It is no longer enough to show compassion to those who suffer injustice—of whatever kind—we must resist and try to change the social structures and cultural mores that cause the injustice in the first place.

There were many contributing factors that expanded the social consciousness of Christians. Modern biblical studies helped to deepen awareness of the Bible's constant call to justice, especially by the Hebrew prophets. Likewise, increased focus on the historical Jesus highlights his opposition to all forms of social oppression and cultural exclusion. In this light, theologians began to embrace social and political concerns, recognizing more clearly the public nature of Christian faith. Various liberation theologies have emerged from struggles against cultural and social oppression (like racism, sexism, homophobia, unbridled capitalism). Such contemporary struggles prompt a rereading of the Bible and of Christian tradition, recognizing the "recessive genes" for justice that have been there all along—but long overlooked or underdeveloped.

In sum, we have come to recognize that both Scripture and Christian tradition are replete with what theologian Johann Baptist Metz calls "dangerous memories." These are stories and texts that challenge social oppression, disturb Christian complacency that settles for an oppressive status quo, and demand that we work for justice for all.

Add, too, the insights of the social sciences that lend greater understanding of how societies and cultures originate and work. Put simply, we have become more aware that our structures and mores did not "come down from heaven" but are human constructs. And just as we made them ourselves, we are capable of changing them toward greater justice for all.

In Catholic social teaching, that first great charter for justice, *Rerum Novarum*, was followed by a steady stream of papal encyclicals and local church documents that widen and deepen the demand on Christians to work for justice. One summary of this now established tradition was the statement that "justice is a constitutive aspect of the Gospel" ("Justice in the World," International Synod of Bishops, 1971). This insists that if Christian teaching, preaching, and praxis do not include a call to justice, then we do not represent the gospel of Jesus Christ. The Church now refers to such social teaching as *doctrine*—placing it atop the hierarchy of truths of Catholic faith.

This call to justice demands that Christians develop antennae that are alert for all instances of injustice and oppression. We need a *critical social consciousness* that can recognize the sources of injustice in cultural mores and public structures, including that of the church. And *awareness* is not enough; Christian social consciousness must prompt us *to act* on behalf of justice for all. Surely we need a *political* spirituality to nurture and sustain such commitment.

The United States Conference of Catholic Bishops offers a helpful sevenfold summary of what is now the Church's social doctrine. It calls for commitment: (1) to the *life and dignity of the human person*—from womb to tomb; (2) to promote the values of *family, community, and participation* in society; (3) to work for the human *rights and responsibilities* of all people; (4) to make an *option that favors the poor and vulnerable*; (5) to recognize and promote the *dignity of work* and *the rights of workers*; (6) to live in *solidarity with the whole human family*; and (7) to *care for God's creation*.

As we read such a listing, it is important that we see them as what the late great Archbishop of Chicago, Cardinal Joseph Bernardin (1928–96) named as a "seamless garment," with each one vital to a Christian commitment to justice. This calls us to work against every injustice, rather than championing some and neglecting others. Pope Francis reiterates this position of consistency when he writes, "Our defense of the innocent unborn needs to be clear, firm and passionate, for at stake is the dignity of human life which is always sacred….Equally sacred, however, are the lives of the poor, those already born, the destitute, the abandoned and underprivileged, the vulnerable infirm and elderly…the victims of human trafficking, of new forms of slavery, and every form of rejection" (*Gaudete et Exsultate* 101). In other words, our commitment to justice must reflect a consistent commitment for life—all across the board.

"Dangerous Memories" and Why Justice: Metz proposes that the most dangerous memories of all for Christians are the *Exodus* and *Calvary*. The Exodus, as we reviewed in chapter 2, reminds that ours is a God who can intervene in human history to set free those suffering oppression. Calvary, then, reflects God's solidarity with all people who suffer and are oppressed, with God's raising of Jesus as the assurance that no injustice can finally prevail. Those two great memories of God's work of liberating salvation within human history can always confront our own complacency and renew our commitment to the justice that God intends for all.

Beyond those two most "dangerous" ones, many other Scripture texts carry such memories. Here we could cite hundreds of compelling quotes, and especially from the prophetic tradition of Israel. For example, "the LORD is a God of justice" (Isa 30:18), "hates" injustice (61:8), and ever opposes oppression and discrimination against "the alien, the orphan, and the widow" (Jer 7:6). The latter is the biblical triad of those who deserve special favor by way of justice. Indeed, worship without justice is "an abomination" before God, whereas true worship demands that we "seek justice, rescue the oppressed, defend the orphan, plead for the widow" (Isa 1:17).

Of the numerous biblical texts that demand the works of justice, none is more compelling than that of Micah 6:1–8. Bible scholars have well portrayed Micah 6:8—the climatic verse—as a summary of the whole prophetic tradition of Israel. However, the context of 6:8 is instructive as well. Beginning in Micah 6:1, it is as if Yahweh puts Israel on trial for its failures to live with justice; the text represents Yahweh as both the plaintiff and prosecutor. God calls the mountains and foundations of the earth as witnesses. God accuses the Israelites of *forgetting*—forgetting especially the dangerous memory of how God freed them from slavery in Egypt.

Israel does not deny the charges but tries, as it were, to buy off the prosecutor, to settle with the plaintiff out of court. God must have a price that can be paid instead of fulfilling the demand for justice; for example, offerings of year-old calves, of thousands of rams, of streams of oil. Israel even wonders if sacrificing its "first born" might placate God (how desperate!). Then, in verse 8, it is as if God looks out over the head of Israel and addresses all humankind as well. "This, O Human-kind is what Yahweh asks of you, only this: to act justly, to love tenderly, and to walk humbly with your God" (Mic 6:8; JB trans.). And scripture scholars note that this triad— of justice, love, and humility—is to work together as one.

Turning to the New Testament, again we could cite many texts and Jesus's clarion call to the reign of *shalom* that God intends for humankind and all creation. However, there is no more summary text for justice than Luke's description (4:14–21) of how Jesus launched his public ministry in the synagogue at Nazareth on a Sabbath day. We already reviewed it (chapter 4) as summarizing all the central themes of Jesus's public ministry; this time, note afresh the politics for justice that Jesus was championing.

Luke says that after Jesus's forty days of struggle and temptation "in the wilderness" (4:1), he was "filled with the power of the Spirit" and "returned to Galilee" (v. 14). Then, on a Sabbath day, Jesus came "as was his custom" (v. 16) to his home synagogue at Nazareth. He was called upon to read and was handed "the scroll of the prophet Isaiah" (v. 17). Jesus unrolled the scroll and searched for the text of Isaiah 61:1–2a to which he would also add, on his feet, an echo from Isaiah 58:6—he must have known it by heart. And then he read, "The Spirit of the Lord is upon me, because he has anointed me to bring good news to the poor. He has sent me to proclaim release to the captives and recovery of sight to the blind, to let the oppressed go free [insert from Isa 58:6], to proclaim the year of the Lord's favor" (Luke 4:18–19).

This last reference is to a Jubilee Year, the fiftieth after seven times seven, a great yearlong Sabbath that mandated the people to let the *land lie fallow, forgive all debts,* and *set free the slaves* (see Lev 25:10–12). Walter Brueggemann, a great Hebrew scripture scholar, says that with this selection from Isaiah, Jesus chose the most radical social justice text he could have found in the Hebrew Scriptures.

Luke says that Jesus "rolled up the scroll, gave it back to the atten-dant, and sat down. The eyes of all in the synagogue were fixed on him" (4:20). Then Jesus made a most dramatic claim, "Today this scripture has been fulfilled in your hearing" (v. 21). Of course, the injustices he listed are still all too prevalent in our world. Yet, because the Spirit has "anointed" (in Hebrew, *messiah*) Jesus for this divine mission of liberating salvation, no injustice can finally prevail. And as long as Christians "fix our eyes"—and hearts—on Jesus, the more likely we are to live for justice as well.

What Justice? All justice is *social*. Yet it can help to distinguish the many levels and forms of justice that Christian faith demands and that a political spiritualty helps to sustain. Its various expressions make the point that justice is a holistic affair, to be realized at every level of relationship—interpersonal, communal, social, and ecological. From the tradition of Western thought, beginning with Aristotle, we can distinguish three types of justice: *commutative*, *distributive*, and *social*. To this I add the renewed concept of *restorative* justice, a summary portrayal of *biblical* justice, and a reiteration of the Church's own need to practice *transitional* justice. The latter is urgent at this time regarding the sexual crimes committed by clergy against children and young adults.

Commutative justice demands honesty in all of our personal relationships, fairness in all dealings between persons or groups. This one-on-one kind of justice is, of course, a necessary foundation for all other forms. Without honesty and truth-telling in people's personal lives, no real justice can be achieved at any level.

Distributive justice requires society to ensure that its social goods—cultural legacy, economic wealth, and political power—are fairly distributed so that all have sufficient for their needs as human beings. This includes access to a good education, to adequate health care, to have dignified work and a living wage.

Social justice, strictly speaking, reflects the responsibility of every society to create structures that protect the dignity of all its citizens and that allow everyone to participate as they desire in the public realm.

Restorative justice is an emerging concept and practice. Biblically inspired, it stands in contrast to the *punitive justice* of our standard legal systems. The latter simply punishes offenders with no attempt at making amends on their part or to redress the suffering of those wronged. Restorative justice proposes that all parties to a conflict or offense come together to resolve collectively how to deal with the aftermath. Perpetrators have the opportunity to admit what they did wrong, to ask forgiveness of their victims, and to make reparation. Victims have their harm or loss recognized and amends made—if possible. With the mediation of such justice, forgiveness may result for offenders. The work of the *Truth and Reconciliation Commission* of South Africa is a notable instance of restorative justice in recent time.

Biblical Justice: For a long time, Christians understood biblical justice simply as sinners being punished for their sins. Now contemporary scholarship makes clear that Bible justice is about establishing right relationship with God, self, others, and creation. As noted earlier, such *right relationship* is the biblical description of both justice and holiness, reflecting the symbiosis between the spiritual and political.

For the Bible, the "rightness" of right relationship is modeled on God's covenant with us. This means that there is a largess, a munificence to God's justice. The image is not of the blind Lady Justice giving "everyone their due" (Aristotle) or "being fair" (John Rawls), but is more like the graciousness of a compassionate mother. Note that the Hebrew Bible term for *compassion*, so often attributed to God, is *rachum*, which is also the word for the womb of a mother. God's justice has the generosity of a mother's womb, granting all we need for nurture and well-being.

As with Jesus, biblical justice has a special favor for "the poor" because God favors those who need the favor most. This awareness has led the Catholic Church to urge a "preferential option for the poor"; as always, the covenant calls us to imitate our Divine Partner. And biblical justice is symbiotic with *peace*. As the Prophet Isaiah well insisted, "The effect of righteousness [justice] will be peace" (32:17).

To this biblical sense of a generous justice, the Christian gospel adds the spirit of *agape*—empathic love that does not count the cost or depend on reciprocity. In sum, *Christian faith demands a munificent justice permeated with generous love.*

For the Church's call to the works of justice to be credible, it must give such witness within its own structures, practicing what it preaches. As *Justice in the World*, the 1971 document from the Second Synod of Bishops, stated perceptively, "While the Church is bound to give witness to justice, she recognizes that anyone who ventures to speak to people about justice must first be just in their eyes." Currently this poses an enormous challenge, and especially apropos the clergy sex abuse scandal and its cover-up, now clearly seen as a systemic injustice within the Church and worldwide.

As elaborated in chapter 7 and worth repeating briefly, it is imperative that the Catholic Church move immediately to "transitional justice" regarding sex abuse by its clergy—the transition being from an ecclesial structure that allowed it to one that prevents it. With at least five aspects, such transitional justice requires the following: (1) that the Church must reach into and root out the causes of such horrendous crimes; (2) that it compensate and help care for the victim/survivors; (3) that it have total truth-telling in the public forum, including reporting all cases to the civil authorities for prosecution; (4) that it memorialize the suffering of the victims and their families to help prevent its recurrence; (5) that it put in place programs of prevention and structures of governance that prevent it from happening again. At this most difficult time, it would seem that the very credibility of the Church's teaching and witness for justice is greatly compromised unless it practices such transitional justice.

PAUSE FOR REFLECTION

- Do you recognize the works of justice as being demanded by discipleship to Jesus? Why or why not?

- How has this review of the categories expanded your understanding of justice? What are some implications?

- Choose one particular demand for justice within your own context at this time. How will you respond?

POLITICAL SPIRITUALITY: PRAYER, PRAXIS, AND PARTICIPATION

Here I propose three forms of spiritual practice that can heighten political consciousness and our commitment to justice. The first is to deliberately *pray* in ways that encourage as much. The second is to engage in a specific Christian *praxis* of justice, doing so in ways that heighten *consciousness* and *action* (both). The third is to *participate* in some form of politics that is effective for the common good of all.

Praying with Commitment to Justice: In response to the question, "What is prayer?", the *Baltimore Catechism* (1885) offered what became a classic definition: "Prayer is the lifting up of our minds and hearts to God, to *adore* Him, to *thank* Him for His benefits, to ask His *forgiveness*, and to beg of Him all the *graces* we need whether for soul or body" (emphasis added). So, as a "lifting up of our minds and hearts to God," prayer is traditionally seen as fourfold: (1) to express worship and adoration to God, (2) to thank God for our blessings, (3) to ask forgiveness for our sins, and (4) to request the graces we need—"whether for soul or body."

All four of those expressions of personal prayer can be intentionally shaped to nurture a spirituality for justice. So, we can *praise* God for the reign of *shalom* that God intends for humankind and creation, hoping that by recognizing justice as God's vision for all will help encourage the same in our own hearts and lives. We can *thank* God for the many works of justice that are constantly realized in our world and for the measure of justice that we experience ourselves; such gratitude can deepen commitment. We can and should ask God's *forgiveness* for our failures to work for justice and likewise for our complicity in systems of injustice and oppressive cultural practices; none of us stand on fully innocent ground regarding justice. And we should surely *ask* God's grace to sustain our commitment to justice at every level. So to consciously "raise our minds and hearts" to a God of justice can encourage our own commitment likewise. To so pray will nurture our political spirituality.

Beyond these traditional modes of personal prayer, we can also practice the rich Christian traditions of meditation and contemplation in ways that help raise political consciousness and commitment to justice. As noted earlier, an easy distinction is to think of meditation as *talking* to God and contemplation as *listening* to God.

The *Catechism of the Catholic Church* describes meditation as "above all a quest…in order to adhere and respond to what the Lord is asking" (no. 2705). So meditation is talking to God in order to discern how best to live as a person of God; this surely entails fulfilling God's mandate of justice. We can craft our conversations with God to help us imagine how to live and promote justice, and with politics effective to this good end.

Then, the *Catechism* likens *contemplation*, quoting the great mystic St. Teresa of Avila (1515–82), as "a close sharing between friends" (no. 2709) and as "God's relationship within our hearts" (no. 2713). For contemplation, our posture is to be more one of listening than talking, opening our hearts to welcome what God is revealing to us personally. Again, if we listen deliberately with our hearts to our God of justice, the consciousness that ensues will surely encourage commitment to live likewise.

So both mediation and contemplation as well as traditional modes of prayer, when suffused with a commitment to justice, can help sustain us to live in right and loving relationship with God, self, others, and creation. We need such prayer to nourish a political spirituality toward justice for all.

Praxis for Justice: We noted already a contemporary retrieval of the ancient term *praxis*—going back to Aristotle. It is helpful here precisely because it includes both *doing* and *reflecting*, whereas *practice* typically refers to action alone. A spirituality to sustain commitment to justice needs both concrete practice and reflection on what one is doing and what is being done in the political realm, all in order to imagine what should get done for justice sake. Let us focus first on the *practice* of justice, and then on the need for *reflection* upon the sociopolitical conditions that cause injustice in the first place.

In recent years, many Catholic parishes, schools, and colleges have mounted programs of "service learning" (by some such name). These bring people into direct encounter with those in need and with situations of injustice. There is ample evidence now that such immediate social action has transformative potential for participants. This should not surprise. As the Bible attests, God's presence is particularly palpable amongst the poor and oppressed; remember Matthew 25: "*I* was hungry and you gave *me* food," etc..

The key for such faith-based service is to find some works of compassion and justice that have personal appeal or are a particular need in one's social context, and to directly participate in them. To encounter through service those suffering poverty or injustice of any kind helps to nurture our political spirituality. Now let us turn to the *reflective* aspect of praxis, so crucial to maximize the potential of service work and programs to encourage a spirituality for justice.

Works of faith-based service will deepen our commitment all the more *if* we reflect critically upon our action and on the political context that causes the need. As noted previously, *critically* does not mean *negatively* but rather with discernment. To reflect critically from a faith perspective is integral to a political spirituality that nurtures commitment to justice.

A critical social consciousness calls us first to recognize and then to analyze the causes of any particular instance of injustice. We are more likely to come to social awareness if we reflect both *contextually* and historically. Thinking *contextually* requires that we recognize the structures involved in a problematic situation, the cultural values (or disvalues) at work, the networks of power that contribute to it, and then to imagine what to do for justice sake. Such contextual thinking is done most readily around a particular issue, and best of all in a community of conversation. Take, for example, climate change.

Just imagine the huge network of industries and conglomerates that are causing negative climate change and destroying the earth's soil, water, air, and the ozone layer over it all. Likewise, consider the cultural disvalues involved, like greed and unlimited profit, even a hard-hearted denial of global warming. When one prayerfully brings a Christian faith perspective to this issue, we remember that God has gifted us with this amazing and beautiful creation and commissioned us to be its good stewards (Gen 2:15). Such analysis from a faith perspective, and particularly when done in conversation with concerned others, can deepen our commitment to preserving our environment.

Thinking *historically*, then, invites us to uncover the *history* behind a particular injustice or oppression—what has produced it over time. From the routine of everyday life, we tend to settle for present arrangements as "given"—as if the status quo is as it should be. Invariably, when we examine the story behind a social justice issue, we detect historical roots and causes. And since people produced it over time, we can help to change it in our time. While history cannot be undone, we can work to rectify its negative legacies.

For example, the exclusion of women from leadership in the Catholic Church betrays the inclusivity of Jesus's original community. Clearly, the Church succumbed to the ethos of its historical context, and the latter, for most of the past two thousand years, excluded women from owning property and from all trades and professions. As recently as 1898, the state legislature of Massachusetts passed a law forbidding admission of women to the medical schools of Boston, claiming that they did not have the emotional stability to be doctors.

Instead of resisting such injustice, the Church embraced it and found Scripture quotes to legitimate it (the Bible, too, reflects its context). Now that we can recognize the historical roots of sexism, Christians must wholeheartedly embrace the radical inclusivity that Jesus modeled. Likewise, we must work for the Church to recognize the full equality of women with men, reflecting this in its structures of ministry and leadership.

It can take time and research to analyze instances of injustice and their history. In immediate circumstances, it can help to ask some ready-at-hand questions. To this end, Peter Henriot and Joseph Holland suggest that of every justice issue and its political context we can ask three revealing questions: *Who decides? Who benefits? Who suffers?* Though simple queries, they can prompt deep social analysis and raise our consciousness and commitment toward justice.

Participate in Politics: Any way that we can make our voices heard for justice's sake in the public realm can be labeled political. We can put our politics to work in our immediate neighborhood, in our local municipality, in our state, or at the national level. Most obviously, this includes the politicians we support and choose to vote for. From recent national elections, there is ample data to indicate that the voting patterns of American Evangelical Christians is deeply shaped by their faith but to favor more conservative political positions, with no commitment apparent to social justice. Mainline Christians must also bring their justice concerns and commitment to the ballot box.

Choosing what politicians to vote for calls for prayerful discernment. It is difficult to find the perfect candidate—one whose politics is totally in keeping with Christian social teaching, all across the board. However, the United States Conference of Catholic Bishops, in their

Forming Conscience for Faithful Citizenship directive (revised 2015), makes clear that the voting choice of Catholics need not be determined by any single issue. Rather, it requires weighing how a politician's negative position on one issue may be offset by their positive position on others. As the Catholic bishops advise, Christians must exercise "prudential judgment" and weigh all the variables to let their faith guide what politicians they vote for and support.

Then, political engagement for justice should go far beyond our voting pattern. We can participate in a movement, lobby group, or organization that promotes good social causes. Such organized efforts need not be overtly political nor explicitly Christian and yet contribute significantly to the realization of justice. I think immediately of organizations like Bread for the Word, Doctors without Borders, Oxfam, Partners in Health. And there are literally hundreds of organizations working against poverty, to end social discrimination, and to preserve the environment. We are more likely to continue in the struggle if we choose organizations with causes that appeal to us personally.

All of such *prayer*, *praxis*, and *participation* in politics amounts to a political spirituality that helps nurture and sustain our commitment to justice.

HOPE FOR OUR HEARTS

Our hearts have a hunger for justice and it requires the heart to sustain such commitment. Of course, we need the critical discernment and social analysis as outlined above. Yet, what keeps us going for justice *is* our hearts. When we have a felt sense of "suffering with" (*com-passio*) people in need or who suffer injustice, we are more likely to respond to their plight. Likewise, our hearts can enable us to "feel with" (*em-pathos*) people who are victims of discrimination or oppression. Compassion and empathy of heart help us to crossover and, as it were, to "walk in the shoes" of the victims of injustice. This encourages solidarity with them.

It seems more imperative than ever in our postmodern era that Christians move beyond a privatized faith and commit to the works of justice in their public realm. This is because we have both the means to know what is unfolding (24-hour news and extraordinary information technology) and likewise the capacity to literally destroy our world; we had neither of these before.

And though we may flatter ourselves in being enlightened, yet old hatreds, bitterness, extremism, division, and greed can raise their ugly heads as readily as ever. It betrays our faith to embrace a political fatalism that settles for the way things are. Though justice requires a long and determined struggle, it can be achieved, if only in slow and inch-by-inch steps. By God's grace, we can always be agents of social transformation for justice.

Christians need to remember that to work for justice is not a matter of philanthropy on our part, nor simply a civic duty. Nor is it only the work of social activists, people who relish being involved in the public sphere. Our motivation is that justice for all *is the law of God*, with Jesus as the model of living for God's reign that disciples must follow. So it is precisely Christian faith that keeps our feet to the fire of justice. Having a politically conscious spirituality can sustain such *living* faith.

We noted earlier the proposal of Johan Baptist Metz that Christians can find in the texts and traditions of Christian faith the *dangerous memories* needed to prompt commitment to justice. However, our hearts will also find motivation by recalling a *dangerous memory* from our own life narrative or from the stories of our immediate family and people.

Most likely all of us have personally experienced injustice of some kind. It will help to recall those encounters and to let them become *dangerous memories* for our political spiritualty. They can challenge us not to settle for a status quo that allows injustice and confront us with our collaboration therein. Personal dangerous memories—as well as the great justice memories of Christian faith—can help to renew commitment when flagging, and to keep on in *living* faith that does justice.

PAUSE FOR REFLECTION

- Think back over your own life or the history of your people. Can you recognize a *dangerous memory* that might inspire your commitment to justice?

- Dwell again in the memory. What status quo or personal complacency does it challenge? How can it inspire you to live justly and work for justice for all?

SPIRITUAL PRACTICE: COMMIT TO A FAVORITE CAUSE

There are oh-so-many issues concerning justice in our societies and cultures. It is simply not possible to take on them all. So a wise spiritual practice is to choose and commit to a particular cause that has personal appeal, like the struggle against sexism or racism, or the need for low-cost housing and a livable minimum wage, or the imperative that all receive a good education (there is high correlation between poor education and incarceration). Your choice might well be suggested by your personal *dangerous memory* or by a pressing issue in your local context. Then commit to that cause at every level of your existence—personal, communal, and sociopolitical.

As suggested earlier, it will help if you join forces with other people of like mind who are engaged in your particular cause. Remember, too, to ask God for the grace you need to keep on in your commitment. And, as we previously noted, when working for the reign of God, even small efforts can be a seed that produces a large tree, or yeast that raises up a huge quantity of dough (see Luke 13:8–21). By God's grace, our efforts can produce up to "a hundredfold" (Matt 13:8) for justice.

FOR FURTHER READING

DeBerri, Edward P., James E. Hug, Peter J. Henriot, Michael J. Schultheis. *Catholic Social Teaching: Our Best Kept Secret*. 4th ed. Maryknoll, NY: Orbis, 2003. A fine review and summary of Catholic social teaching, beginning with *Rerum Novarum* (1891) and down to 2003.

Holland, Joe, and Peter Henriot. *Social Analysis: Linking Faith and Justice*. Rev. ed. Maryknoll, NY: Orbis, 1983. A helpful handbook on developing a sociopolitical consciousness that links faith and justice.

Pope Francis. *Laudato Si': On Care for Our Common Home*. Rome: Libreria Editrice Vaticana, 2015. Pope Francis's clarion call to develop environmental stewardship as an integral aspect of *living* Christian faith.

Postlude

Growing in Faith by Giving It Away

Like Sowing a Seed

Maureen, a student in one of my courses, mentioned in passing that both of her sisters are also working in pastoral ministry. Before moving on to discuss her thesis essay, I paused and wondered aloud how her parents had been so effective in sowing the seeds of faith—in all three of their daughters' souls. I needed to learn from her success!

First, Maureen explained that her mother was a single mom, and then told of how she had taken them to Mass every Sunday and involved them in parish catechesis and youth programs. But lots of parents do as much and we don't have such success, so I still wondered, "Yes, but what was key to her sowing the seed so effectively?"

After some more reminiscing, Maureen excitedly announced, "Oh, I think I know," and went on to explain. Her mom worked two jobs to raise her three children. Yet no matter how tired she was, every night before they went to bed, she would take each daughter, individually, in her arms for a hug. Her closing ritual was to look them in the eye and say, "God loves you, I love you, and Jesus is your best friend." This took no more than a minute or two with each child. Yet Maureen and I agreed, that nightly ritual was most likely how her mom had sown the seed of faith in her and her sisters.

ALL CHRISTIANS TO EVANGELIZE

The early Christian communities understood evangelization as *sowing* the initial seeds of faith, while catechesis was *growing* those seeds with more in-depth instruction and formation. Christians need both sowing and growing to sustain a lifelong journey into *living* faith. Here, however, we will focus on the *sowing* because it is the responsibility of every Christian. Planting the initial seed typically requires some intentional move by a person of faith; it is much like the common cold—caught from someone who has it already. For families, the seed is most likely sown by its faith practices; they can be as simple as the night ritual of Maureen's mom with her daughters.

Catholics, at least, have typically thought of evangelization as the work of missionaries sent from faith communities to faraway places and people who have not yet heard the gospel. However, the Second Vatican Council began a great broadening of evangelization, insisting that every Christian person and community has a responsibility to share their faith with others, and likewise that all of us need ongoing evangelization. The genius of this "new" evangelization is that our efforts to share Christian faith will help to grow our own.

The mandate for all Christians to share their faith goes back to that great commission that the risen Christ gave to the little remnant community on a hillside in Galilee (check again Matt 28:18–20). Note well that the mandate was given to all there present; in other words, the responsibility to evangelize lies with every disciple and with every Christian community; it comes with baptism. As Pope Francis summarized in his well-named exhortation *Evangelii Gaudium* ("The Joy of the Gospel"), "Each Christian and every community must go forth to reach all in need of the Gospel" (*EG* 20). Or to cite again his compelling phrase, all Christians are called to be "missionary disciples" (no. 120).

Note, too, in that commission to the first Christian community, the risen Christ mandated that they "evangelize" *and* "teach," to both sow and grow the seeds of faith. Now every Christian is not directly involved in teaching the faith in a formal way, for example, as a parish catechist or school religious educator. However, baptism commissions *every* Christian to evangelize, to help sow the seeds of faith in the lives of others, and this as needed to nurture one's own.

As explained in chapter 9, faith is first in the ever-circulating flow among the great triad of virtues—with *faith* grounding *hope* to be realized through *love* that flows back into *living* faith. Their symbiosis means that to share either one of the three is to encourage the other two as well. In any given circumstance we can discern what is most needed—a word of love, of hope, or of faith—confident that with any one, we are nurturing all three. And we have nothing more valuable to share with others. Note well how more life-giving it is to share a seed of faith rather than doubt, of hope rather than despair, of love rather than hatred. With the help of the Holy Spirit, we can all be instruments of God's grace to sow such seeds in the hearts of others.

Oftentimes what we sow may seem very small, perhaps a passing word of faith, hope, or love into a person's life, especially when needed. In Mark's Gospel, Jesus's encouraging parable of the mustard seed that can grow into a tree (4:30–32) follows after one of a farmer who simply scatters seeds and they grow of themselves, "he does not know how" (4:26–29). In other words, we are responsible for sowing the seeds; as St. Paul echoed wisely, some plant, others water, but it is "only God who gives the growth" (1 Cor 3:7).

Given our responsibility to be evangelizers of *living* Christian faith, the two pressing questions are *what* seeds to sow and *how* to intentionally sow them.

PAUSE FOR REFLECTION

- Think back if you can to who first planted the seed of Christian faith in your life. How did they do so? What can you learn from the memory?

- What do you recognize as the core of Christian faith—the seed that can become a large tree? Imagine how to share it as good news with others.

WHAT FAITH TO SHARE:
THE GOOD NEWS OF JESUS, THE CHRIST

We sow more effectively the more convinced we are that Christian faith is deeply life-giving, that it reflects the best good news ever heard, the greatest story ever told. No one in our time has encouraged this positive approach to evangelizing more than Pope Francis. Instead of being like people who have just "come back from a funeral" (*EG* 10), Christians must enter into "the joy of evangelizing" (no. 13). We must reflect *good news* instead of appearing "like sourpusses"—the bearers of bad news (no. 88).

Note, too, the Church's increased awareness that evangelizing is not to be simply of individual persons. As reviewed in chapter 10, Christians must bring gospel values into their public life as well. As Pope Paul VI so well taught in *Evangelli Nuntiandi* (1975, in English "The Evangelization of Peoples"), Christians must integrate the gospel of "liberating salvation" into "every strata of society," helping to renew humanity "from within" (*EN* 9, 16). Rather than focusing only on bringing nonbelievers into the Church, the new evangelization intends to bring Christians out of the Church and into the world with a *living* faith that helps to transform their social contexts and promote the values of God's reign. Going out into the world with such values may be the best way to attract people into the Church.

So, *what* faith to share in evangelization and catechesis? The comprehensive answer to be realized eventually is all of Christian faith as mediated through its Scripture and Tradition. At least over time, people deserve to have access to the whole Christian Story as a grand narrative of God's liberating salvation in Jesus, mediated now in myriad different ways—through scriptures, sacraments, and symbols, through dogmas and doctrines, values and virtues, and so on.

Following on, every instance of the Christian Story should be presented as prophetic, as calling people to live faithfully into their covenant with God as disciples of Jesus. It is not just an "old" story from times past but an ever-fresh invitation and challenge for now. In other words, there is always a Vision to the Christian Story, a prophetic challenge to live into the responsibilities and possibilities that discipleship to Jesus demands of and offers to people's lives.

Sharing the whole Story/Vision of Christian faith, however, is something that religious educators and catechists are to do over time, with scope and sequence that is appropriate to age level, sociocultural context, and so on. It surely cannot—and should not—be attempted in the initial evangelization that sows the first seeds of faith. So what might be at the heart of the faith that Christians are to share, the first and most attractive seed to entice people to grow the whole tree?

Here, Pope Francis gives wise counsel to evangelizers: "To actually reach everyone without exception or exclusion, the message has to concentrate on the essentials, on what is most beautiful, most grand, most appealing and at the same time most necessary" (*EG* 35). What, then, is "most beautiful, most grand, most appealing" about Christian faith? Or, we might ask, what is its "canon within the canon"—its defining core that permeates and guides our understanding of every other aspect?

The imperative response, of course, is "Jesus, the Christ." As noted in the prelude of this work, the centrality of Jesus is a growing awareness for many Catholic Christians. The polemics of the Reformation shunted Catholics to emphasize the dogmas and doctrines of their faith, its rules and regulations, the authority of its leaders, especially the pope. Though important, none of these are the core. Here I cite again the summary statement from the *Catechism* regarding Christian faith: "At the heart we find a Person, the Person of Jesus of Nazareth, the only Son from the Father" (*CCC* 426). And note again the dual emphasis; evangelizing needs to represent both "the Jesus of history" *and* the "Christ of faith."

So, evangelizers must share the story and stories of Jesus, that carpenter from Nazareth turned teacher, who walked the roads of Galilee, announcing the inbreaking of God's reign of unconditional love, mercy, compassion, justice, and peace. We can share stories of his working miracles to feed the hungry, cure the sick, comfort the sorrowing, and drive out evil. We can tell of how he welcomed everyone to the table, insisted on the dignity of all people, and his full inclusion of women among his core community of disciples. And we must tell again the stories that he told—the prodigal son, the Good Samaritan, the persistent widow, and

more. As we share the Jesus story, we must raise up its vision as well—
how it calls us to live as disciples for God's reign. And we must ever
craft our presentation to engage the hungers of people's hearts.

Likewise, we are to share the story of the Christ of faith, the One
who was God among us as one of ourselves, revealing *who* our God is
and *how* God is for us with unconditional love. We must witness to our
conviction that by Jesus's life, death, and resurrection, God has effected
humankind's liberating salvation, freeing us from overpowering sin and
evil, even from death. And we must raise up the vision that Jesus's paschal mystery brings to people's lives, encouraging them to experience
the enduring hope it offers to all in every circumstance.

Even as we share the story/vision of Jesus Christ as the heart of
Christian faith, it will be most persuasive for evangelization if we can
filter it through our own faith story and vision. As we personally appropriate and make our own the stories of Jesus and the hope that the risen
Christ means for our lives, we are all the more likely to plant the seeds
of faith effectively. There is nothing more persuasive than a personal
faith narrative of embracing Jesus Christ into one's life.

The *General Directory for Catechesis* well summarizes that the
intent of all evangelization is "to put people in communion and intimacy with Jesus Christ (*GDC* 80). However, this is not a warm, fuzzy
feeling toward Jesus but demands "full and sincere adherence to his
person and the decision to walk in his footsteps" (no. 53). Our own
story of Christian faith must include a prophetic vision to so live.

Because the gospel of Jesus Christ is such *good news*, we can
approach its evangelizing with an apologetics of persuasion. As admitted already, there have been times, indeed, when the Church used a
coercive apologetic, appealing solely to its teaching authority and
demanding unquestioning assent. But in our time we need to mount a
persuasive apologetic that invites people to *see for themselves* the truths
and wisdom—the treasure—of Christian faith and freely decide to
embrace it as good news for their lives. Again, as Pope Francis advises
on this point, we should never "impose the truth but appeal to [peo-
ple's] freedom" (*EG* 165).

Such persuasion requires evangelizers to be deeply convinced
that "we have a treasure of life and love which cannot deceive, and a

message that cannot mislead or disappoint" (*EG* 265). As Pope Francis repeats often, in Jesus we can recognize our God as One "of infinite tenderness" and mercy (no. 275). Sharing with people the story/vision of a God of tenderness and mercy as revealed in Jesus is the heart of Christian evangelizing.

PAUSE FOR REFLECTION

- When you think about your own faith, is Jesus Christ the very "heart" of it all? If not, what adjustments might you need to make?

- As you imagine sowing seeds of Christian faith in some particular person, how might you craft the conversation?

A LIFE TO FAITH TO LIFE CONVERSATION

When we begin to imagine *how* to share our faith effectively, we can well recall the often-quoted phrase attributed to St. Francis, "Preach the Gospel at all times; when necessary, use words." The best source of evangelization will always be our own *living* faith. Yet we are also called to evangelize by human discourse. This is best crafted as a *conversation*, with all the give and take, questioning and sharing, listening and responding that a good conversation entails.

When crafting a conversation to sow seeds of Christian faith, only *you* can discern when to engage in explicit faith talk and when to be more subtle, perhaps with a word of hope or love for now. Often there is need for *preevangelization* that asks questions or tells stories that turn people toward the hungers of their hearts. We can prepare the ground for the seed of faith by developing trust, asking soul-engaging questions, listening well, and always showing deep respect for a person's own faith journey.

Life to Faith to Life: Whatever the circumstance, I propose that we can find a powerful model in *Jesus's way* of evangelizing. In the prologue, we highlighted Jesus's conversation with the Samaritan woman at the well (John 4) as an instance of his pedagogy. Here I elaborate his evangelizing as inviting people "from *life to Faith to life* (in faith). We can portray Jesus's *life to Faith to life* approach as unfolding in five distinguishable movements. Though they are often subtle in Jesus's praxis, we can detect an overall pattern. I call them "movements" because they are fluid rather than lockstep; yet, for clarity, I lay them out here as sequential.

Movement One: Beginning with Life. The historical Jesus most often began his evangelizing by turning people to look at some experience, practice, issue, or concern in their daily lives. So, he could refer to catching and sorting fish, or a farmer sowing seed, or a day laborer digging in a field, or a merchant in search of fine pearls, or a vineyard owner hiring workers, or a woman pleading with a judge, or a traveler going down from Jerusalem to Jericho, or a woman baking bread or losing a coin, or just the birds of the air or the lilies of the field or the buds on a tree, and the list goes on and on. All of his some forty parables and twenty metaphors somehow engaged people's daily lives, initiating his pedagogy with what the great educator Paulo Freire called people's own *realidad* in the world.

Movement Two: Reflecting Critically on Life. While Jesus began with people's own lives, he regularly encouraged them to question their attitudes and taken-for-granted assumptions, often to "see" in a whole new way. So the Samaritan becomes the neighbor, the prodigal is welcomed home, workers who began at day's end are paid the same as those who worked all day, and Lazarus goes "to be with Abraham" while the rich man goes to "Hades" (Luke 16:19–31). Much of his evangelizing, especially by parables, called for such in-depth reflection, appealing to the hungers of people's hearts while encouraging a much more discerning perspective on their lives in the world.

Movement Three: Teaching his Gospel. Then, into the midst of people's own reality, Jesus proclaimed his gospel and the inbreaking of God's reign *now*. From the beginning of his public ministry, he did so "with authority" (Mark 1:27). Jesus was far from being just a discussion leader. That God must come to reign in people's lives and world, as noted many times, was the central commitment of Jesus's life; he taught and witnessed to this gospel with great authority and, as events proved, at grave risk to himself.

Movement Four: To See for Themselves. Jesus's constant invitation was for people to come to live as disciples by *the way* he taught and modeled. His clear intent was that would-be disciples *come to see for themselves* and embrace with conviction the good news of his gospel. His call to discipleship was ever by invitation, leaving people free to discern and decide for themselves.

Movement Five: Decision for Discipleship. The intended outcome of Jesus's evangelizing was always that people respond to his overall invitation "Come follow me" and choose to live as disciples for God's reign. Many so decided and many did not.

Sometimes Jesus would appear to have done all the movements of *life to Faith to life* in just a one-verse parable. For example: "Look at the birds of the air [movement 1]; they neither sow nor reap nor gather into barns [movement 2], and yet your heavenly Father feeds them [movement 3]. Are you not of more value than they?" [movements 4 and 5; Matt 6:26]. However, Jesus's way of crafting an evangelizing conversation is writ large in the modeling of the risen Christ on the Road to Emmaus. Let us turn briefly to that text, Luke 24:13–34, to observe the Master Evangelist at work—and to learn from him.

The Road to Emmaus: Two disciples (Cleopas is named, v. 18; his companion was most likely his wife, Mary, see John 19:25) are departing Jerusalem for Emmaus on Easter Sunday morning, too traumatized to recognize their new traveling companion. Instead of introducing himself, however, the Stranger is content to *accompany* them along the way; Pope Francis often speaks of *accompaniment* as the ideal style of evangelizers.

The Stranger inquires what they are talking about in such a lively fashion. When they hesitate, incredulous that anyone would not know of the tragic events that had just taken place in Jerusalem, he asks, "What things?" (Luke 24:19). What an amazing pedagogical move since no one knew better than he; his clear intent was to turn them to look at, name, and reflect upon their own painful reality. They proceed to tell him their story of "the things about Jesus of Nazareth" (v. 19), how he was crucified, and they share their shattered vision: "We had hoped that he was the one to redeem Israel" (movements 1 and 2, v. 21).

Only now does the Stranger proceed to share with them the Story and Vision of their faith community. "Beginning with Moses and all the prophets, he interpreted to them the things about himself in all the scriptures" (v. 27) and explained that "the Messiah should suffer these things and then enter into his glory" (movement 3, v. 26).

At this point in what proves to be a daylong conversation, their own painful story and shattered vision and the Story and Vision of their faith community are accessed into the conversation. Yet the Stranger still does not tell them what to see. Clearly he wants them to come to see for themselves as if this is essential to renewing their battered faith and lending renewed hope.

The recognition comes with their offer of hospitality and the Stranger's acceptance; a friendship has emerged out of the conversation, a sense of community. As the three sit at table, regarding the bread, the Stranger *takes*, *blesses*, *breaks*, and *gives* it to them (the same four verbs as at the Last Supper). With this their eyes are opened, and they recognize the One in their midst. They have integrated their own story/vision with the Story/Vision of their faith community and come to a deep level of personal *recognition* (the Greek there, *epiginosko*, reflects the bond between friends) (movement 4).

Whereupon the risen Christ vanishes from their sight. Why vanish now? Was *his* work here complete with their "coming to see" for themselves—and many more Emmaus roads awaited? Amazed at how he had set their "hearts burning" with the evangelizing upon the road, the two disciples get up immediately and return to a renewed life of faith in the Jerusalem community. This would have been a hazardous journey at night; such recognition, however, becomes urgent to share (movement 5).

In Jerusalem, they rejoin the community of disciples, reassembling and now trying to get their heads and hearts around what is nigh unbelievable: that God had raised their Jesus from the dead. The two are greeted with, "The Lord has risen indeed, and he has appeared to Simon" (v. 34). So, a new story of faith is gathering, the Christian Story and its Vision of a risen Savior. While receiving this amazing *good news* from the community, the two from the road have their own faith narrative to share: "Then they told what had happened on the road, and how he had been made known to them in the breaking of the bread" (v. 35).

Their story, surely, was of how the risen Stranger had moved them *from life to Faith to life-in-faith.* The Holy Spirit continues the same good work today through the efforts of every Christian evangelizer.

CRAFTING THE CONVERSATION

We can now summarize the dynamics of a *life to Faith to life* (in faith) approach to evangelization. Let me reiterate that all education-in-faith must engage people's lives, and not simply as a pedagogical ploy but because their own experiences are an immediate source of God's presence and invitation to them. So beyond engaging people's interests (though imperative to do), turning them to "life" as an opening move in evangelizing encourages recognizing God's presence to them already and the mystical potential of their own lives in the world.

As a conversation among friends, a *life to Faith to life* approach will go back and forth and, indeed, will unfold with varied sequences. Yet the commitments that undergird each of the five movements outlined above can suggest our crafting of an evangelizing conversation, and especially the questions that carry it along. Let us imagine it as unfolding with one other person or a small group of people.

Movement 1: Begin the conversation by engaging what matters to people, the generative themes of their own lives. This can be the joys and sorrows, hopes and fears, and everyday concerns that occupy them. The key here is to appeal to their desires, to pose questions that turn people to the hungers of their hearts. This can be as simple as saying, "So tell me about yourself" or asking "What's going on for you?" or simply, "How are things?"

Movement 2: As the conversation unfolds, invite them to go deeper, to probe their life issues, to bring their reason, memory, and imagination to reflect on their present reality around the conversation theme. Such reflection can be both personal and social, inviting them to share the sources of their feelings and desires, and how their context, past or present, impinges upon them now and going forward. Again, this is most likely prompted by good questions that invite people to go deeper and to reflect critically on what is shaping their present reality. These first two movements can be well summarized as inviting people to share their own stories and visions. Indeed, few people can resist the invitation, "so tell me your story."

Movement 3: As appropriate, be alert for an opportune moment to share something of Christian faith, and especially of Jesus. The key is to access persuasively Jesus's teachings and stories that are most likely to resonate with these participants' hearts and the concerns of their lives. We ever need to craft the Christian Story/Vision to respond to people's situations in life. Again, our personal narrative of Christian faith is most likely to echo in the hearts of others.

Movement 4: Now is the time for reflections that encourage people to *see for themselves*, to make their own and take to heart—however they do so—what the resources of Christian faith might offer to their present lives. Again, this can most likely be done by questions that encourage their own appropriation of its truths and spiritual wisdom. It can be as simple as asking, "So what do you think now?" or "What are your own thoughts about what we have shared?"

Movement 5: The best ending is to gently invite to some glimmer of Christian faith. Reflecting the aspects of *living* faith, the invitation can be about what to believe or probe further, what to trust, pray for, or take to heart, or a particular action or moral choice to make. The key is that any emerging decision be truly the person's own for how they might embrace *living* Christian faith.

In summary, a *life to Faith to life* (in faith) conversation is disarmingly simple—though never simplistic or a sure formula. It invites people to share their own stories and visions, gives them persuasive access to the Christian Story and Vision, and then invites them to integrate the two sources—life and Faith—toward *living* faith.

A Sample: Let me close with a sample (*example* would overclaim) from my own evangelizing efforts. It took place on an extended plane ride with the stranger beside me, with whom I struck up a conversation. After the usual chitchat and noticing that I was reading a book with Jesus in the title, he inquired of my work. When he heard I was some kind of theologian, he volunteered that his own life had too many worries and problems to think much about God, much less theology, though he had grown up Catholic. Assuring him that I did not mean to be invasive, I invited, "Would you be comfortable to share some of those worries?" (movement 1).

Quite willingly he proceeds to recount a host of painful struggles about a failing marriage and broken relationships with a twenty-two-year-old son and a teenage daughter. As he talked on, I posed an occasional question, not to pry but to help him to reflect deeper. So I asked him to recount why and how he thought the difficulties had begun, the key causes, and yet what might be his best hopes for those family relationships—his heart's desire (movement 2). He talked on very willingly.

After a while, I volunteered that what I find most helpful in the midst of my life struggles is to bring them to God. I explained that I pray for help but often just to talk to God about what is "going on" and how best to respond. I also asked if he could imagine what might be God's desire for him in the midst of his pain. He seemed surprised by this question—as if God would not care—and then opined that God would likely punish him for his failures. I pushed back that this is not the God I know and talked about Jesus's emphasis on God's enduring love and mercy for us all (movement 3).

My friend admitted that he "never prays any more"—though he had enjoyed some prayer ways in his Jesuit high school. I asked if he might consider "giving it a go" again, if only to ask God's help and guidance with all the burdens he was carrying (movement 4). At this, he fell silent and we said no more.

Soon we were ready to land in Boston. To ask *him* to make a decision seemed premature to the flow of conversation. Instead, when saying goodbye, I said that I would pray for him and that my prayer would be that *he* might pray as well. He seemed to welcome this arrangement. He asked for my business card, with apparent interest in continuing the conversation (movement 5). We parted as friends in the moment and went our separate ways. I've never heard from him since. Yet by God's grace, I might have sown or revived a seed of faith in his heart. I hope someone else will water and I pray that God will give the growth.

PAUSE FOR REFLECTION

- What is your response to the proposal of a *life to Faith to life* approach to crafting an evangelizing conversation?

- Think of someone in your life at this time who seems particularly in need of a seed of faith, perhaps to begin with a word of hope or love. How might you create an evangelizing conversation with them?

SPIRITUAL PRACTICE: SHARE YOUR OWN FAITH STORIES

For Christians, the first and authoritative source of divine revelation is the Bible and then the long-established traditions of faith that have developed from the biblical sources down through history. Christian faith also attests, however, that the Holy Spirit can speak personally to our own hearts and souls as we reflect upon our lives in the world, with our own story revealing God's most intimate word for us. As encouraged before, we must carefully discern how the Holy Spirit is moving in our lives at any given time and how best to respond. Yet with good discernment *we can* recognize God's personal word to us through our own experiences, drawing upon their spiritual and mystical potential.

Cumulatively over time, from integrating the Christian Story/Vision with reflection on our own life experiences, we craft our own "faith story." It reflects God's word to us as particular persons. Though our faith stories are intensely our own, they have a unique potential to lend spiritual wisdom to others as well. Of course, we must be careful not to impose our faith experiences as if normative for everyone else. Yet sharing our own story in faith can echo all the more effectively as a "word of God" in other hearts as well.

With some reflection, all people can recognize specific experiences of God's personal invitation to integrate life and Christian faith

294

into *living* faith and can tell the story. So look back over your life-in-faith and recognize a few of your favorites. Then, without imposing or pontificating, imagine with whom and how you might share those faith stories. By God's grace, the telling can renew your own faith and plant a seed in others as well.

At this closing, a personal faith story that comes to mind for me is of a childhood Christmas long ago, and overhearing my father sing with great gusto the lovely Irving Berlin song:

> If you're worried and you can't sleep.
> Just count your blessings instead of sheep
> And you'll fall asleep
> Counting your blessings.

And thanking God—as I do now—I hope readers may be as blessed from reading this book as I have been by writing it.

FOR FURTHER READING

Groome, Thomas. *What Makes Us Catholic: Eight Gifts for Life*. San Francisco: Harper One, 2003. An overview of the deep currents that make up the great river of Catholic identity in Christian faith.

Treston, Kevin. *The Wind Blows Where It Chooses*. Melbourne, Australia: Coventry Press, 2018. The subtitle, *The Quest for a Christian Story in Our Time*, summarizes this short and readable masterpiece from a senior scholar in religious education.